Summer Bridge Activities™

Kindergarten to 1st Grade

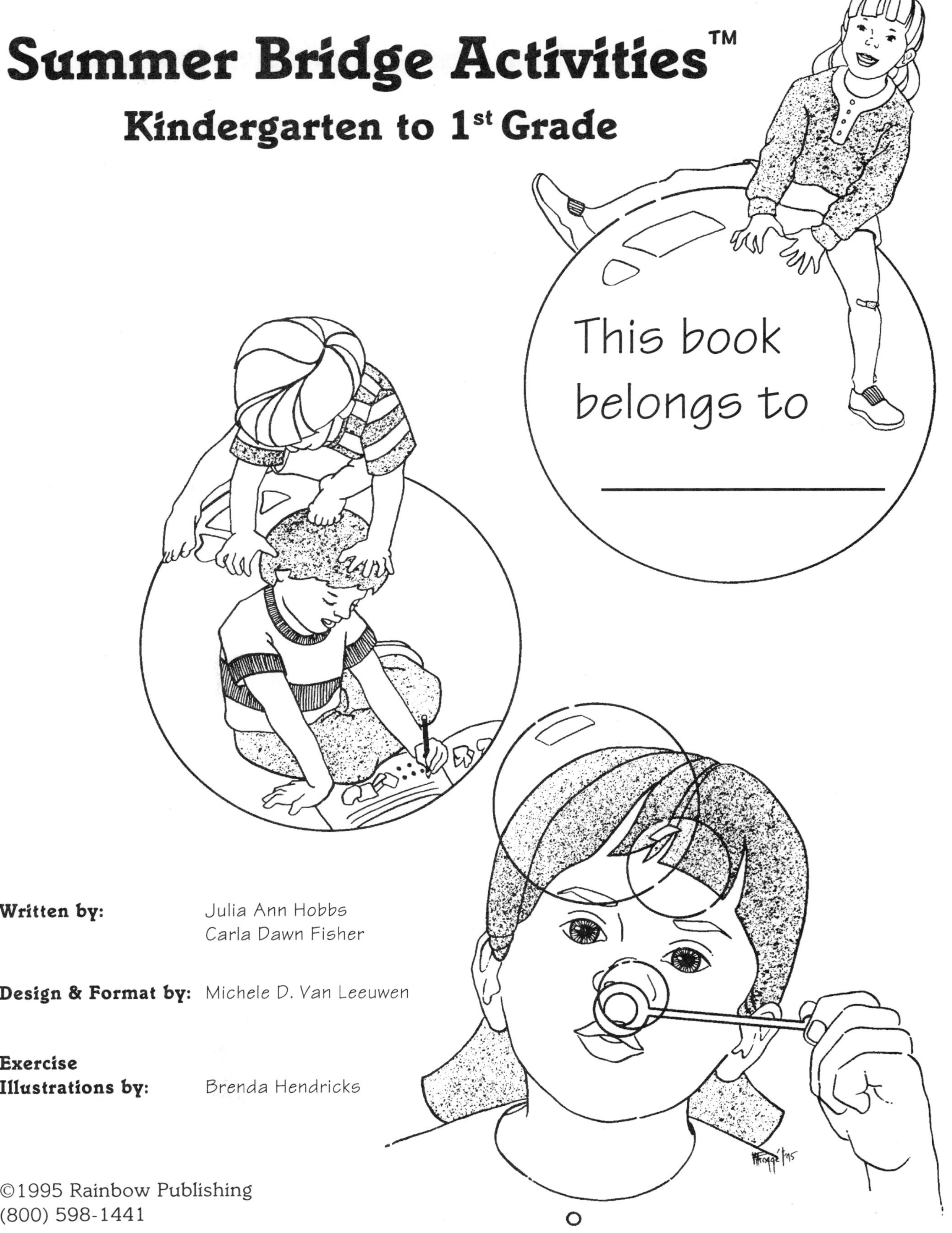

Written by: Julia Ann Hobbs
Carla Dawn Fisher

Design & Format by: Michele D. Van Leeuwen

Exercise Illustrations by: Brenda Hendricks

(800) 598-1441

Summer Bridge Activities™
Kindergarten to 1st Grade

Published in cooperation with Rainbow Publishing, 1994.

For information, write: Rainbow Publishing, Inc.
332 West Martin Lane, Salt Lake City, Utah 84107
801/268-8887

PRINTING HISTORY
First Printing 1992
Second Edition 1995
Third Edition 1996
Fourth Edition 1997

For orders call 1-800-598-1441
Discounts available for quantity orders

ISBN: 1-887923-03-9

PRINTED IN THE UNITED STATES OF AMERICA.
10 9 8 7 6 5 4 3 2 1

Table of Contents

You're TERRIFIC!
Do You Know Why?

Dear Parents,

You're terrific because you've become involved in your child's education. Picking up this workbook clearly shows your child their education is important. Something to value. Welcome to *Summer Bridge Activities*™!

Let me tell you how this unique series of workbooks came to be. As a parent of a 1st grader, the summer was quickly approaching. I was concerned the skills he had worked so hard to develop would take a good licking if I didn't do something to support them. In addition, I was apprehensive about his adjustment to school in the fall after three months of playing.

I went to his teachers for help. In speaking with them, other school administrators, and parents, I found I wasn't alone with my concerns. In fact, I was told approximately 80 percent of what children are taught in school is lost within a month, unless that knowledge is reinforced quickly and continuously. I certainly didn't want that to happen to my child.

The search began. I looked all over for appropriate workbooks. Oh, yes…I'm sure you'll agree, if you've ever gone out looking, there are lots to choose from. But they're either too hard or too simple, or usually didn't match what he had learned in school. I wasn't looking for perfection, but it sure seemed that way. I simply wanted to buy something that correlated with the curriculum guidelines from the department of education.

I found myself back in front of my son's teachers, asking where I could find such materials. They knew of none. So…

With a team composed of award-winning teachers, informed educators, and concerned parents, we put our own books together. You have in your hands the results of literally thousands of hours of work. All of the activities—over 240 in each book—follow the

Please turn to page viii

curriculum guidelines I mentioned earlier. And we've taken it one step further—*Summer Bridge Activities*™ has been successfully tested on thousands of children.

And what about my son—or better yet, how about your son or daughter? If you'd like to find them thinking while having fun,
motivated by a desire to learn,
confident and excited when the new school year rolls around,
use *Summer Bridge Activities*™ as suggested.
Yes, we've got many testimonials to the workbooks' successes.

And what about me—or better yet, what about you? If you'd like to:

- reach your goal of keeping your child active the smart way,
- successfully bridging the gap over the summer
- with an easy-to-use daily program—
- all without hassles—
- yet, producing the results of busy, happy, and learning children,

it can now be accomplished.

Again, it's terrific you're involved. Thank you for your purchase. We at Rainbow Publishing would love to hear about your success. Call 1-800-598-1441 with your story.

Best to you,

Michele D. Van Leeuwen

P.S. *Summer Bridge Activities*™ also works great for those students who are off-track from year-round school. Try it.

Parents' Guide
"Getting the Most From the Workbook"

You, as a parent, are the most important teacher your child will ever have. *Summer Bridge Activities*™ offer a guided daily workbook to help you succeed in this role.

Studies indicate the basic learning skills are more readily learned early in life. Small triumphs can have a lifelong effect on a child's accomplishments. The more often you tell your children they are intelligent, the more likely they are to become just that.

Educational opportunities to make such comments present themselves every day in every way with your child, and summer or off-track breaks are the perfect times.

Maximize your child's development by involving them in what you do when cooking. For example, point out what ingredients you use and what effect they have on the meal—you've taught vocabulary and science. Take time to explain the newscast—you've taught social studies. Take your child shopping and point out price, brand, and weight differences—you've taught math, economics, and consumer skills. Take a few hours to help your child start a collection of leaves, bugs, rocks, etc. Identify them—you've taught your child vocabulary and biology.

This workbook contains:

- Over 240 specially designed, self-motivating activities which will keep your child busy, happy, and learning. It's divided into four daily activities, one in each of the subject areas of reading, writing, arithmetic, and language. Sixty days in all, with pages numbered by day.
- A Parents' Guide, which you are now reading. It contains helpful hints on how to get the most out of the program.
- A carefully selected and researched book list, full of works children love to read.

Please turn to page x

- An Incentive Contract to motivate and reward your children's efforts.
- A "Discover Something New" list of creative ideas for when your child says the inevitable: "What can I do? I'm bored."
- A comprehensive Word List. Words to sound, read, and spell are located at the end of each section to reinforce and challenge.
- A frameable Official Certificate for successfully completing the workbook activities.

As you can see, *Summer Bridge Activities*™ has hundreds of ideas for extracurricular activities, as well as fun and challenging math, reading, writing, spelling, and identification exercises that will take your child a step ahead—a step to the head of the class.

Summer Bridge Blueprint for Success

Books Children Love Reading

- A suggested list of reading books (see page xvii).
- It is recommended that parents read to their Pre-Kindergarten and Kindergarten-1st Grade children 5-10 minutes each day and ask questions about the story. For older children the recommended time for reading each day to maintain reading skills are: Grades 1–2, 10–20 minutes; Grades 2–3, 20–30 minutes; Grades 3–4, 30–45 minutes; Grades 4-5, 45-60 minutes; and Grades 5-6, 45-60 minutes.
- It is suggested that parent and child decide the amount of reading time and fill it in on the Summer Activity Incentive Calendar.

Summer Activity Calendar

- The calendar is located at the beginning of each twenty–day section.
- It is suggested that parent and child sign an agreement for an incentive or reward before the child begins each section.
- When the child completes one day of ***Summer Bridge Activities***™, he/she may color or initial the "☆" star.
- When the child completes the agreed reading time each day, he/she may color or initial the "📖" book.
- The parent may initial that the activities have been completed.
- Let your child explore and experiment with the **Discover Something New** activities list.

Sections of Summer Bridge Activities™

- There are three sections of ***Summer Bridge Activities***™.
- Each section becomes progressively more challenging.
- Each section includes twenty pages of activities.
- There are four activities each day.

Continued on page xii

- The activities are numbered by day.
- Your child will need a pencil, eraser, crayons, and ruler to complete the activities.

Words to Sound, Read, and Spell

- At the end of each section there are words to sound out, read, and spell (in K–1 there are flash cards). Activities are suggested word games you may want to play with your child.
- Together you and your child can:
  - Write your favorite words on flash cards. Make two sets and play the matching game (in order to keep the two matching cards, you have to know their meaning or spelling).
  - Draw pictures of exciting words.
  - Use as many words as you can from the list to make up five questions, statements, or explanations.
  - Write a story using as many words as you can from the word list.
  - Write a list of colors.
  - Write a list of words you have a hard time spelling.
  - Write a list of action verbs.
  - Close your eyes, try to remember as many words as you can from the word list, and write them down.
  - Practice writing each word five times.
  - Write a list of words you find while traveling to the mountains, on vacation, or on the way to a friend's house.

10 Helpful Hints on How to Maximize *Summer Bridge Activities*™

1. **First, let your child explore the book.** Flipping through the pages and looking at the activities will give your child an idea about the book.

2. **Help select a good time for reading or working on the activities.** Suggest a time after your child has played outside and before he/she is too tired.

3. **Provide any necessary materials.** A pencil, ruler, eraser, and crayons are all that are required.

4. **Offer positive guidance.** Children still need a lot of guidance. Remember, the activities are not meant to be tests. You want to create a relaxed and positive attitude toward school. Walk through at least one example on a page with your child. "Think aloud" and show your child how to solve problems.

5. **Give your child plenty of time to think.** You may be surprised by how much children can do on their own.

6. **Stretch your child's thinking beyond the page.** If you are reading a storybook, you might ask, "What do you think will happen next?" or "What would you do if this happened to you?" Encourage your child to name objects that begin with certain letters, or count the number of items in your shopping cart. Also, children often enjoy making up their own stories with illustrations.

7. **Reread stories and flip through completed pages occasionally.** Completed pages and books will be a source of pride to your child and will help show how much has been accomplished over the weeks.

8. **Read and work on activities while outside.** Take the workbook outside, in the back yard, the park, or camping. It certainly can be fun!

9. **Encourage siblings, babysitters, and neighboring children to help with reading and activities.** Other children are often perfect for providing the one-on-one attention so necessary for children who are beginning to read.

10. **Give plenty of approval!** Stickers and stamps, or even a hand-drawn funny face are effective for recognizing a job well-done. When the child has completed the book, hang the certificate of completion where everyone can see it. At the end of the summer, your child can feel proud of his or her accomplishments and will be eager for school to start.

36 Amazingly Simple, Yet Fun & Educational Activities For Parents and Children to Do Together

1. Have a safety planning meeting with your children. Help them understand proper procedures in case of fire, earthquake, tornado, etc.
2. **Organize materials for your child to decorate a box—a "treasure box" for storing art projects and school awards.**
3. Visit a playground with your child. See who can swing the highest.
4. **Give your child a bear-hug and a compliment daily.**
5. Go through the calendar with your child and mark any special days—birthdays, family events, etc.
6. **Make plans to visit your local high school or college. Find a football or gymnastics practice to watch.**
7. Count with your child by twos to twenty, threes to thirty, fours to forty, and so on.
8. **Choose a story from the newspaper. Ask your child to circle all the proper nouns.**
9. Have your child stay very still and listen to the sounds around him/her for three minutes, then have your child share all the things he/she heard.
10. **Go through your old toys together and carefully choose some to be donated to charity.**
11. Bake cookies with your child. Wrap some and take them to a neighbor.
12. **Have your child read aloud to you. At some point in the story, ask the question: "What do you think will happen next?"**
13. Present your child with an IOU card, such as "Good for one trip to the zoo."
14. **Make a list of errands to run. Give the list to your child. Let him/her decide the order in which to run the errands and the shortest and fastest way to get around town.**
15. Read a newspaper with your child. Cut out current articles and talk about them.
16. **Go to the library and check out books about your child's favorite animal. Help him/her make a picture book about it with drawings.**
17. Ask your child to describe as many feelings as he/she can, completing sentences like "Happiness is..." or "Sadness is..."
18. **Work together with your child listing ways to save electricity at home. Try to implement those ideas immediately.**
19. Have your child complete some fun rhymes, for example: "I saw a pig wearing a wig. I saw a cat wearing a..."

20. Ask specific questions about your child's day: "What was the most fun? What did you like the best?"

21. Go on a penny hike. At each corner, flip a coin—tails go left, heads go right.

22. Make plans to attend something musical with your child—a ballet, the symphony, a concert in the park.

23. Unplug your telephone and let your child practice making an emergency call.

24. Take a nature walk to enjoy the season. Come home and have your child write about or draw what he/she experienced.

25. Take some time to read with your child today.

26. Encourage your child to develop a hobby—photography, rock or stamp collecting, model building, museum exploring.

27. Put a special "I love you" note in your child's lunch or backpack.

28. Plan a few minutes to play a game with your child—cards, board games, catch, hide-and-seek.

29. Is there a swimming pool in your area that offers lessons? Check it out this week and sign your child up.

30. Both you and your child select something to read silently. After a period of time, summarize for each other what you read.

31. Find out which science subjects interest your child—astronomy, sea life, the environment. Check out books from the library and read together.

32. Plan a picnic at a large park with trails, ponds, trees, and animals. Take a walk and look for signs and sounds of summer.

33. See how many words you and your child can write in five minutes that end in "all." Score one point for four-letter words, and three points for five-letter and six-letter words.

34. Take your child somewhere to observe the clouds. Are they all the same? Can you find any shapes in the clouds?

35. Let your child experiment with watercolors. Suggest a landscape or a still life.

36. Make a list of some fun and exciting beginnings for stories. "A little purple man landed in my soup..." or "A hairball with legs walked into my class..." Give the list to your child and encourage him/her to tell or write and illustrate stories using these beginnings.

How to Encourage Children to Voluntarily Pick Up a Book and Read

You can help your child develop good reading habits before school begins. Most experts agree, reading with your child is the most important thing you can do. Start your child's summer reading off right with the books included in the *Summer Bridge Activities* book list.

Set aside time each day to read aloud to your child at bedtime or after lunch or dinner. Let your child take a break from playing, and stretch out with a book from the list which follows. Read some of the books you enjoyed when you were their age.

Visit the library to find books that meet your child's specific interests. Ask a librarian which books are popular among children of your child's grade. Take advantage of summer storytelling activities at the library. Ask the librarian about other resources, such as stories on cassettes, videotapes, records, and even computers.

Encourage a variety of reading materials. Help your child read house numbers, street signs, signs in store windows, and package labels. Encourage your child to tell stories using pictures.

But best of all, show your child you like to read. Sit down with a good book. After supper, share stories and ideas that might interest your child from the newspapers and magazines you're reading.

Books Children Love Reading

Kindergarten to 1st Grade Level

Easy Readers

Galdone, Paul
- Little Red Hen

Gregorich, Barbra
- The Fox in the Box

Hillert, Margaret
- A House for Little Red
- Circus Fun
- Dear Dragon books
- Little Puff
- The Cookie House
- The Funny Baby
- The Three Bears

Modern Press (*see list)
- Max series

Seuss, Dr.
- Cat in the Hat
- Fox In Socks
- Green Eggs and Ham
- One Fish, Two Fish

The I Can Read books:
- Danny the Dinosaur, etc.

Wildsmith, Brian
- Cat on the Mat

*Modern Curriculum
Set 1—Short Vowels
- Fun with Gus
- Gus
- Hop On, Hop Off
- Hot Rocks
- Jet Bed
- Jim Wins
- Max
- Red Hen
- Sam and Al
- Six Kids

Modern Curriculum
Set 2—Long Vowels
- Bike Hike
- Dave and his Raft
- Dune Bug
- I Like What I Am
- Joe and Moe
- Katie and Jake
- Mr. Jones and Mr. Bones
- Pete and his Beans
- Sue and June
- Zeke

Modern Curriculum
Set 3—Blends
- At the Pond
- Brag, Brag, Brag
- Glen Wit
- Glub, Glub
- Here Comes the Bride
- Hunk of Junk
- Miss Swiss
- Scat, Cat
- Squire's Square Deal
- Stan the Squid

Modern Curriculum

Set 4—Diagraphs

At the Beach
Bath Time
Black Ducks Wind Ding
Gretch the Witch
Jack's King
Mush? Mush!
Sh!
Smith's Store
The White Whale
Whiz Kid
Trucks
The Puffins are Back

Books To Read to Children

Berenstain, Stan & Jan
The Berenstain Bears series

Bridwell, Norman
Clifford the Big Red Dog series

Dorros, Arthur
Follow the Water From Brook to Ocean

Duvoisin, Roger
Petunia

Gibbons, Gail
New Road

Hawes, Judy
Fireflies in the Night

Jordan, Helen J.
How A Seed Grows

Joyce, William
Bently and Egg

Numeroff, Laura Jaffe
If You Give A Mouse A Cookie
If You Give A Moose A Muffin

Parish, Peggy
Amelia Bedelia books

Sendak, Maurice
Where the Wild Things Are
Outside Over There
In the Night Kitchen

Ward, Lund
Biggest Bear

Happy Reading!

Summer Activity Contract & Calendar

Month______________________

My parents and I decided that if I complete 20 days of *Summer Bridge Activities*™ and read ______ minutes a day, my incentive/reward will be:

____

Child Signature______________________ Parent Signature______________________

Day	I have completed one day of activities (Color the Star)	I have completed ______ minutes of reading (Color the Book)	Parent Initials
1	☆	📖	
2	☆	📖	
3	☆	📖	
4	☆	📖	
5	☆	📖	
6	☆	📖	
7	☆	📖	
8	☆	📖	
9	☆	📖	
10	☆	📖	

Day	I have completed one day of activities (Color the Star)	I have completed ______ minutes of reading (Color the Book)	Parent Initials
11	☆	📖	
12	☆	📖	
13	☆	📖	
14	☆	📖	
15	☆	📖	
16	☆	📖	
17	☆	📖	
18	☆	📖	
19	☆	📖	
20	☆	📖	

Have a Fun Day...Discover Something New!

Fun Activity Ideas to Go Along with the First Section

1. Sign up for summer classes with the community education or local parks department.
2. Make a chart for summer chores with incentives.
3. Write to a relative about your summer plans.
4. Check the library for free children's programs.
5. Boost reading—make labels for household objects.
6. Start a journal of summer fun.
7. Zoo contest—find the most African animals.
8. Shop. Use a calculator to compare prices per pound.
9. Tune up those bikes. Wash 'em, too.
10. Attend a brown bag concert downtown.
11. Play flashlight tag.
12. Check out a science book. Try some experiments.
13. Make up a story at dinner. Each person adds a new paragraph.
14. Summer solstice. Time the sunrise and sunset.
15. Bubble fun: One-third cup liquid dishwashing soap, plus two quarts water. Use cans or pipe cleaners for dippers.
16. Arrange photo albums.
17. Find bugs in the park.
18. Learn American Sign Language or Morse Code.
19. It's going to be hot—go swimming.
20. Do some stargazing up a local canyon.

When using a pencil, REMEMBER to:

1. Hold your pencil correctly.
2. Sit up straight with both feet flat on the floor.
3. Make your letters with even circles, curves, and straight lines.
4. Space the letters in your words evenly.
5. Space your words evenly on the line.
6. Make your writing neat and easy to read.
7. Practice writing fast as well as neat.
8. Some people write right-handed and other people write left-handed.

Left-handed   Right-handed

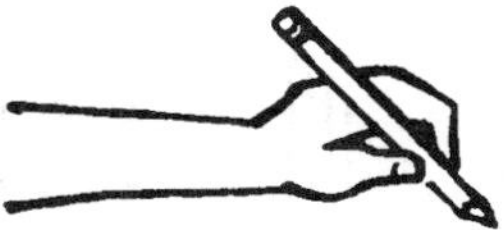

The thumb and first finger form a good "o."
The middle finger supports the pencil.

A good position helps make good writing habits.

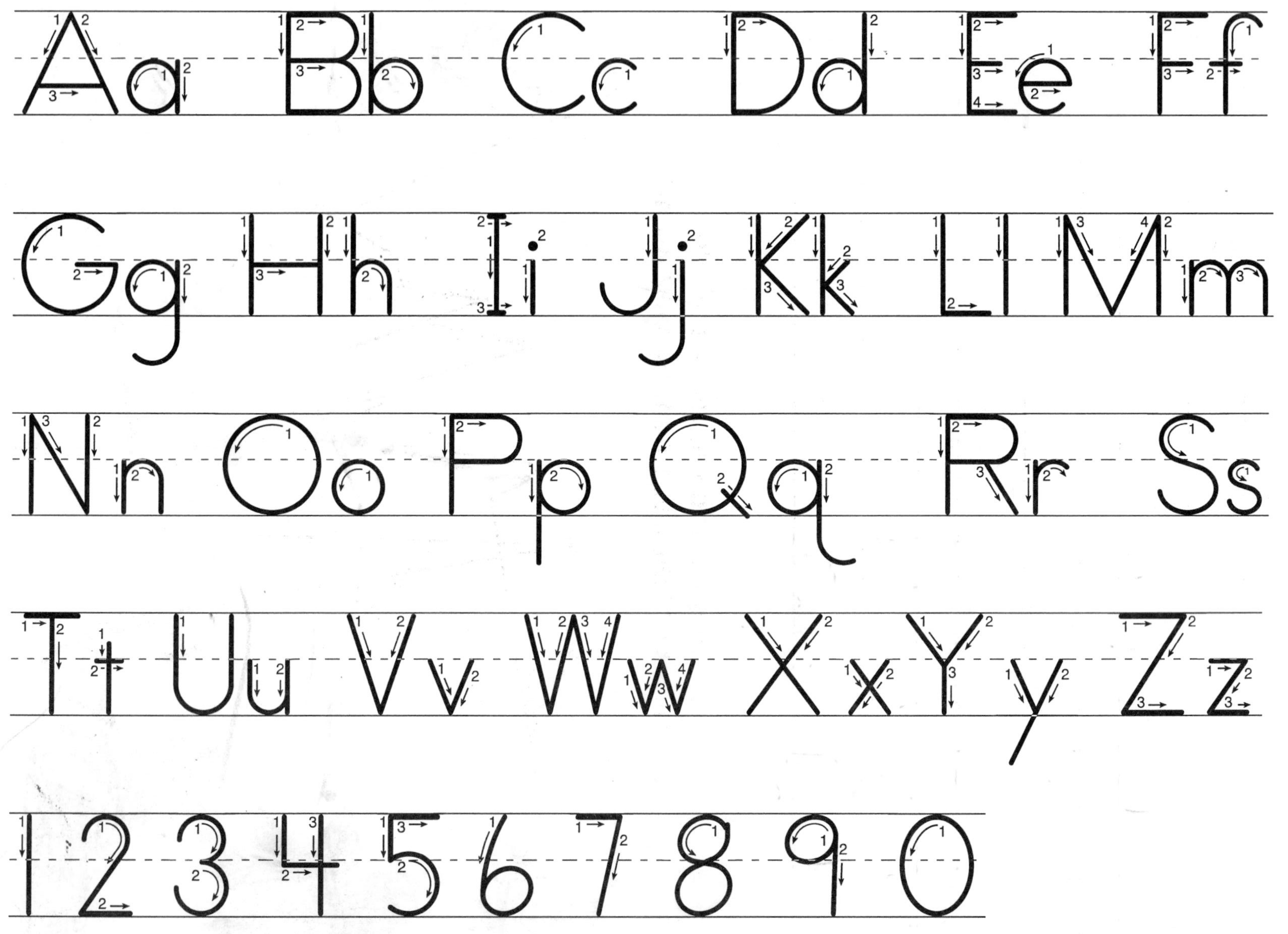
Aa Bb Cc Dd Ee Ff
Gg Hh Ii Jj Kk Ll Mm
Nn Oo Pp Qq Rr Ss
Tt Uu Vv Ww Xx Yy Zz
1 2 3 4 5 6 7 8 9 0

Writing numbers can be fun. Remember to always write your numbers beginning at the top.

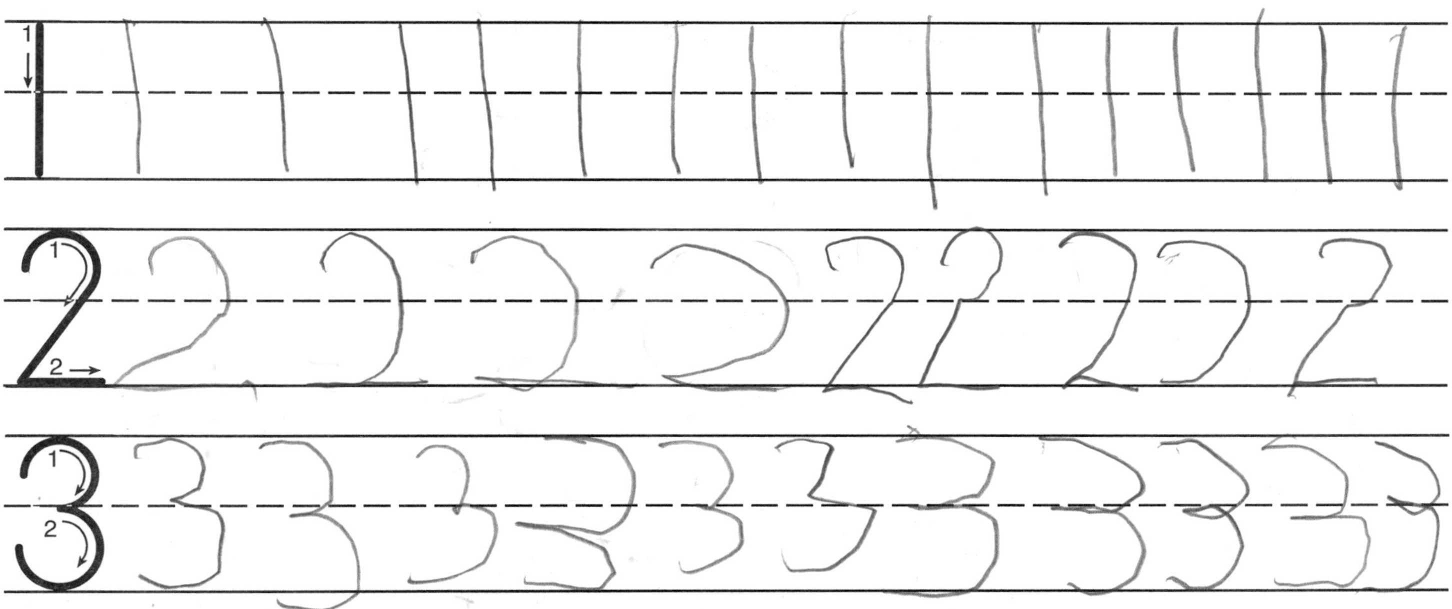

Color the fish green, the octopus orange, and the whale blue. Trace a path in the same color to help the sea creatures find their way home.

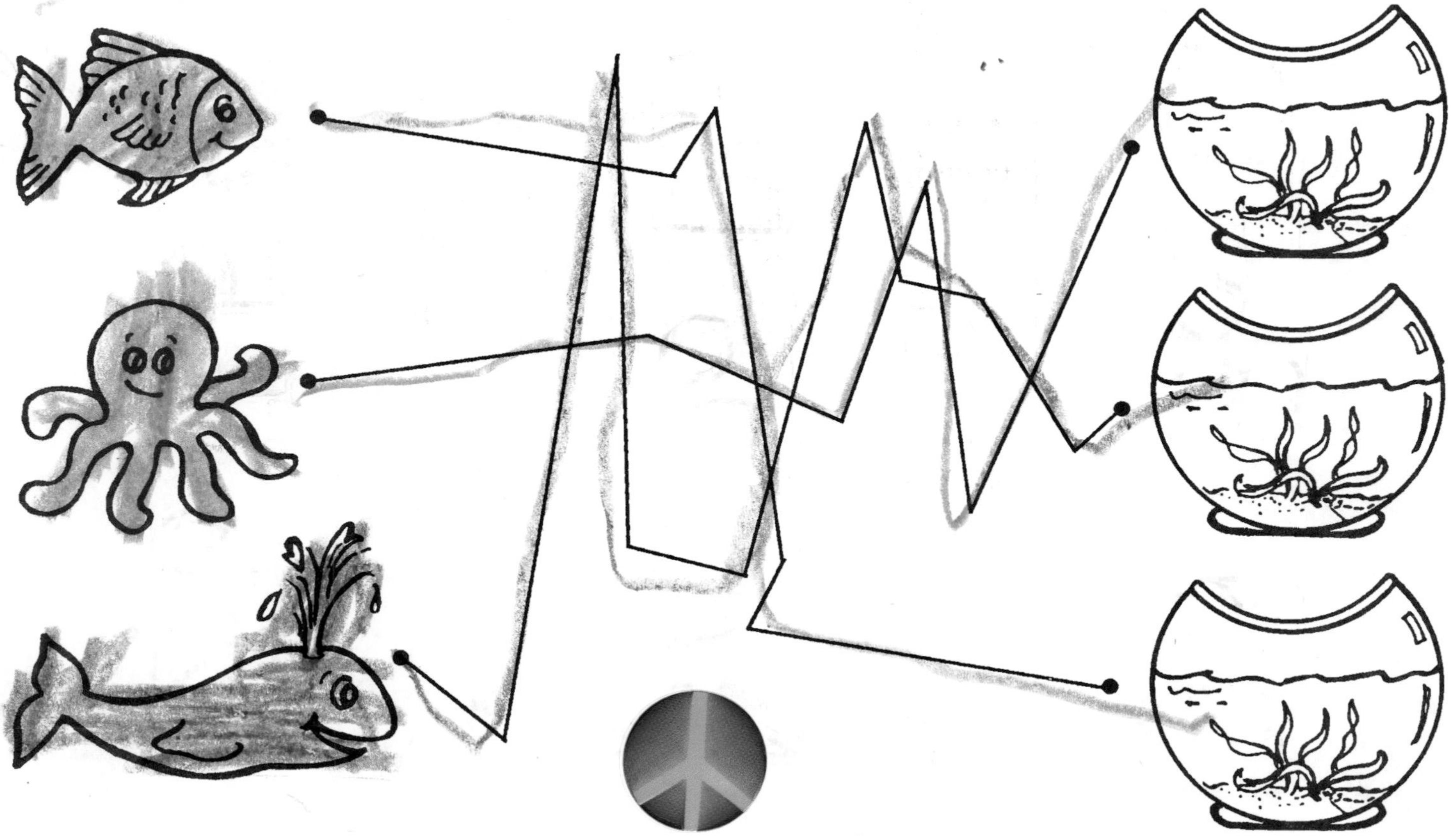

Say the alphabet in order, then choose a letter and say it aloud. Make sure you know the difference between capital and lowercase letters.

Aa Bb Cc

Dd Ee Ff Gg

Hh Ii Jj Kk

Ll Mm Nn Oo

Pp Qq Rr Ss

Tt Uu Vv Ww

Xx Yy Zz

Another fun thing to do is to have an adult in your family say a letter. You find it and put a marker on it (a button, bean, etc.). Continue this until you have covered all the letters.

Now, here are some numbers to write. Remember to write numbers beginning at the top.

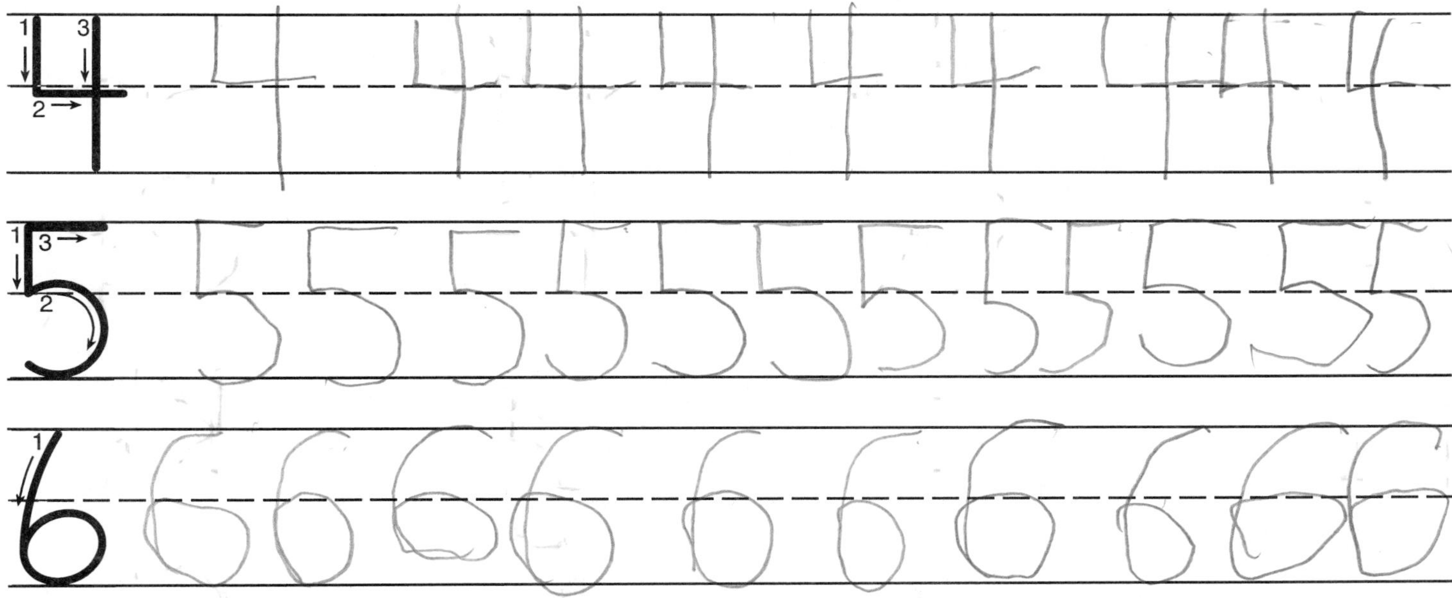

Circle the shape that is different in each box.

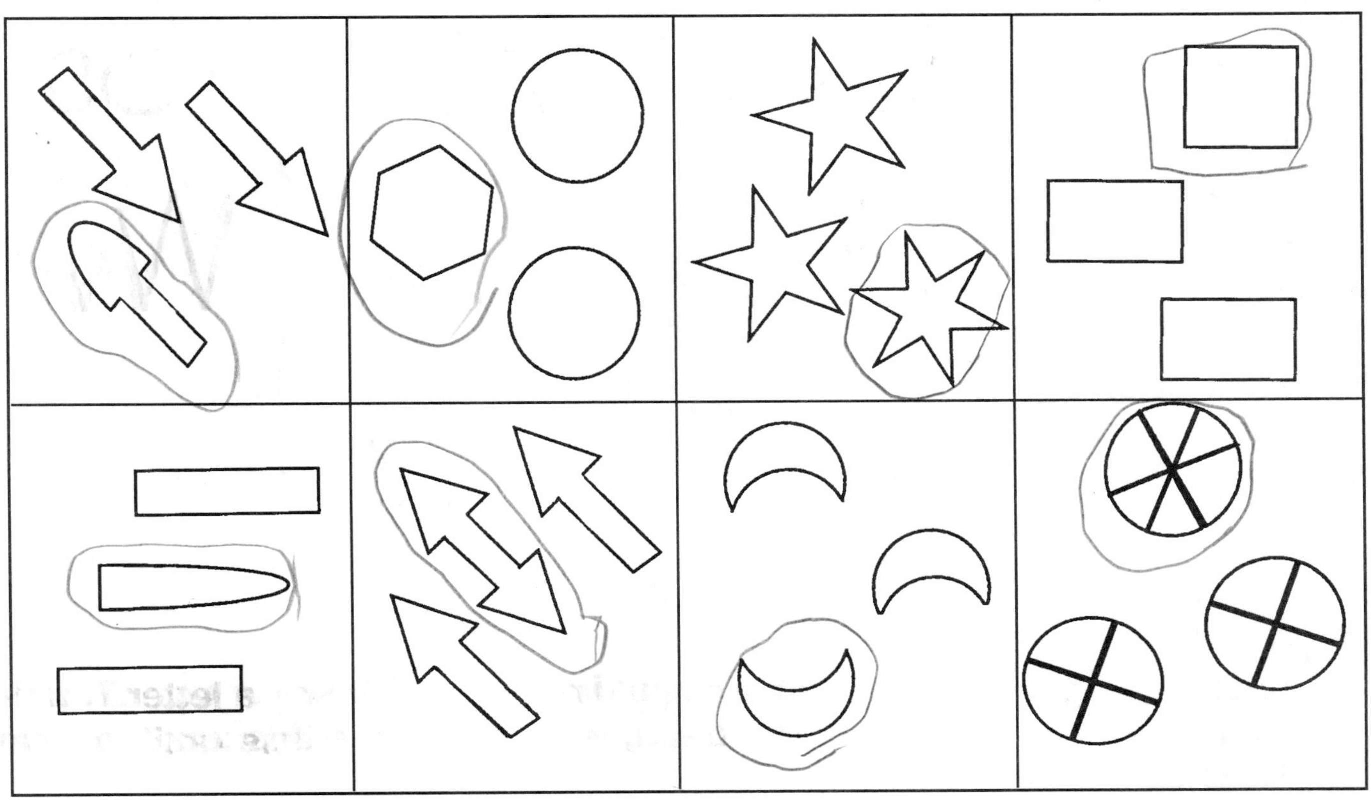

Bat and ball begin with the sound of (b). Color the bat, then practice writing capital and lowercase (b's).

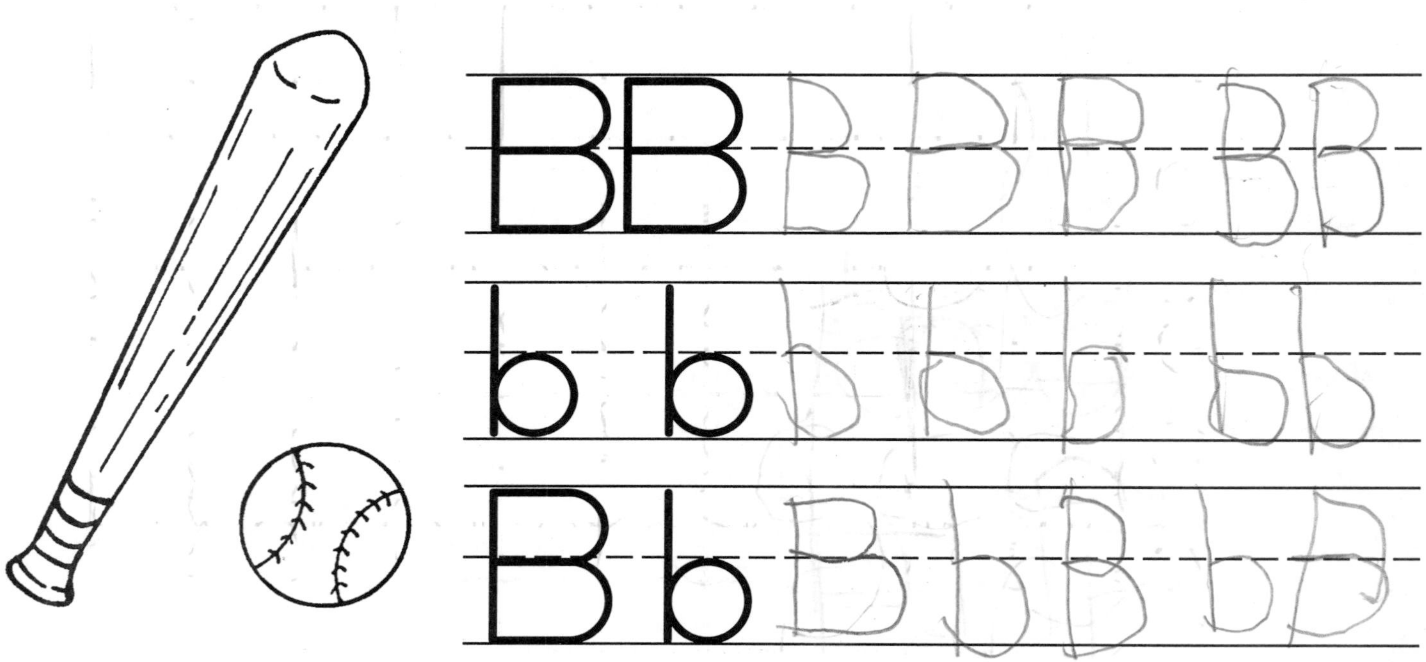

Now color all the objects below that begin with the sound of (b), like bat and ball.

Color the number of squares to match the number at the beginning of each row.

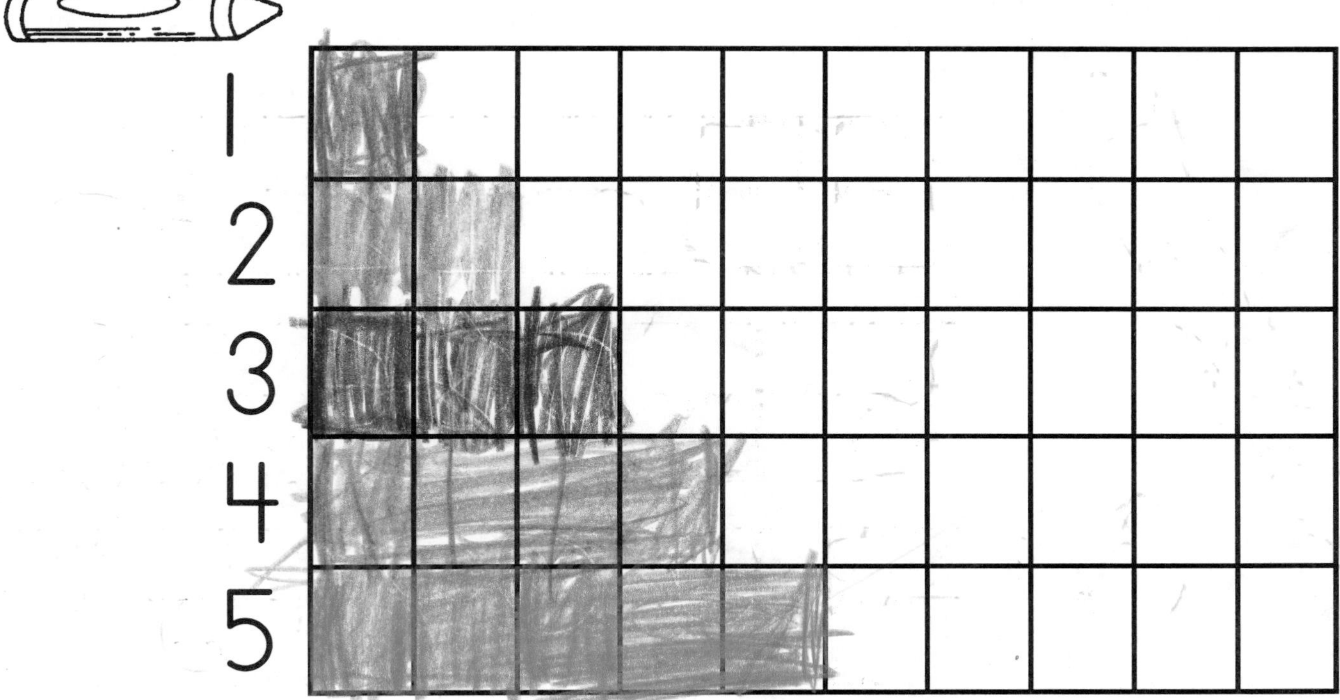

Trace over each capital letter.

A B C D E F G

H I J K L M N

O P Q R S T U

V W X Y Z

Carrots begin with the sound of (c). Color the carrots, then practice writing capital and lowercase (c's).

Now color all the objects below that begin with the sound of (c), like carrot.

Can you draw and color the correct number of beads?

Example: 2

Trace each lowercase letter.

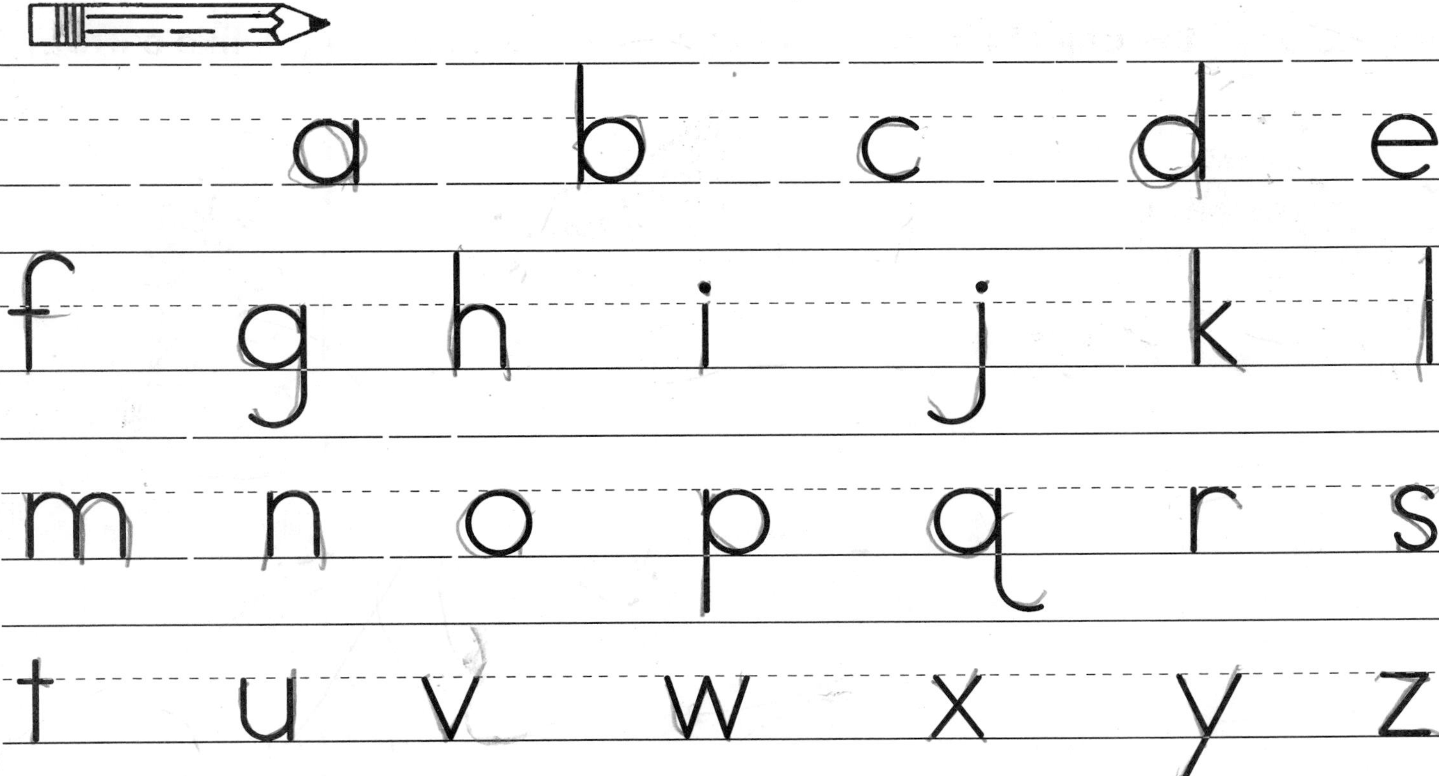

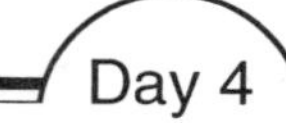

Duck begins with the sound of (d). Color the duck, then practice writing capital and lowercase (d's).

D D

d d

D d

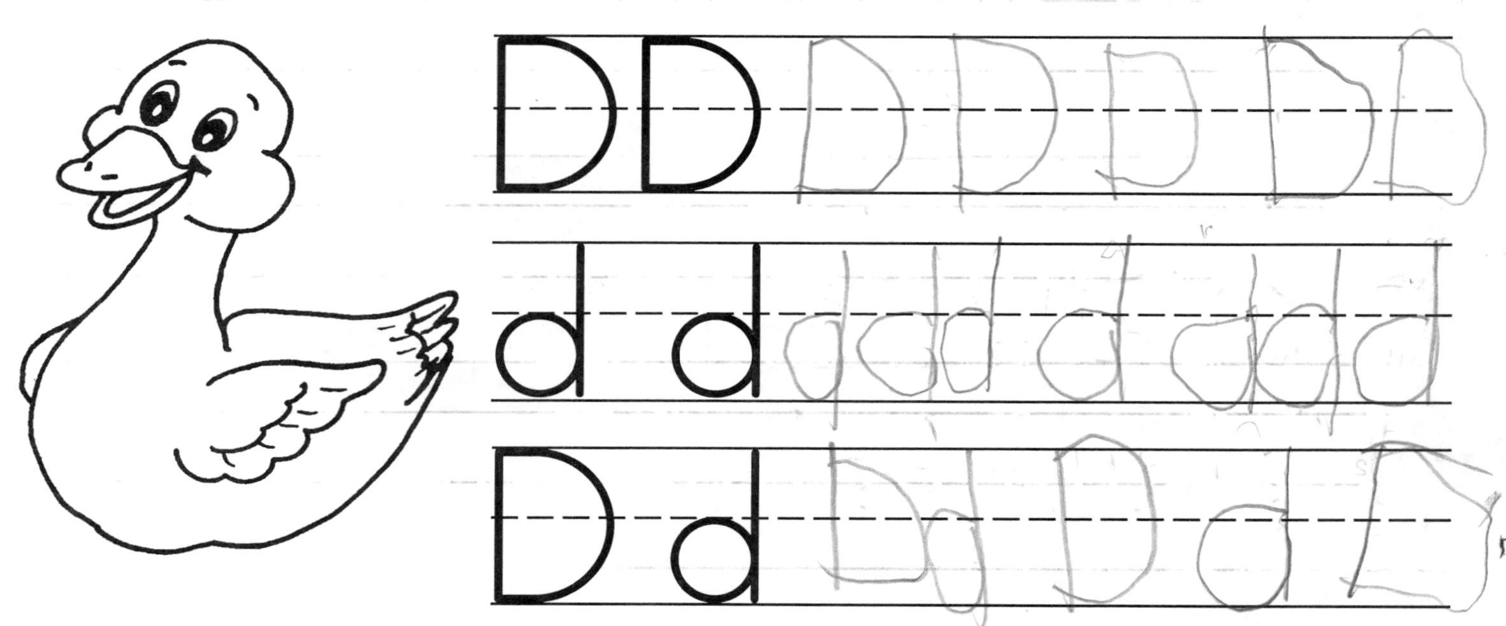

Now color all the objects below that begin with the sound of (d), like duck.

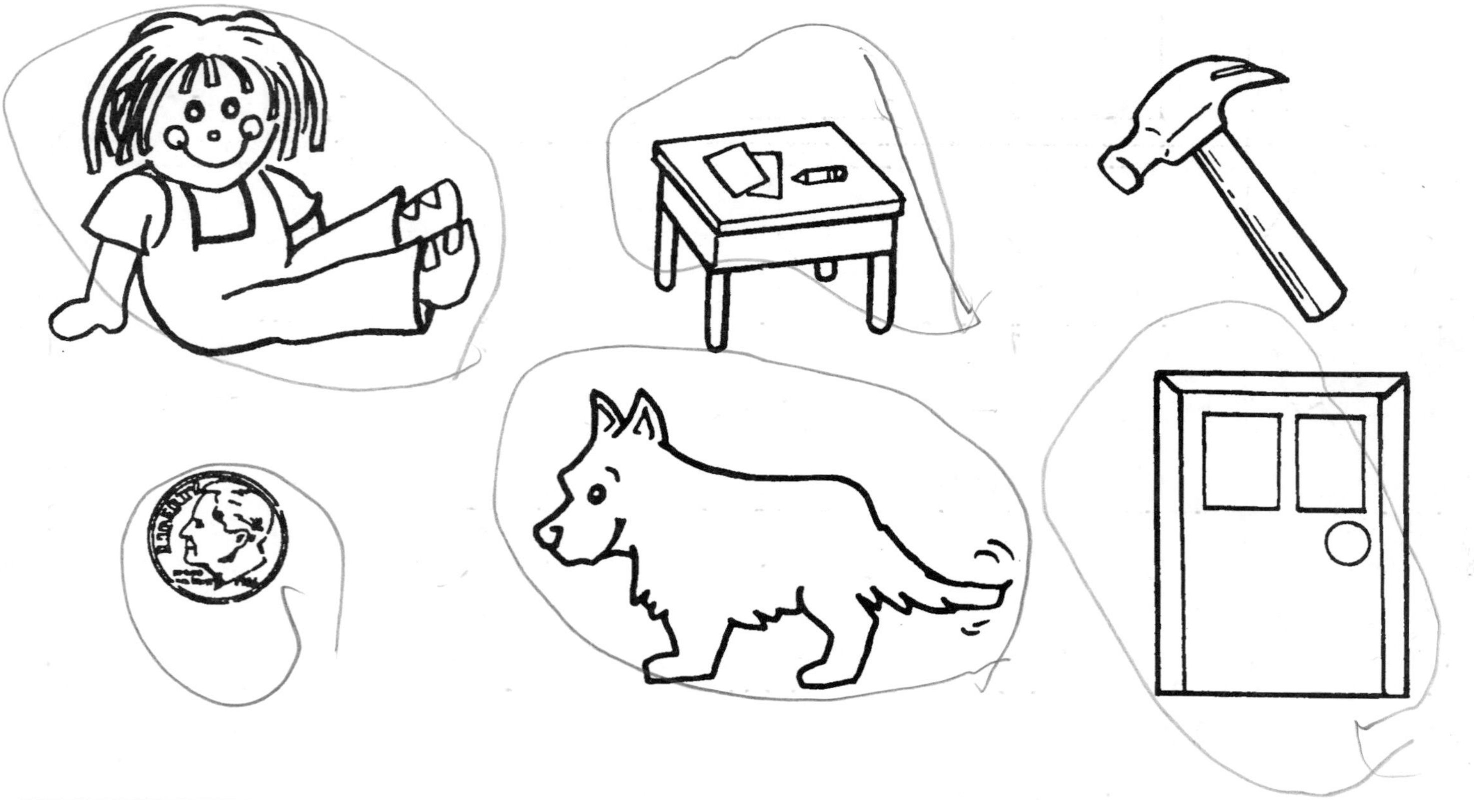

1, 2, 3, 4, 5, 6, we are not ready to quit! Now try numbers 7, 8, and 9. Remember to write numbers beginning at the top.

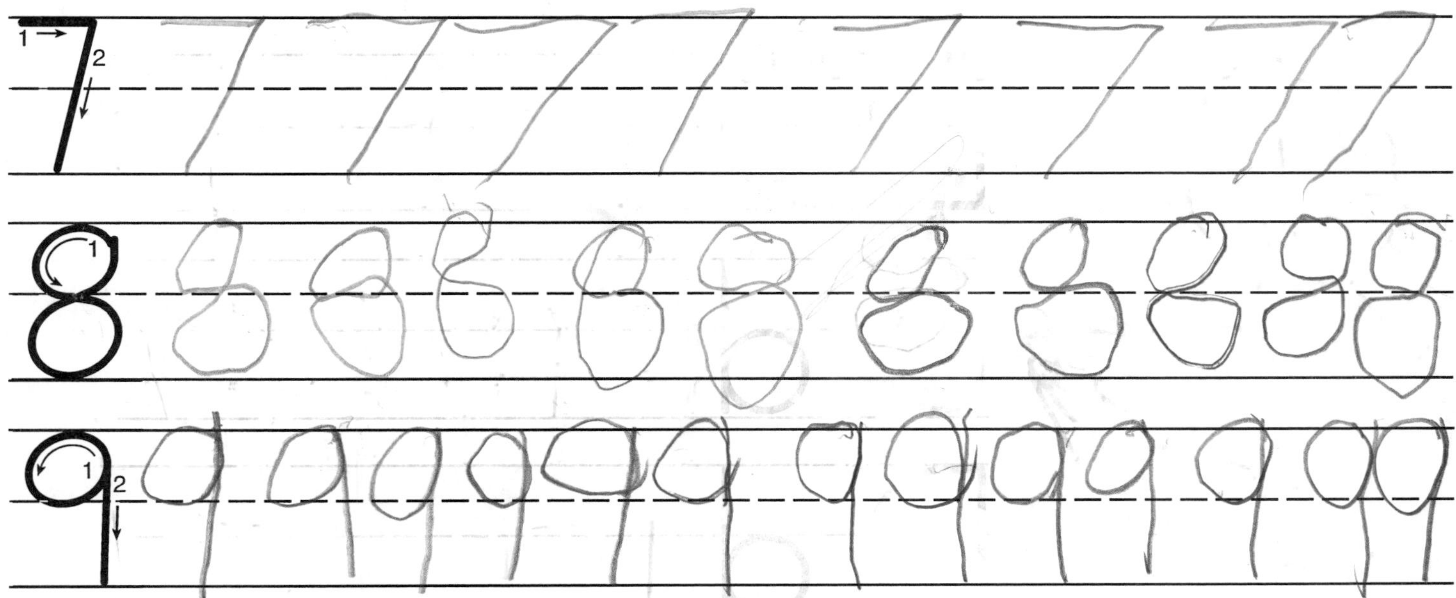

Make each picture look exactly the same as the first one in each row.

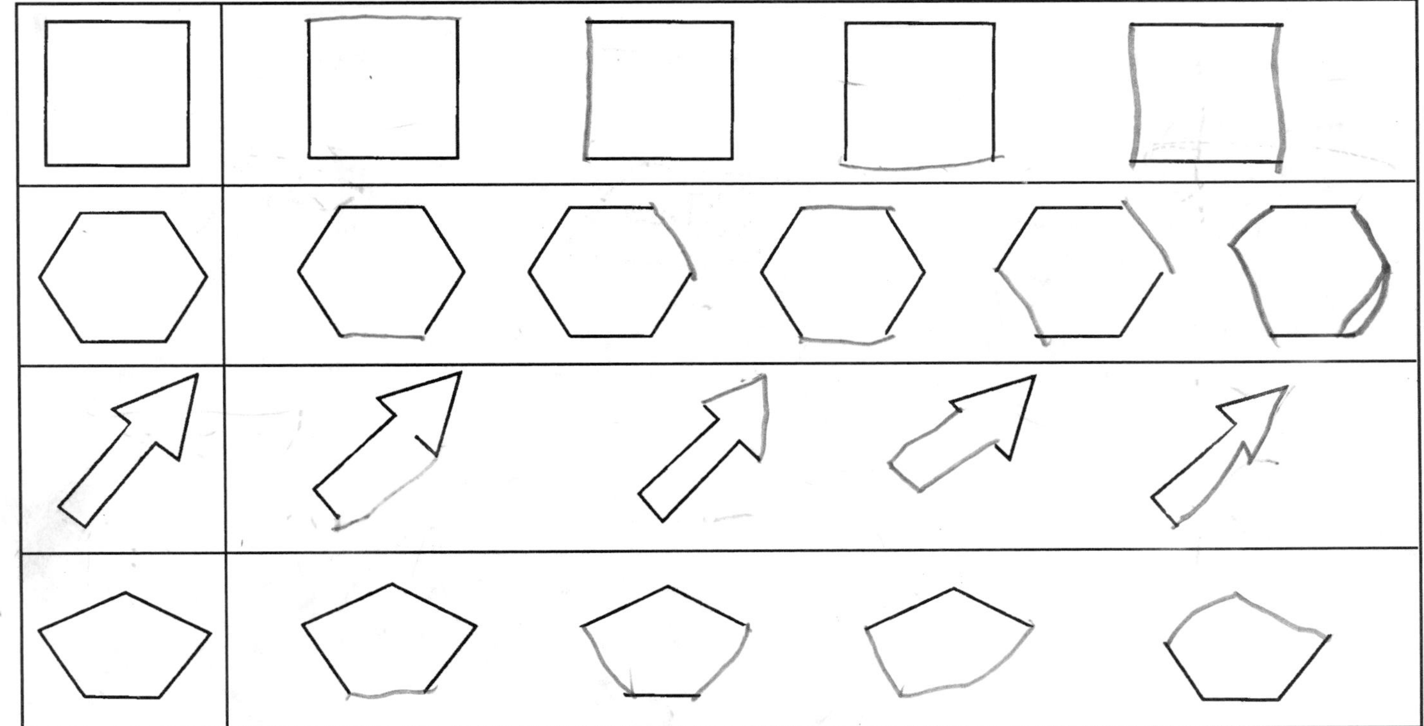

Fish begins with the sound of (f). Color the fish, then practice writing capital and lowercase (f's).

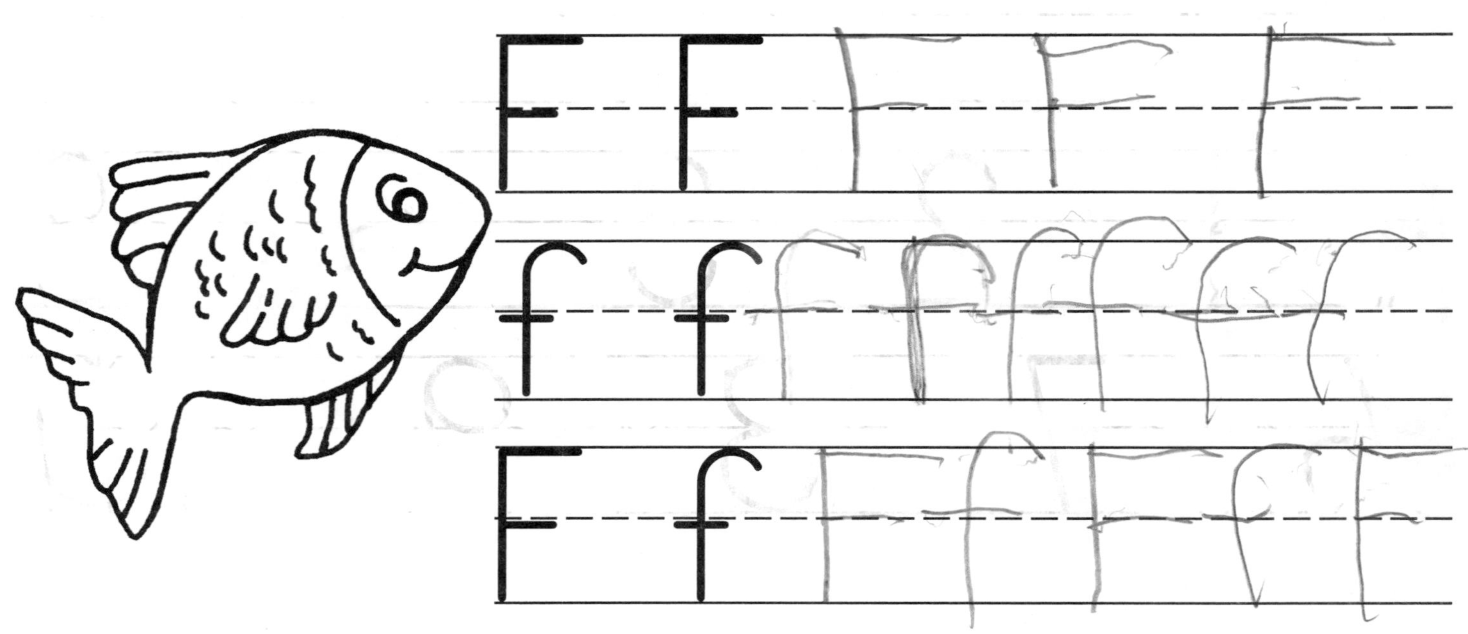

Now color all the objects below that begin with the sound of (f), like fish.

Don't forget the rule. We *always* write our numbers beginning at the top. Finish the line of (0's). Trace over the numbers from 1-10.

Circle the letters that are exactly like the letter in the first box of each row.

n	m	n	r	n	h	n	m	r
b	b	a	b	d	b	b	d	p
f	f	t	f	f	h	f	f	t
v	x	v	w	v	v	x	w	v
u	u	n	a	u	v	u	a	v
a	o	a	c	a	d	a	a	c

Girl begins with the sound of (g). Color the girl, then practice writing capital and lowercase (g's).

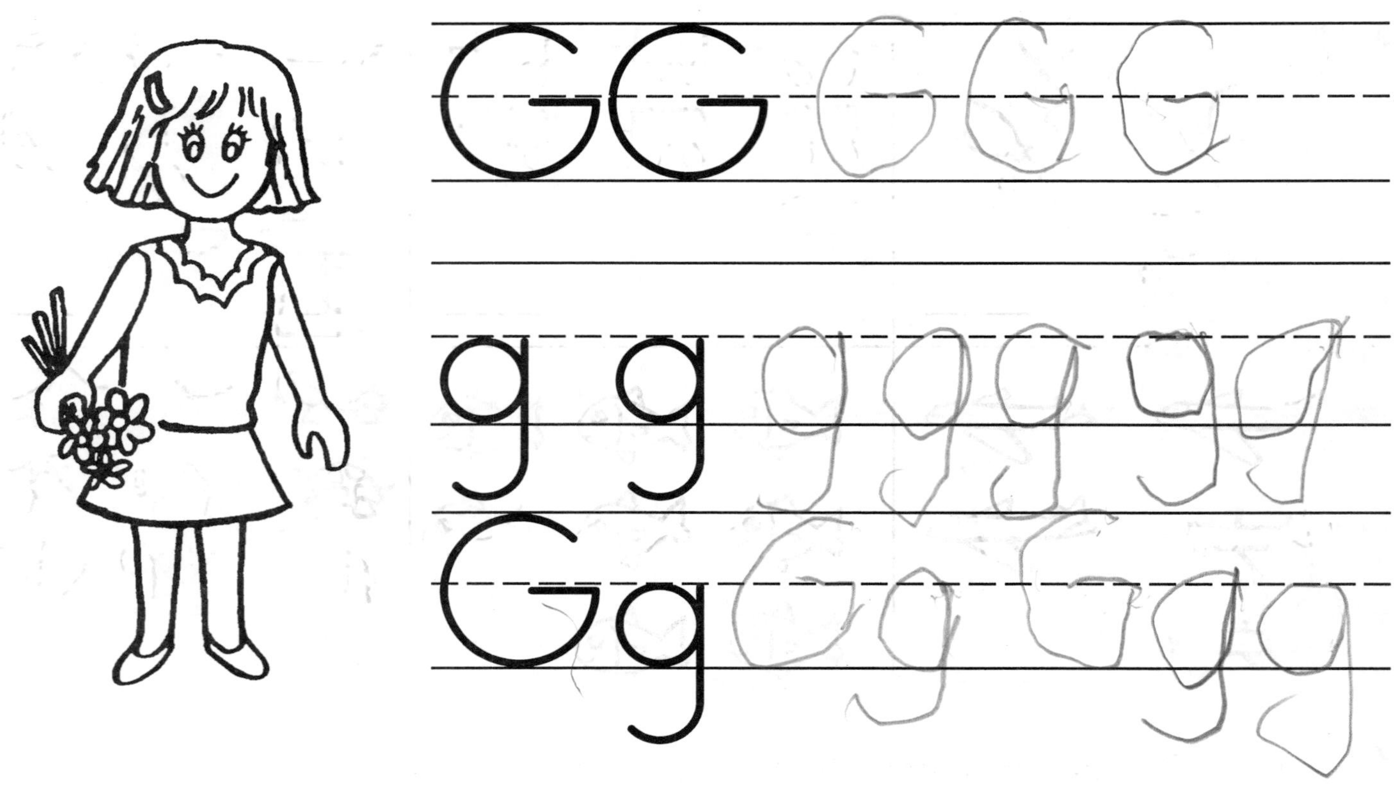

Now color all the objects that begin with the sound of (g), like girl.

Write the number telling how many objects are in each box.

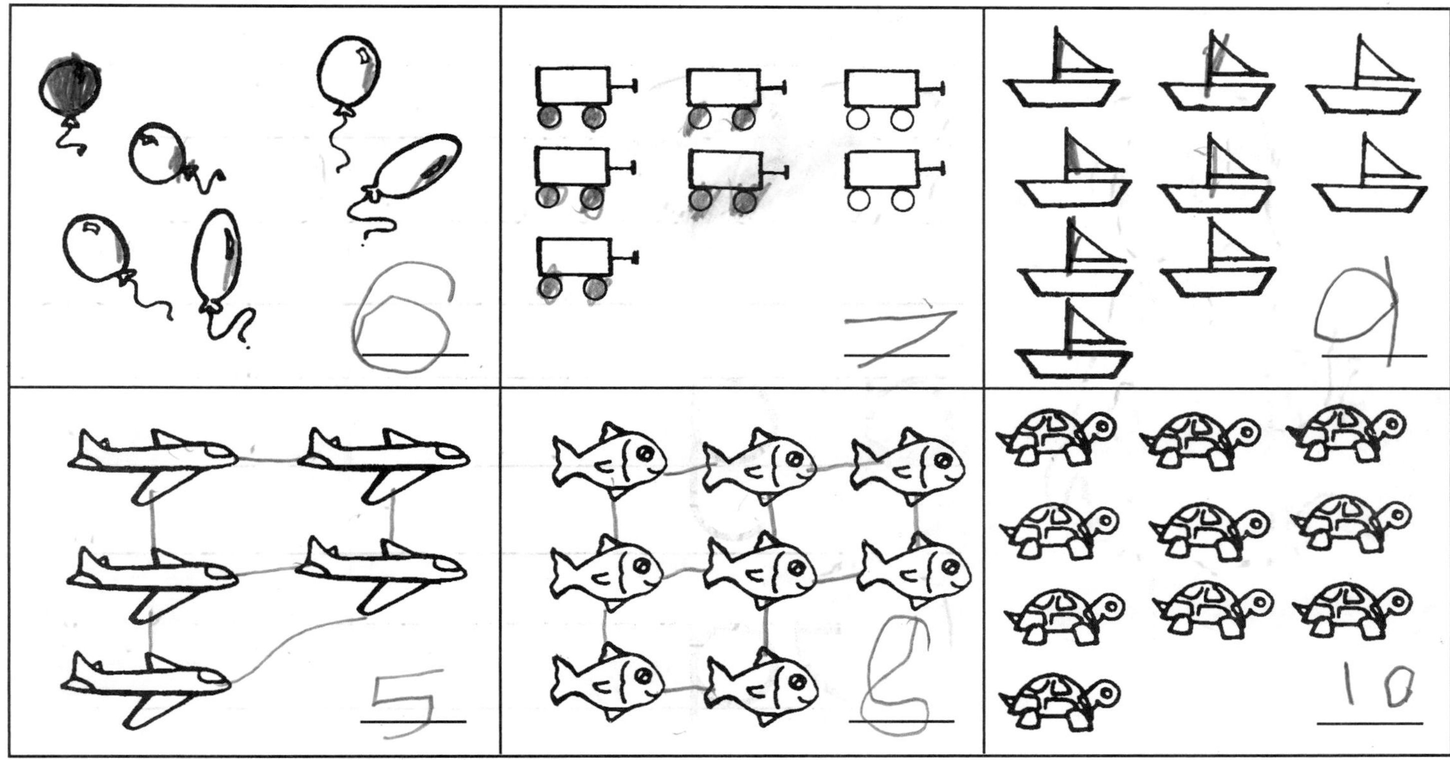

Write the missing capital letters in the empty squares.

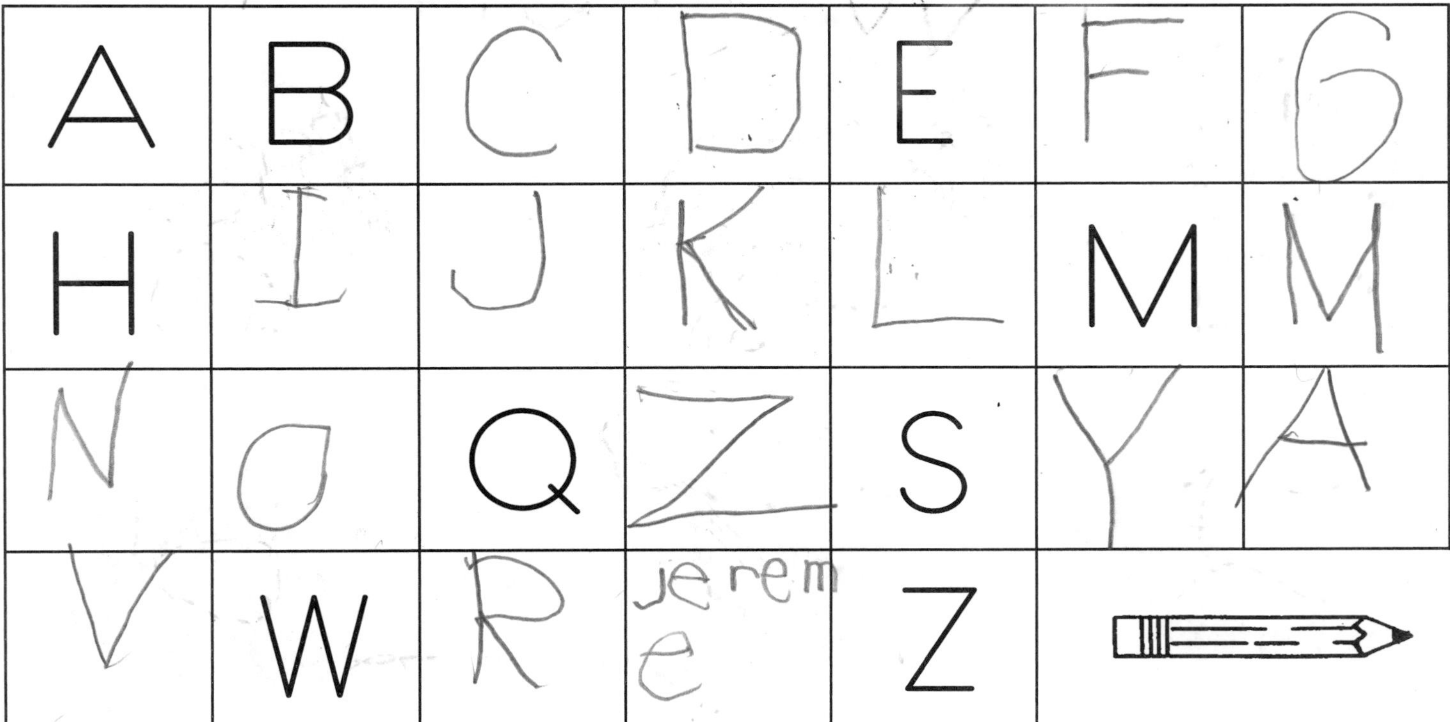

Horse begins with the sound of (h). Color the horse, then practice writing capital and lowercase (h's).

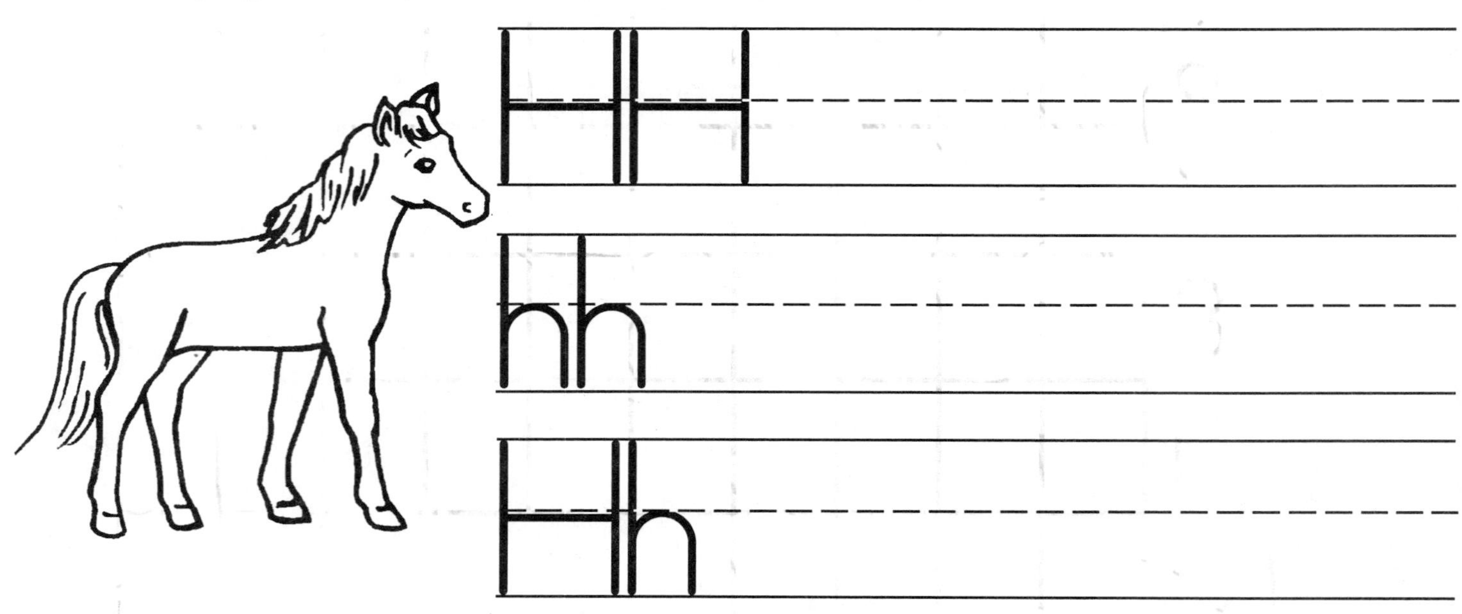

Now color all the objects below that begin with the sound of (h), like horse.

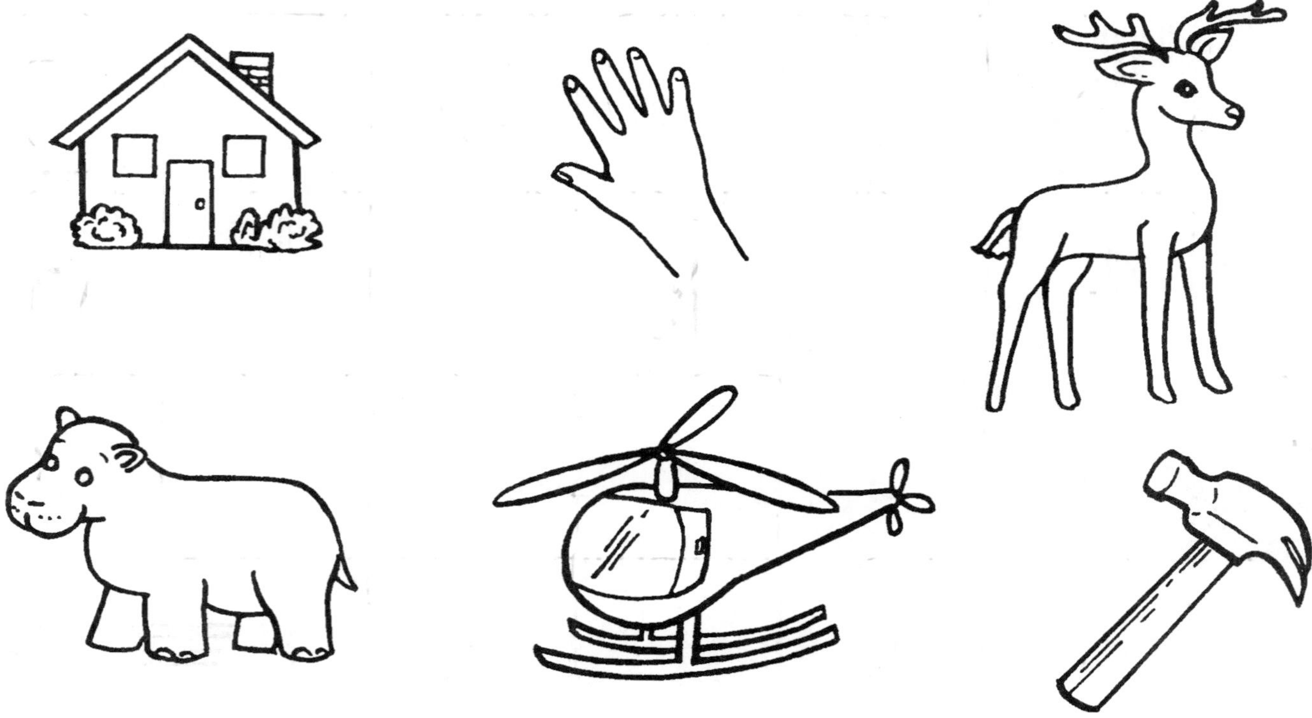

Color the number of squares to match the number at the beginning of each row.

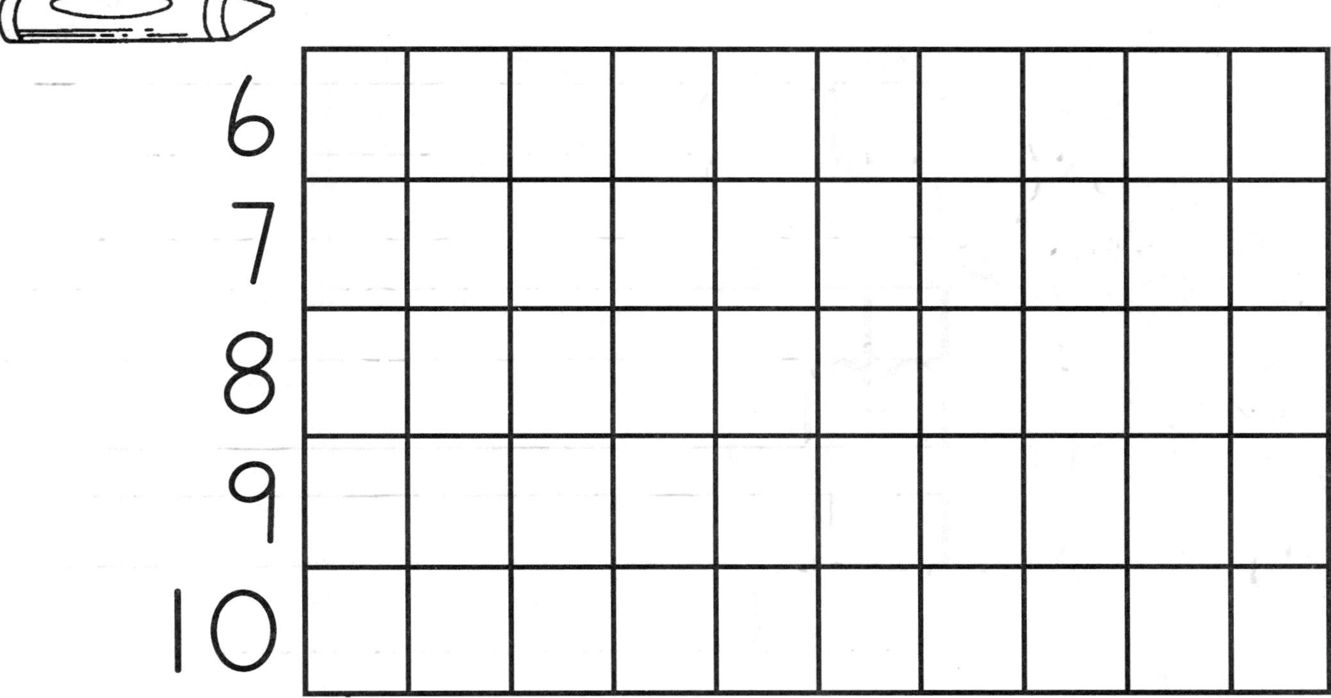

Write the missing lowercase letters in their boxes.

a	b			e		g
	i		k			n
o		q				u
v				z		

Jack-in-the-box begins with the sound of (j). Color the jack-in-the-box, then practice writing capital and lowercase (j's).

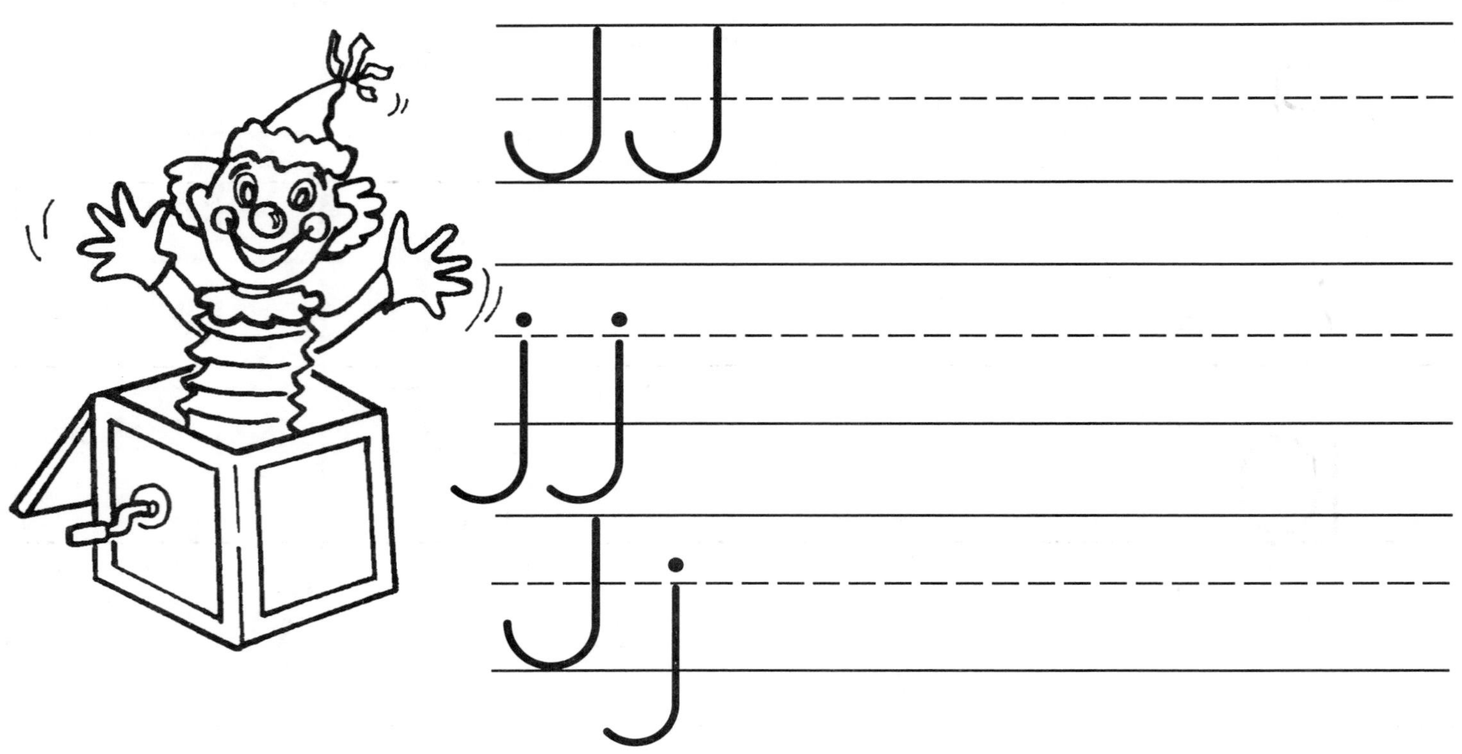

Now color all the objects that begin with the sound of (j), like jack-in-the-box.

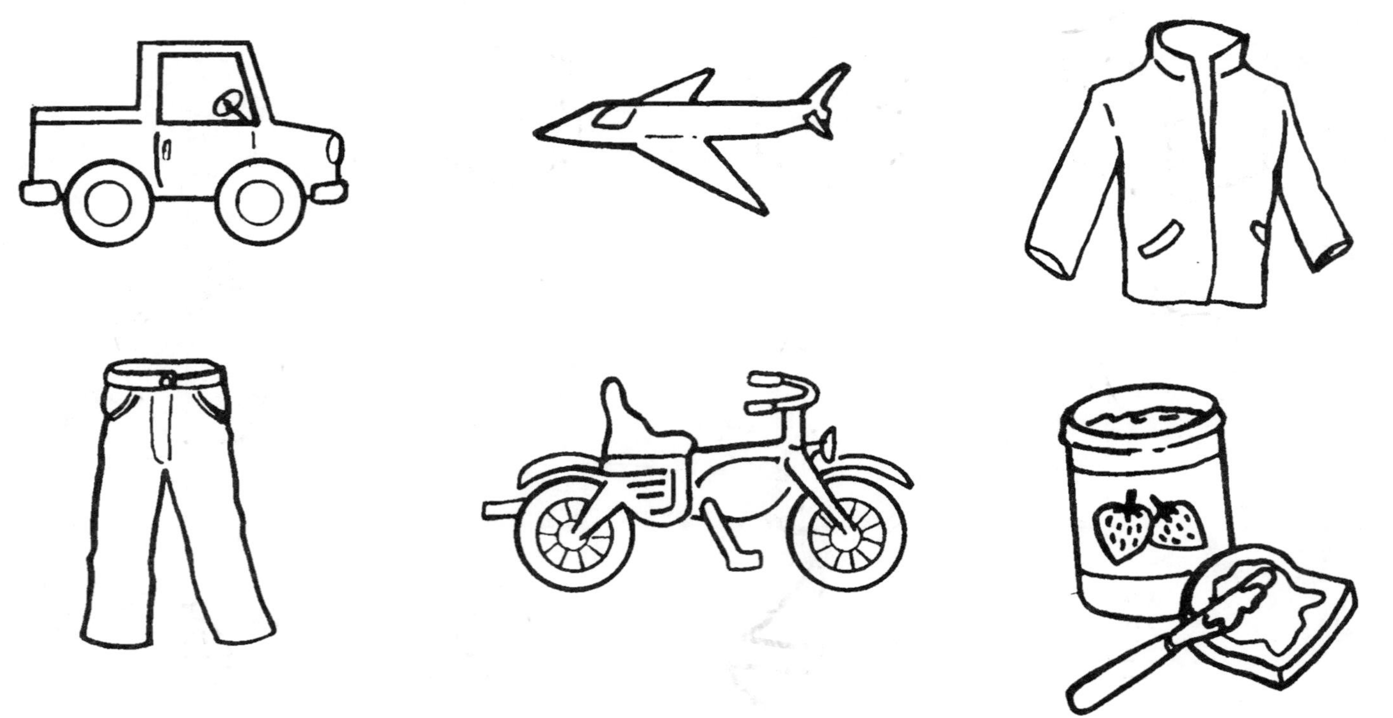

Can you draw and color the correct number of apples?

Example: 4 

9

6

7

Find the two objects in each row that are exactly the same size. Circle them.

Kangaroo begins with the sound of (k). Color the kangaroo, then practice writing capital and lowercase (k's).

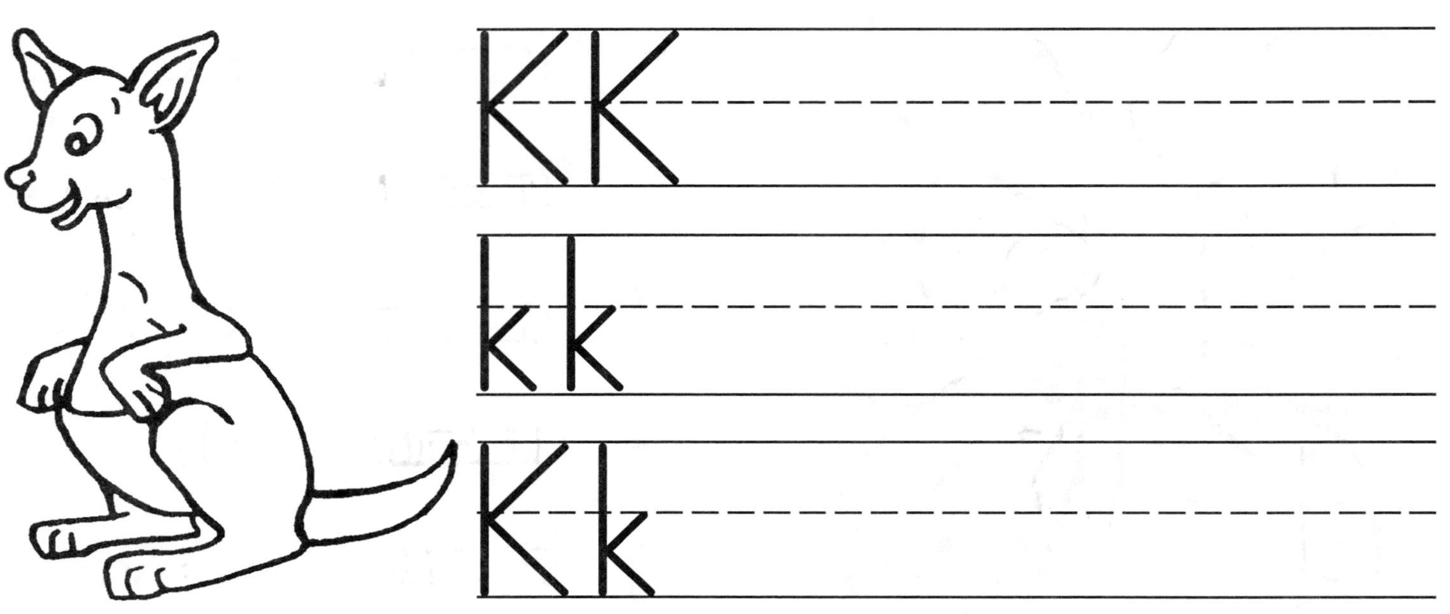

Now color all the objects below that begin with the sound of (k), like kangaroo.

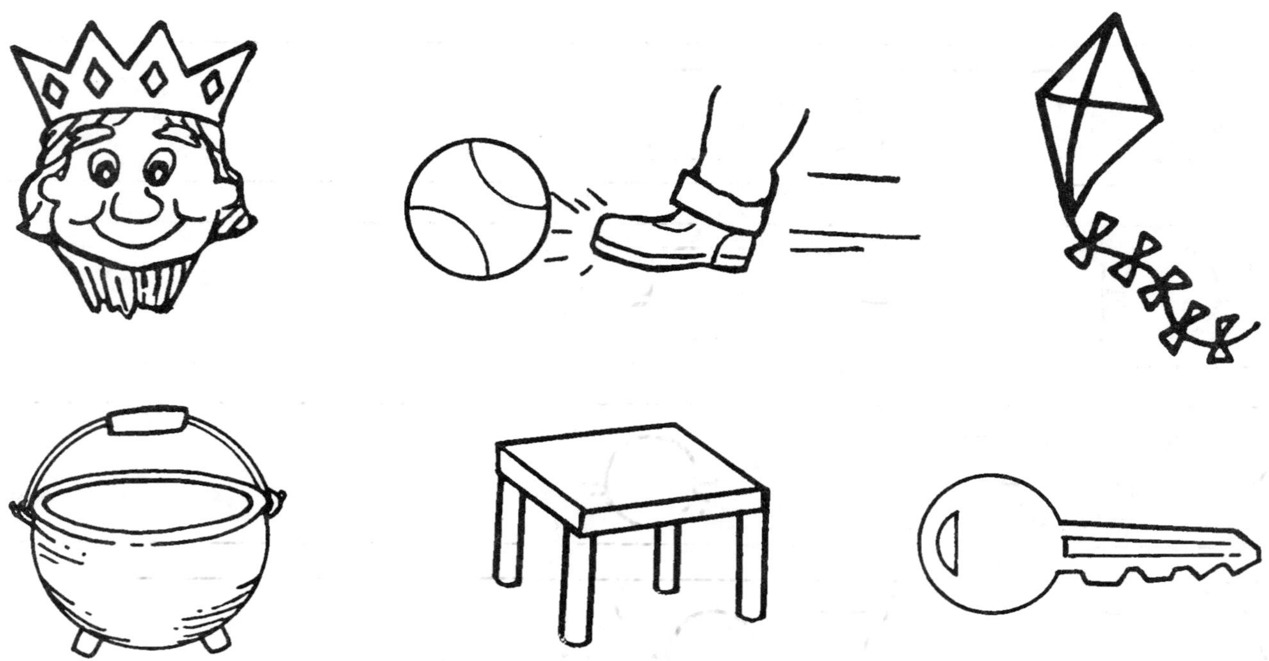

Color the butterfly by matching the number of dots in each shape to the numbered crayon.

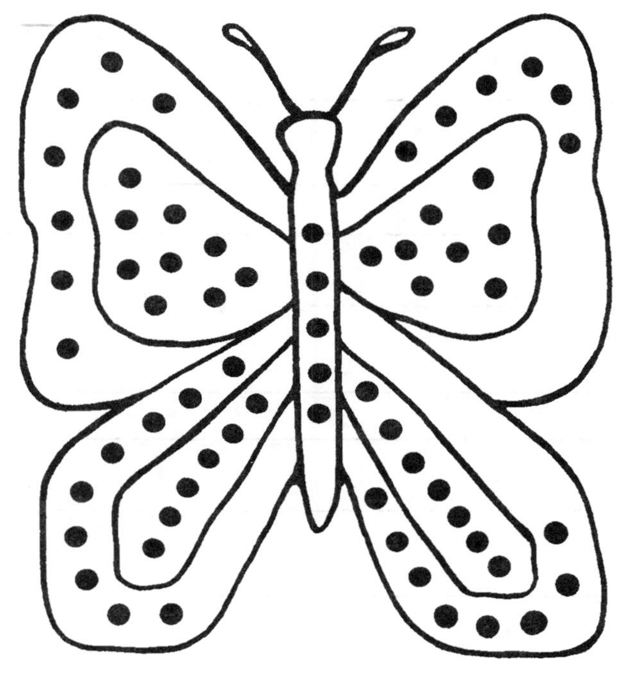

5 black

6 orange

7 yellow

8 blue

9 green

Complete the pattern in each row.

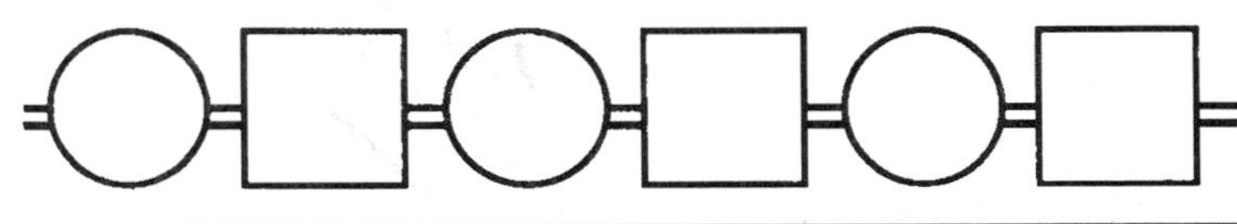

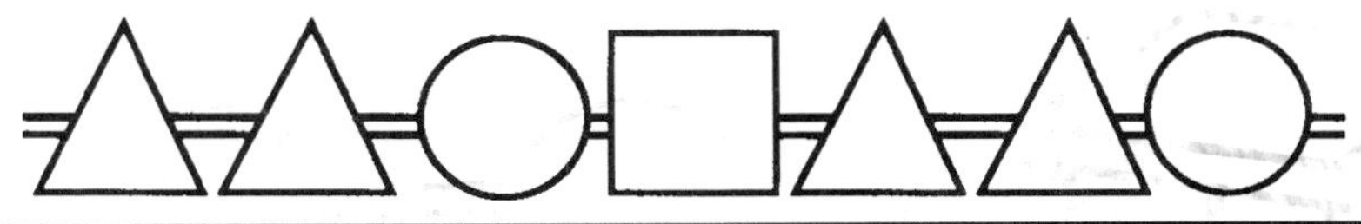

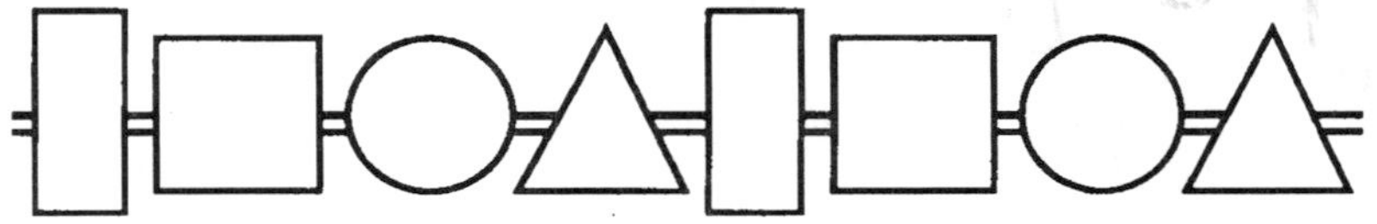

Ladybug begins with the sound of (l). Color the ladybug, then practice writing capital and lowercase (l's).

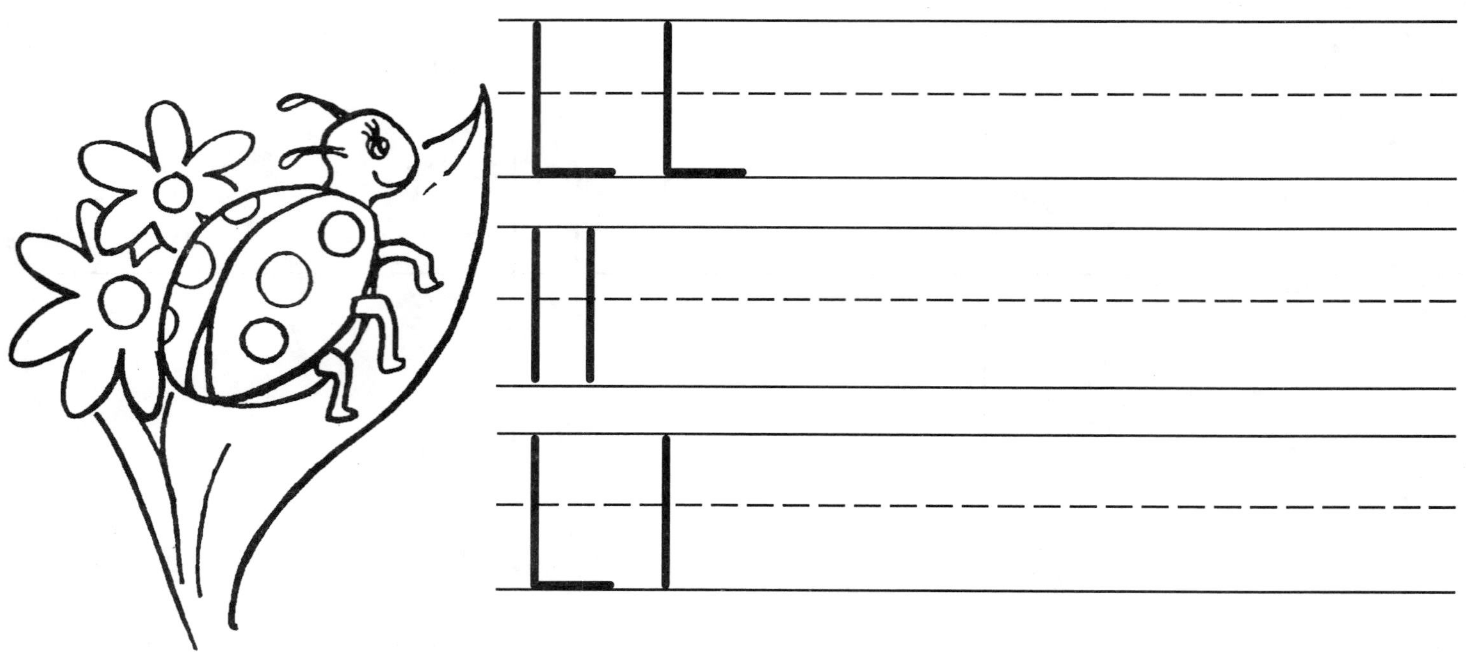

Now color all the objects below that begin with the sound of (l), like ladybug.

Draw and color as many objects as the number shows.

Draw a line from the capital letter to the matching lowercase letter.

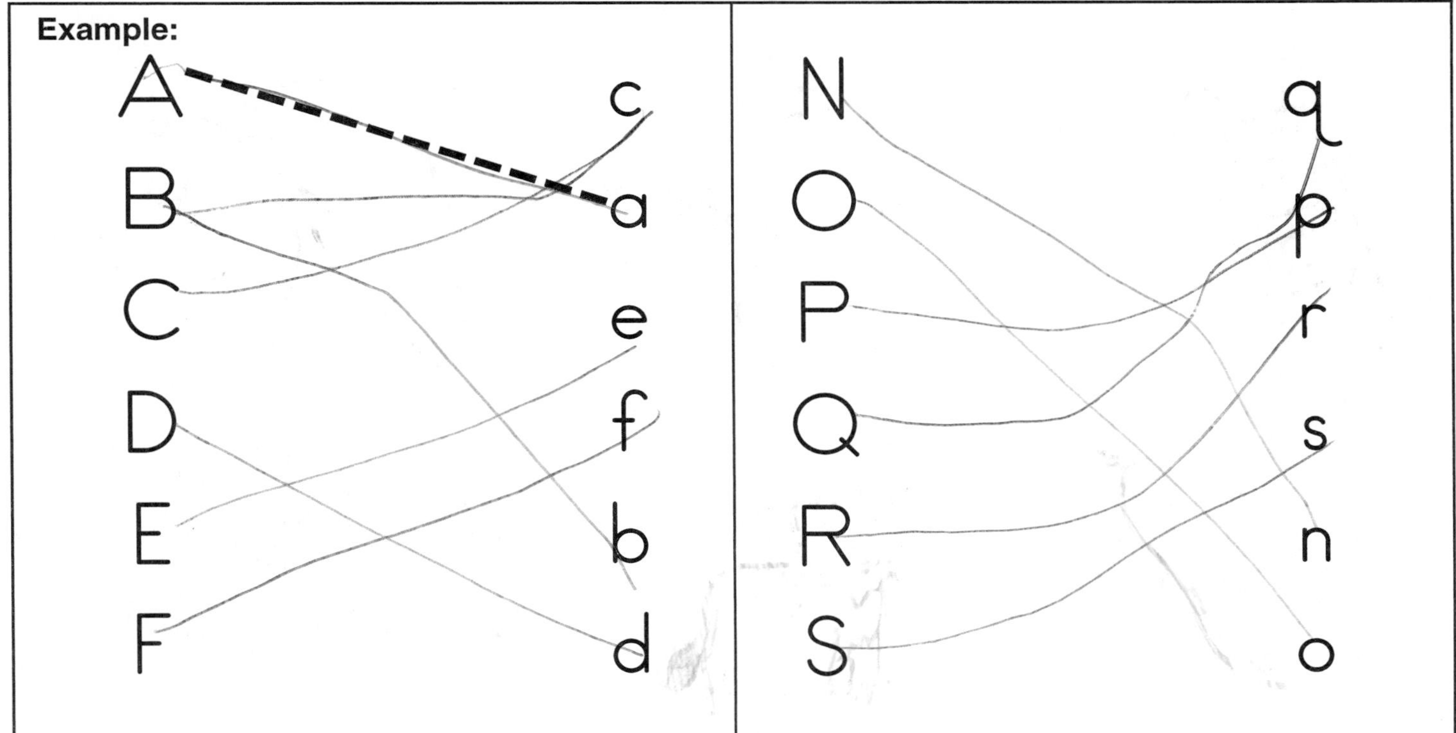

Mouse begins with the sound of (m). Color the mouse, then practice writing capital and lowercase (m's).

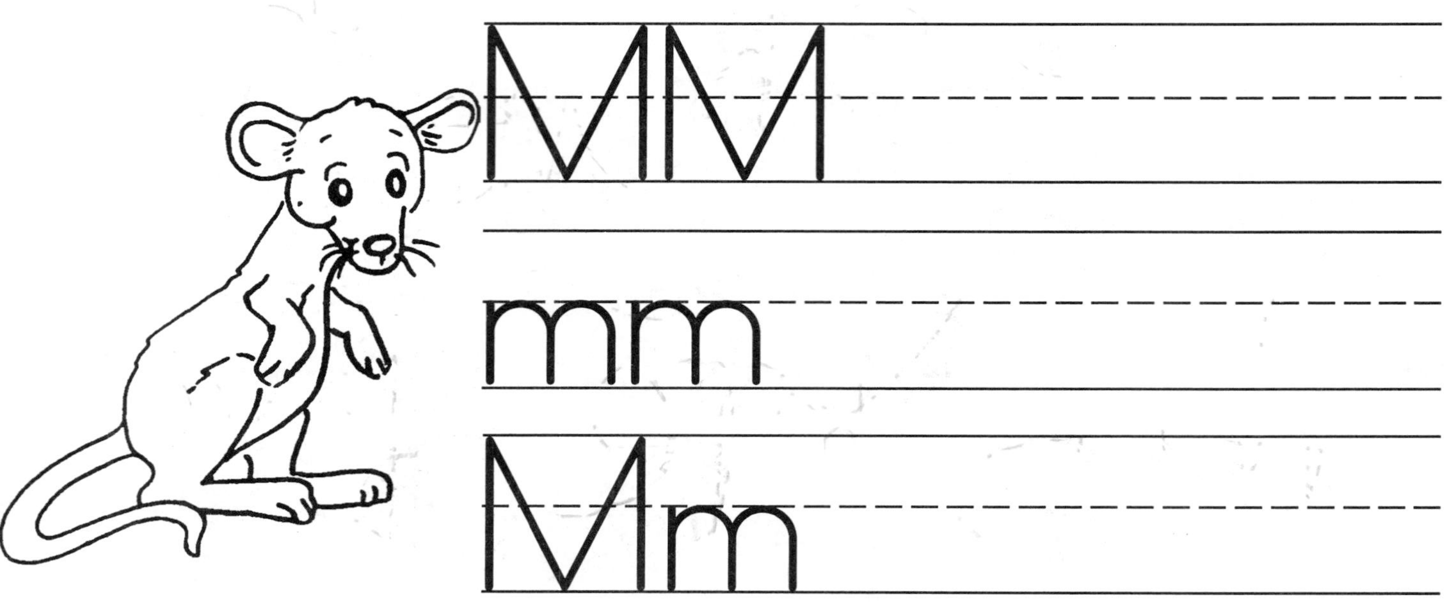

Now color all the objects below that begin with the sound of (m), like mouse.

Help Mother bird lay the right amount of eggs. Draw and color as many eggs in each nest as the number shows.

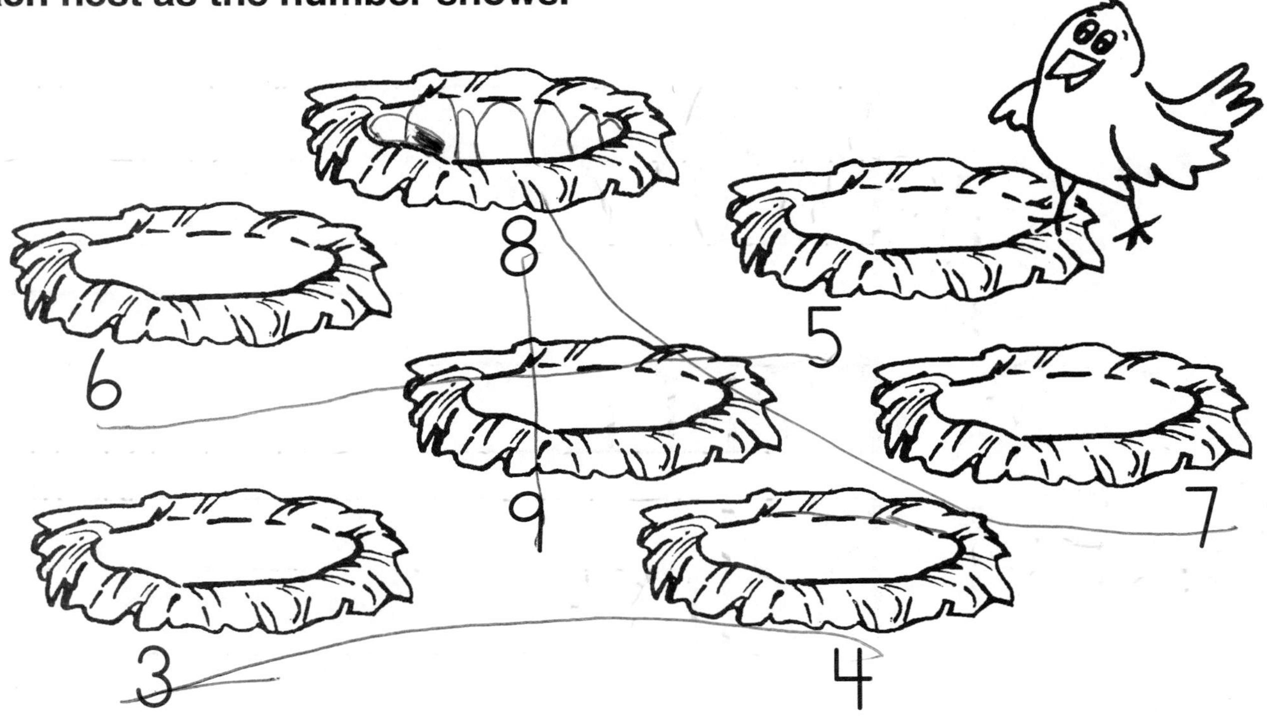

Draw a line from each capital letter to the matching lowercase letter.

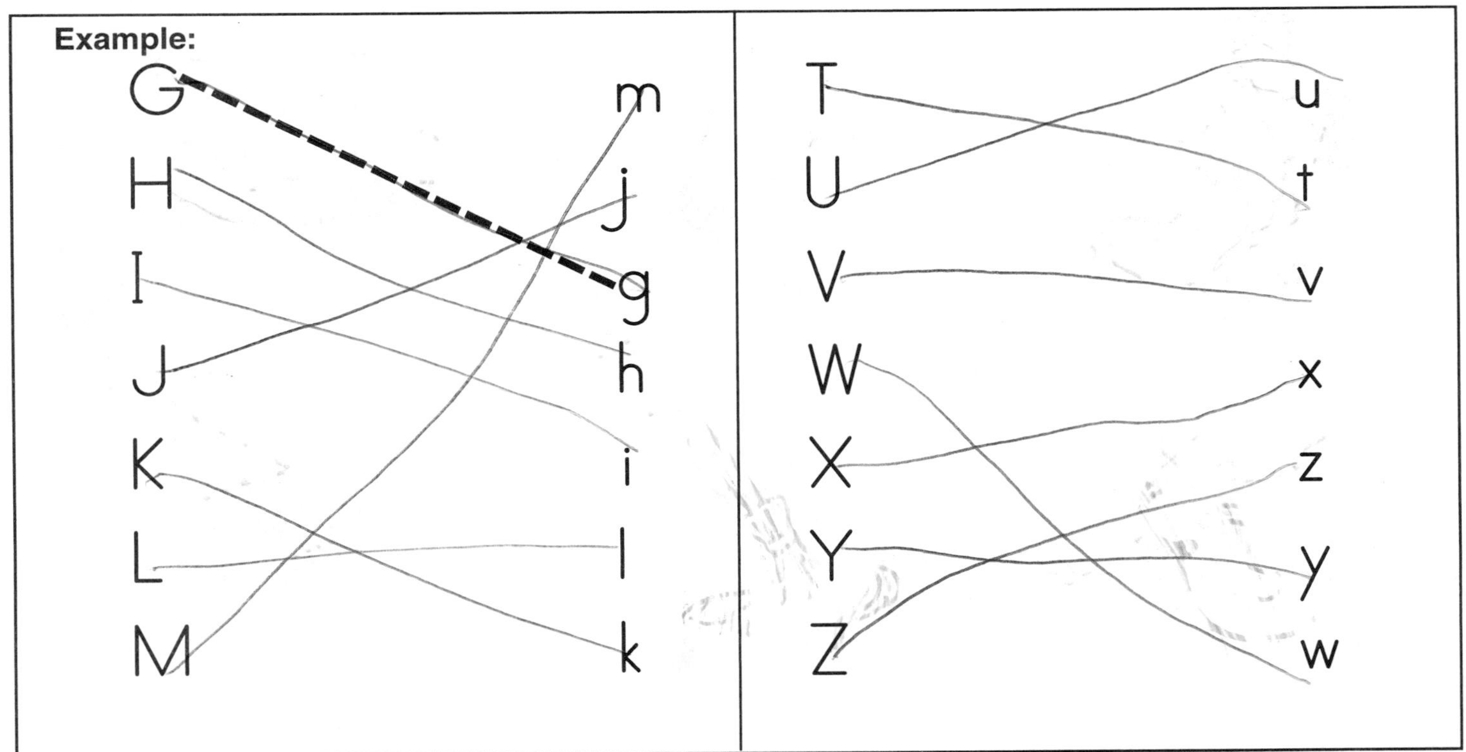

Nurse begins with the sound of (n). Color the nurse, then practice writing capital and lowercase (n's).

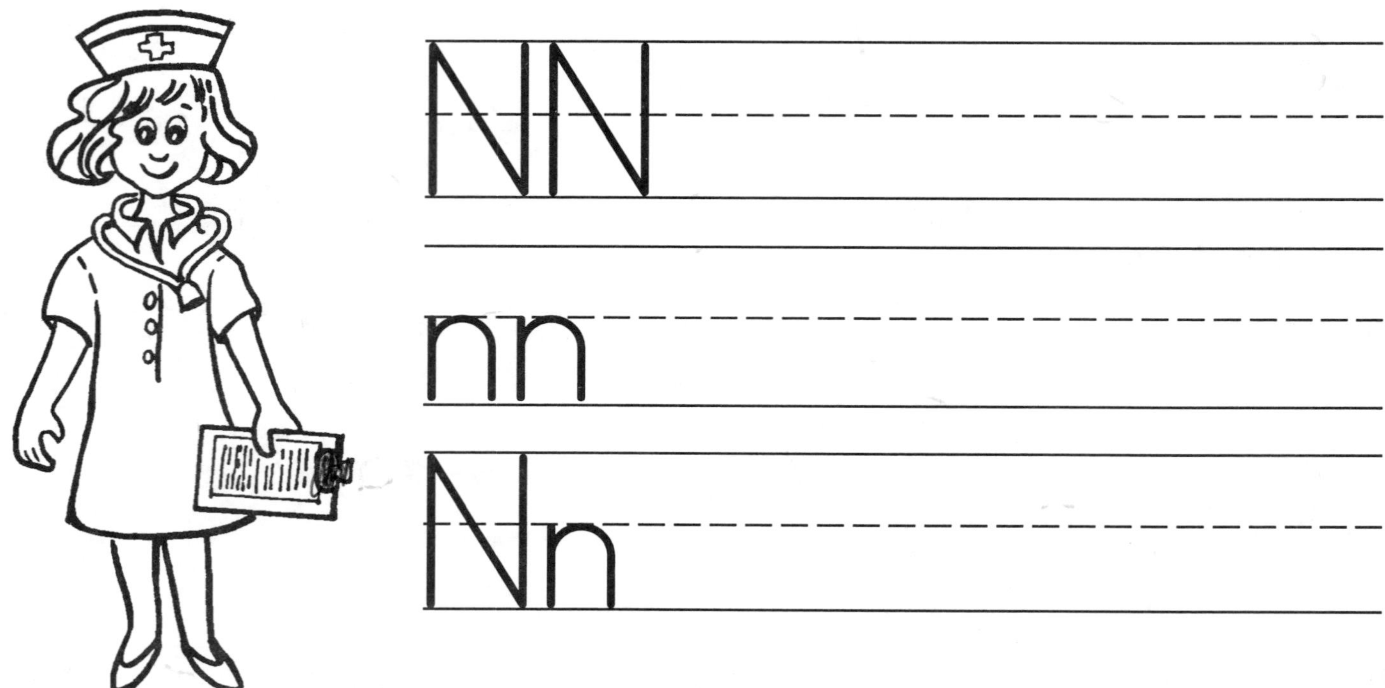

Now color all the objects below that begin with the sound of (n), like nurse.

Number recognition. Put a green circle around all of the 6's and an orange circle around all of the 9's.

3 6 7 2 6 9 6 9

6 4 9 3 9 5 0 2

9 6 8 6 9 9 6 9

Trace over the capital letters and write the matching lowercase letters beside them.

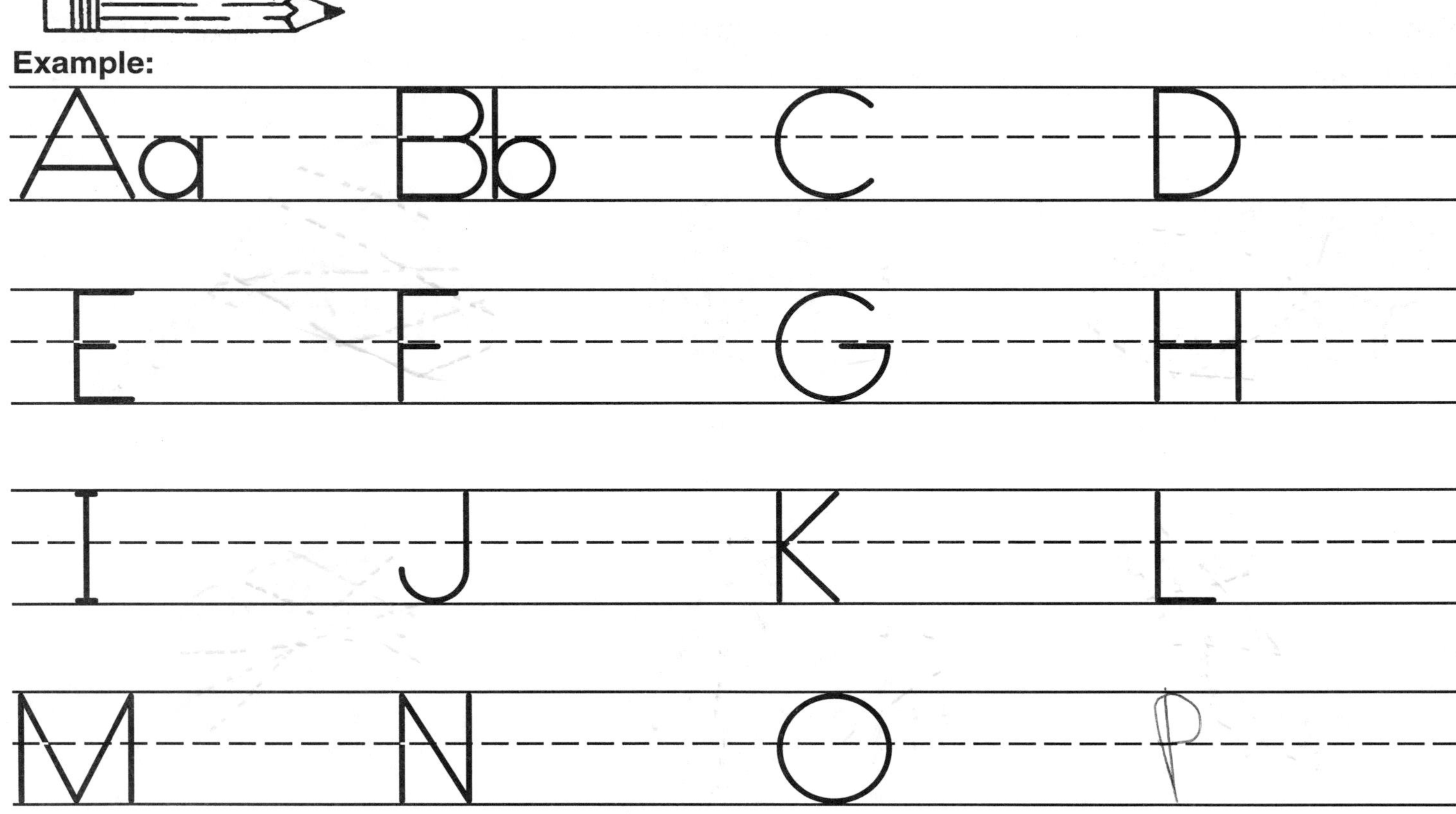

Peanuts begin with the sound of (p). Color the peanuts, then practice writing capital and lowercase (p's).

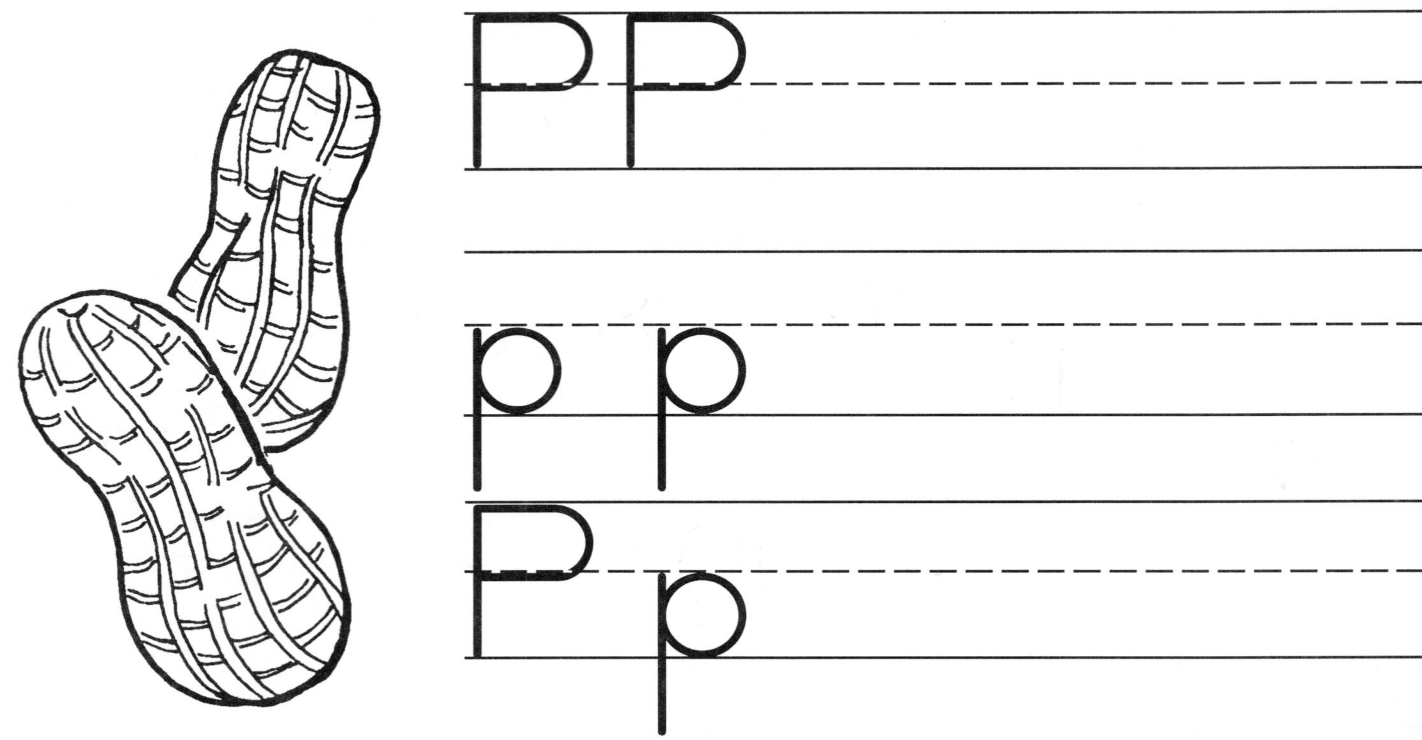

Now color all the objects below that begin with the sound of (p), like peanuts.

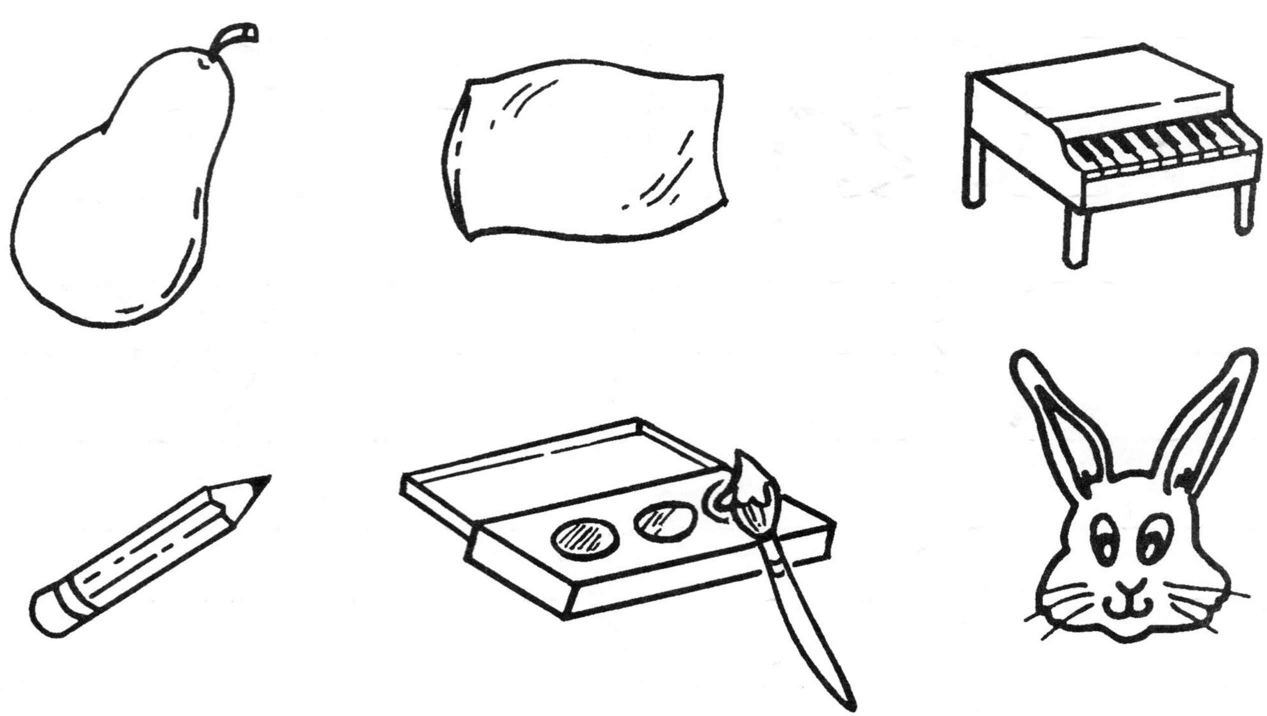

Number recognition. Say each number aloud.

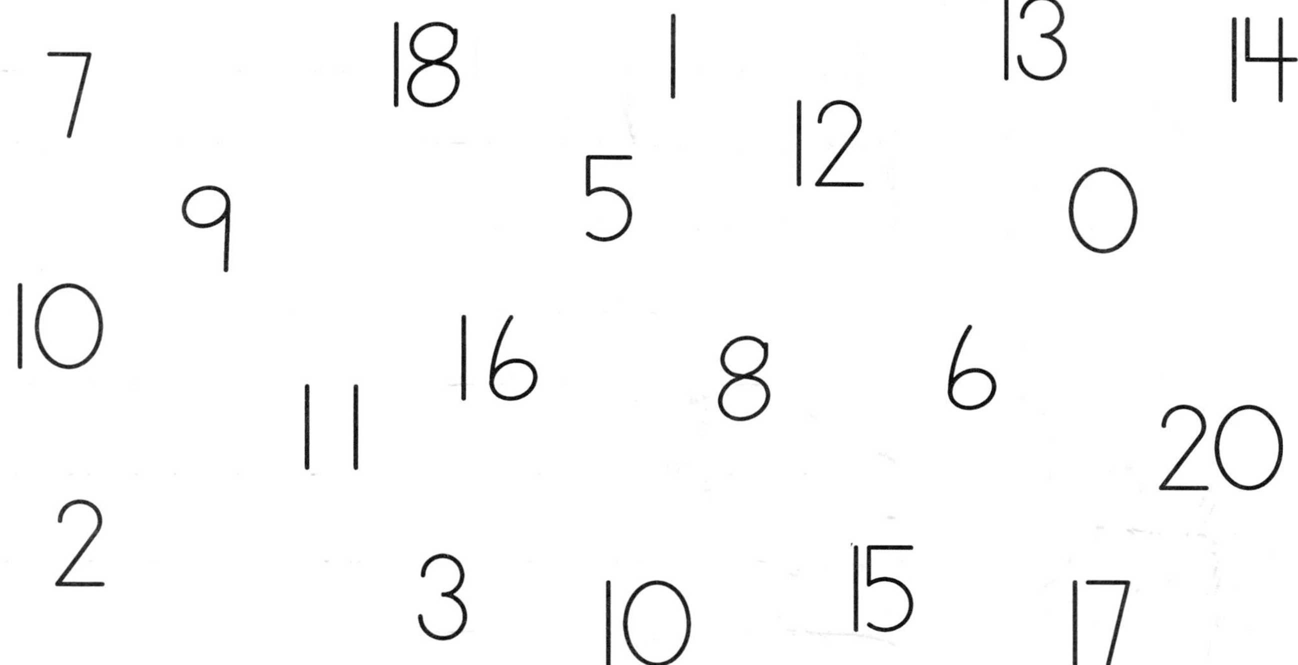

Trace over the capital letter and write the matching lowercase letter beside it.

Example:

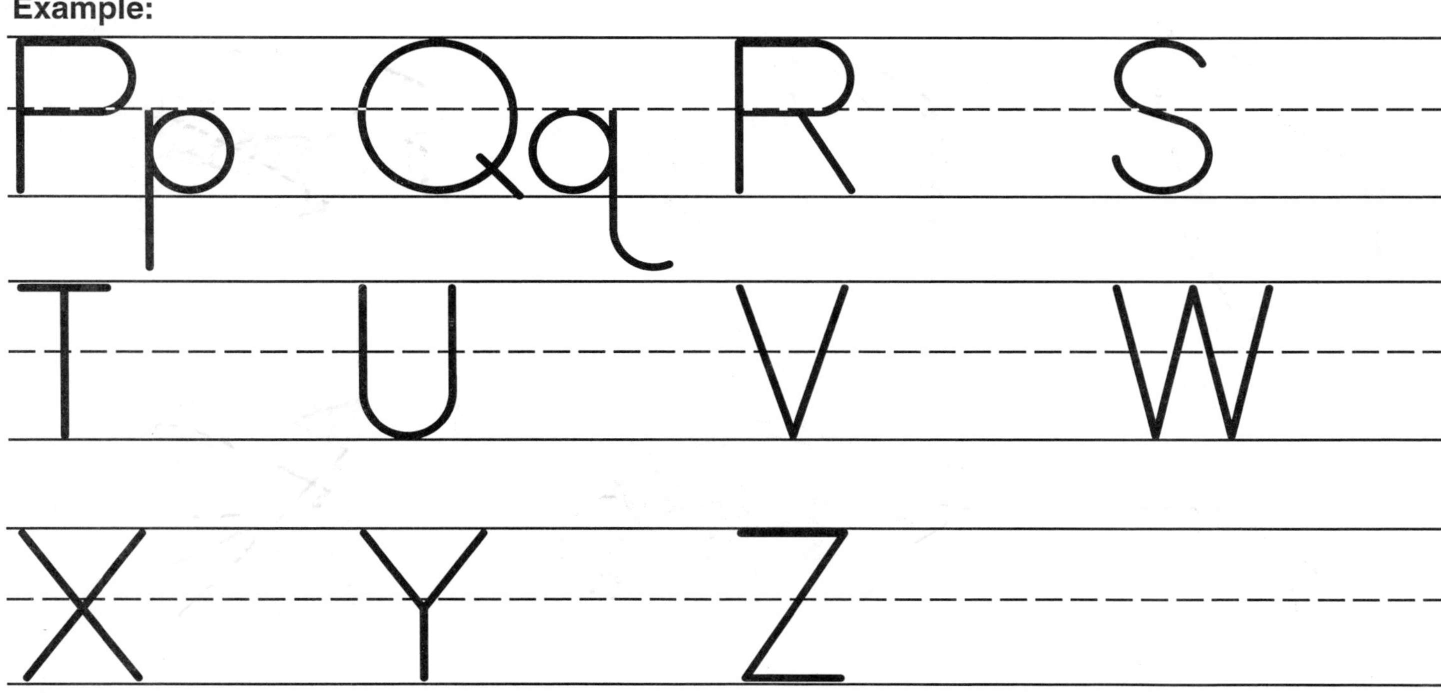

Queen begins with the sound of (q). Color the queen, then practice writing capital and lowercase (q's).

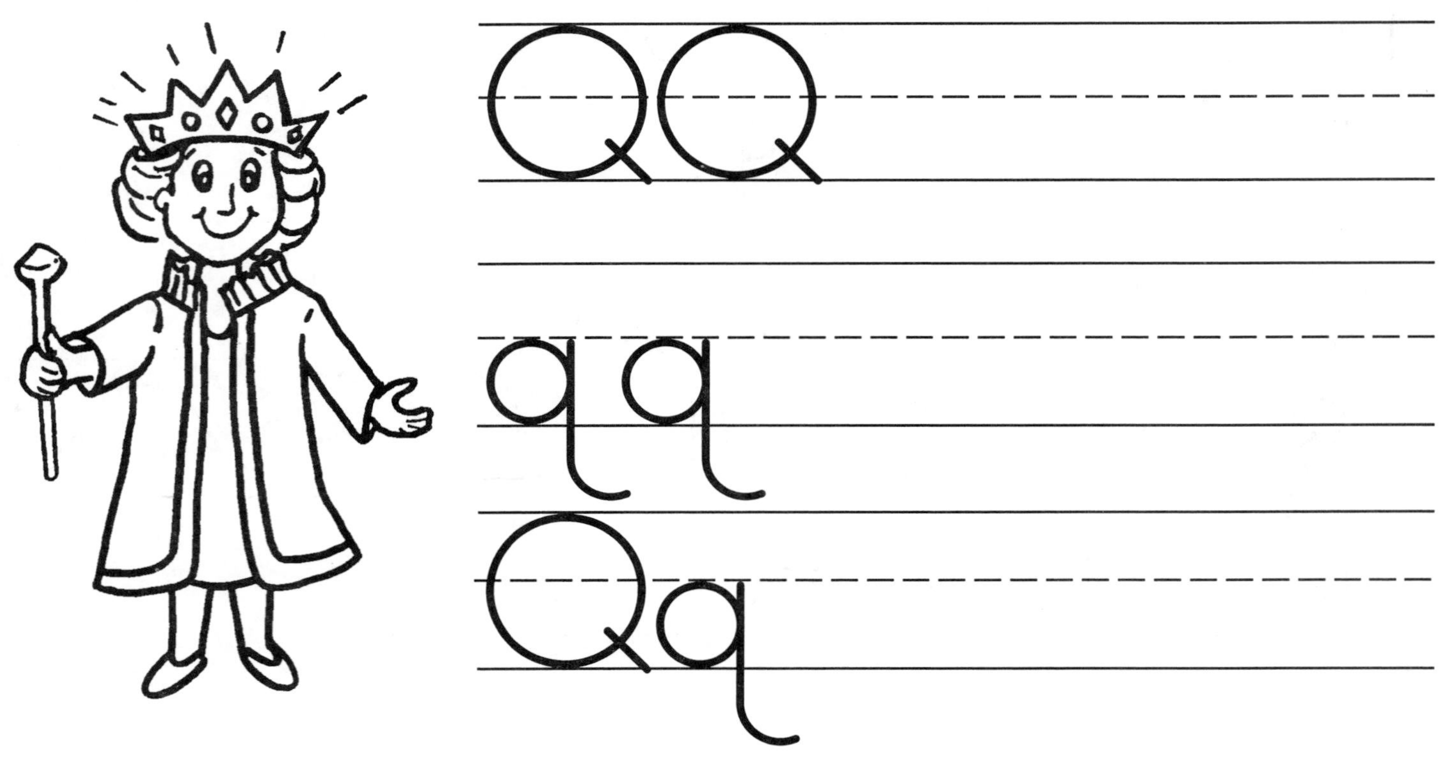

Now color all the objects below that begin with the sound of (q), like queen.

Write the number that comes next.

1 2 3 4 5 6 ___ ___

5 6 7 8 ___ ___ 11

0 1 2 3 4 ___ ___ ___

8 9 10 11 12 ___ ___

16 17 18 ___ ___ 21

Color the letters green and the numbers blue.

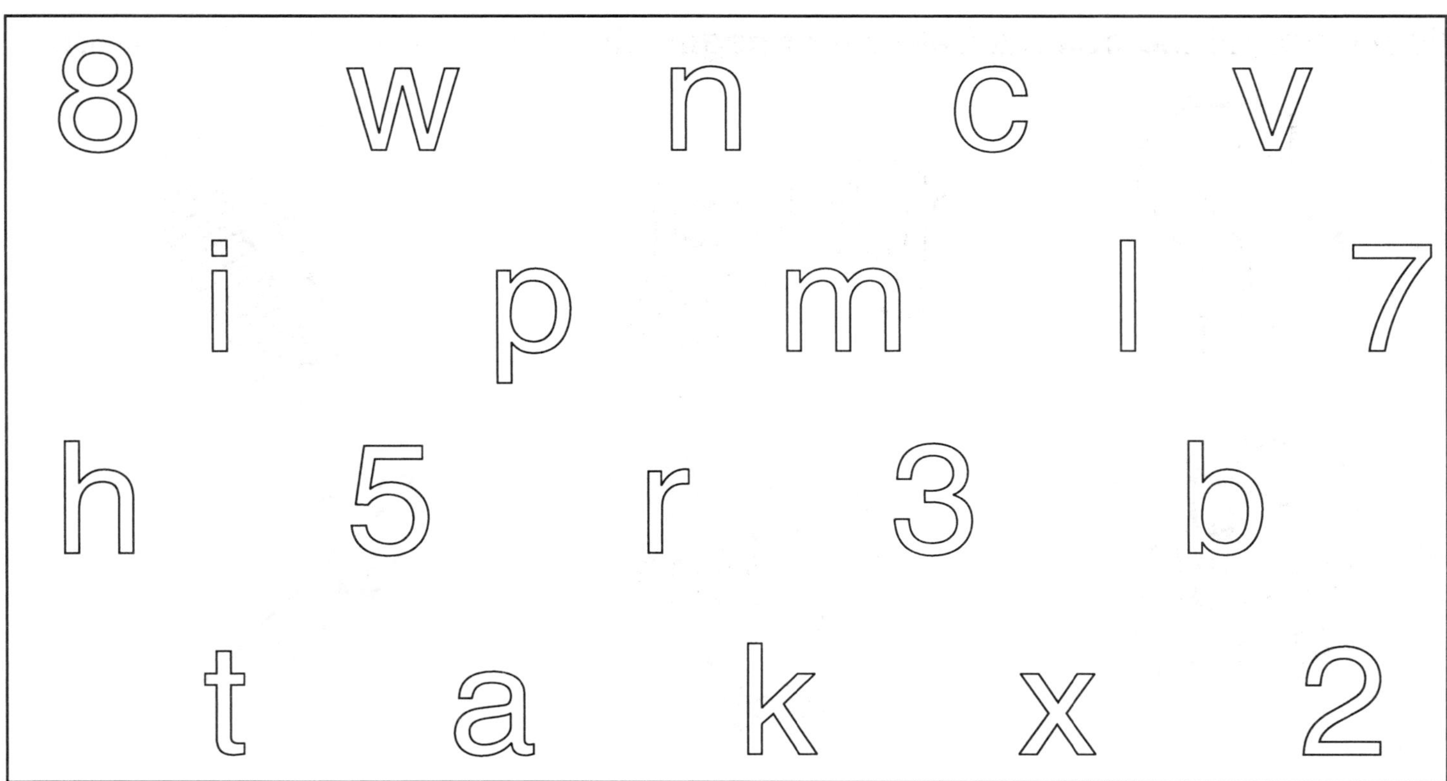

Ruler begins with the sound of (r). Color the ruler, then practice writing capital and lowercase (r's).

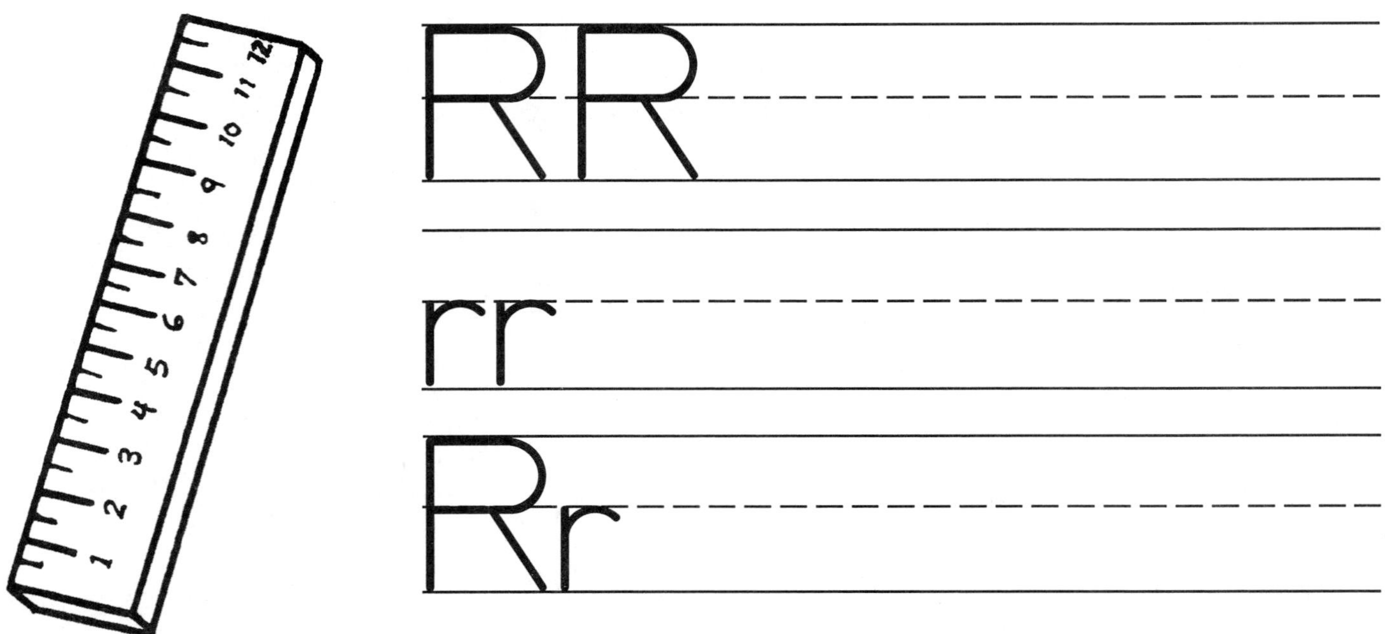

Now color all the objects below that begin with the sound of (r), like ruler.

Count the blocks and write the number in the blank provided.

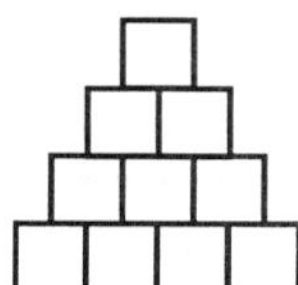 ________

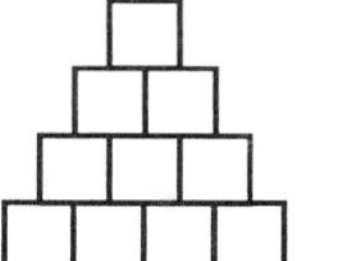 ________

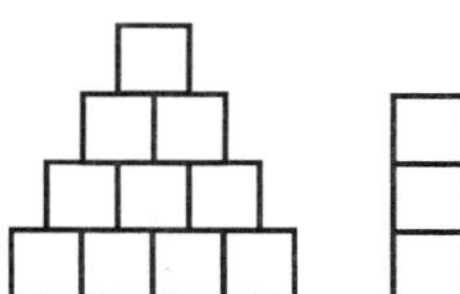 ________

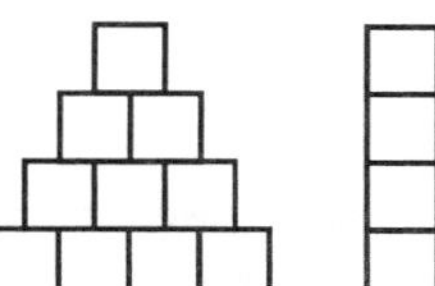 ________

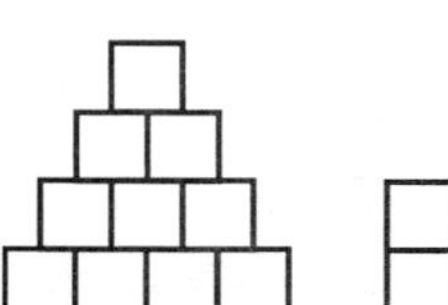 ________

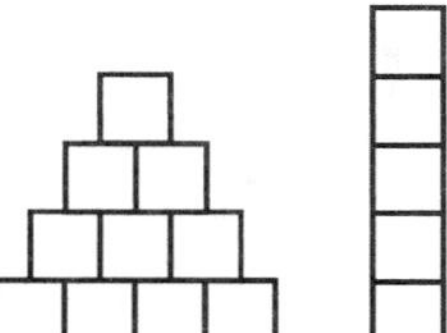 ________

Color the stars with matching capital and lowercase letters in them.

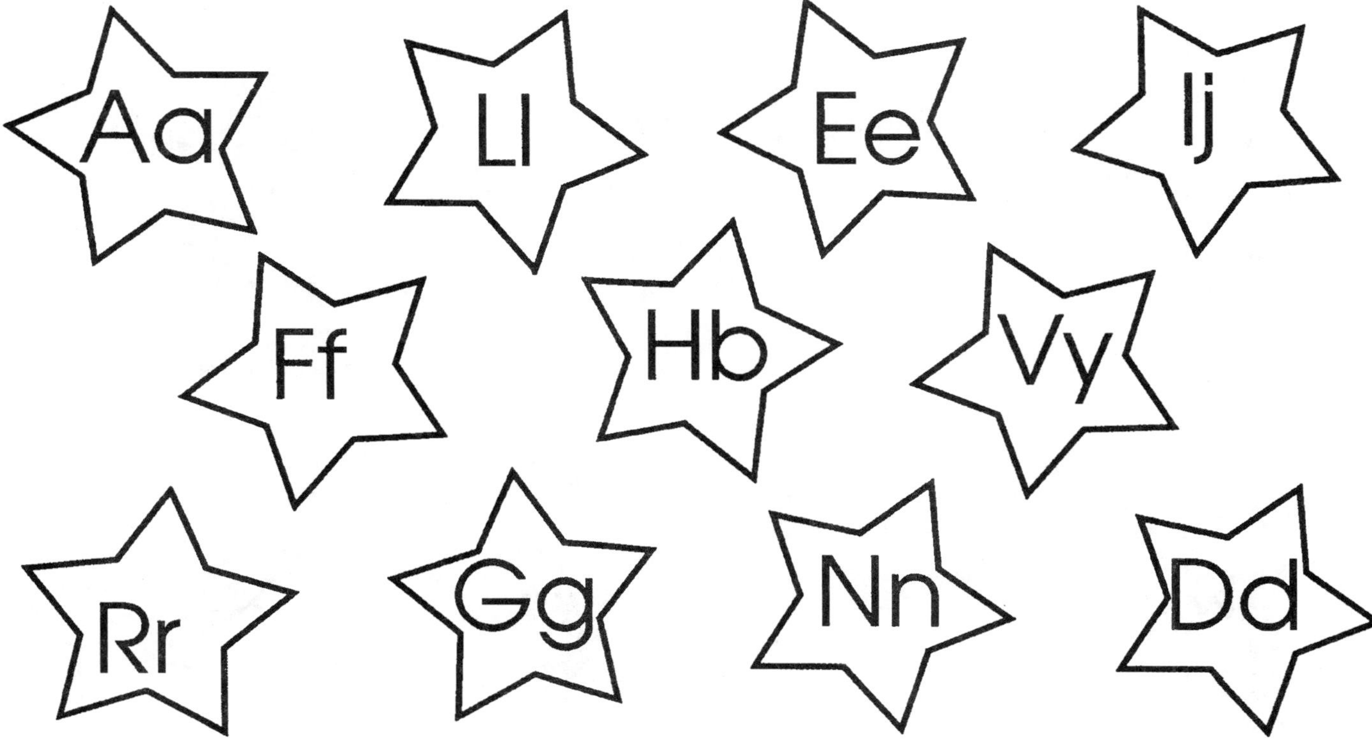

Sandwich begins with the sound of (s). Color the sandwich, then practice writing capital and lowercase (s's).

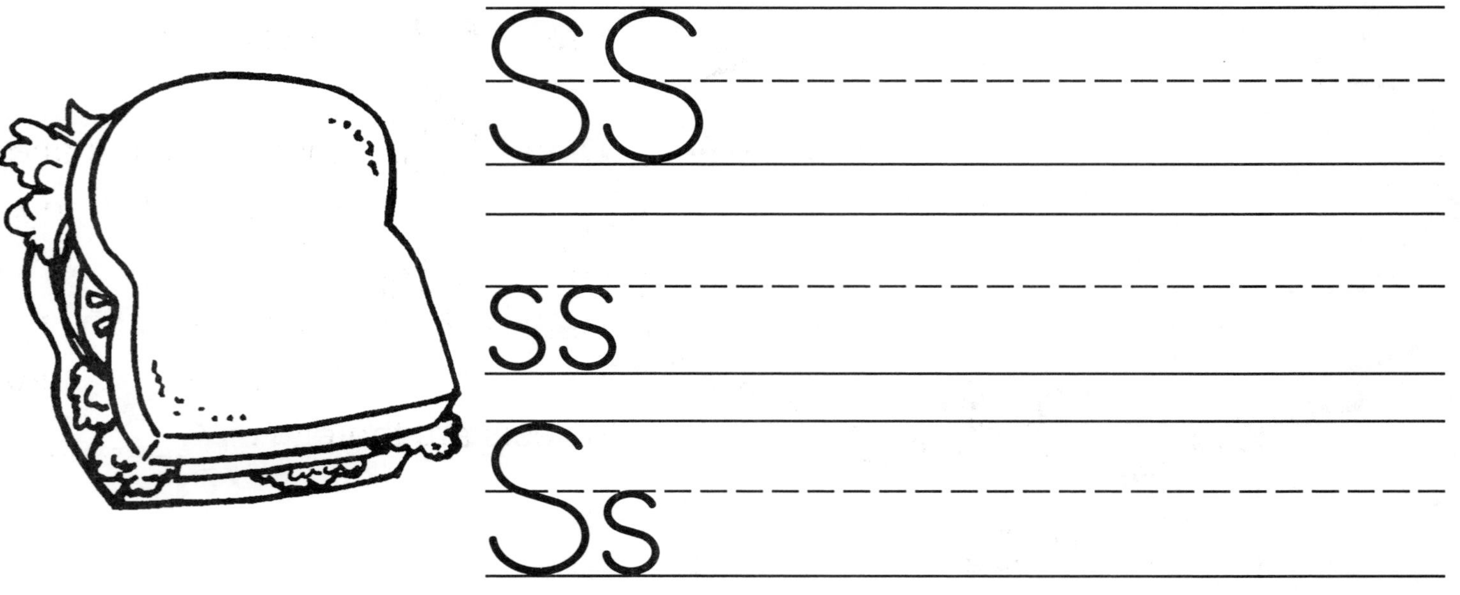

Now color all the objects below that begin with the sound of (s), like sandwich.

Draw and color.

Draw 9 apples in the tree.

Draw 3 nests in the tree.

Draw bird in the tree and 4 more birds flying.

Draw 7 flowers and color your picture. How many pictured objects are there in all? ________

Write the capital letter on the blank line that follows each letter in the alphabet.

Example:

A B ____ K L ____ C ____ X ____

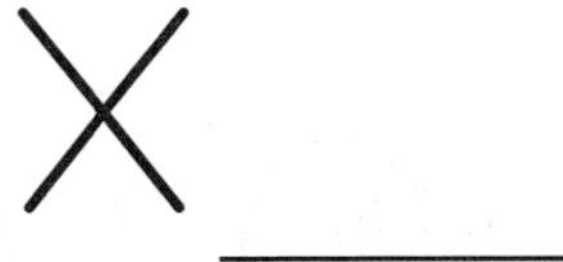

Q ____ E ____ N ____ L ____

G ____ U ____ I ____ O ____

D ____ M ____ S ____ Y ____

Television begins with the sound of (t). Color the television, then practice writing capital and lowercase (t's).

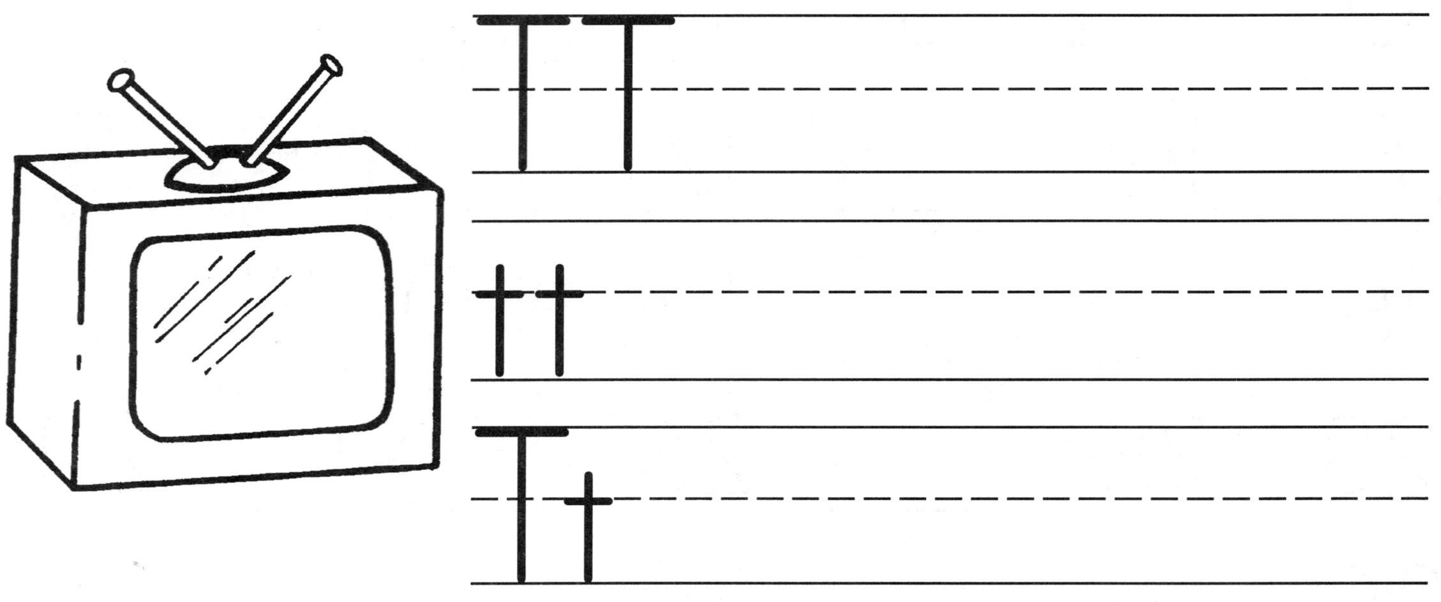

Now color all the objects below that begin with the sound of (t), like television.

Write the missing numbers.

0 1 2 3 4 ___ 6 7 ___

9 10 ___ 12 ___ 14 15

16 ___ ___ 19 20 21 ___

23 24 ___ 26 ___ ___ 29

30 31 ___ 33 ___ ___ 36

Draw the faces in each row that come next to finish the pattern.

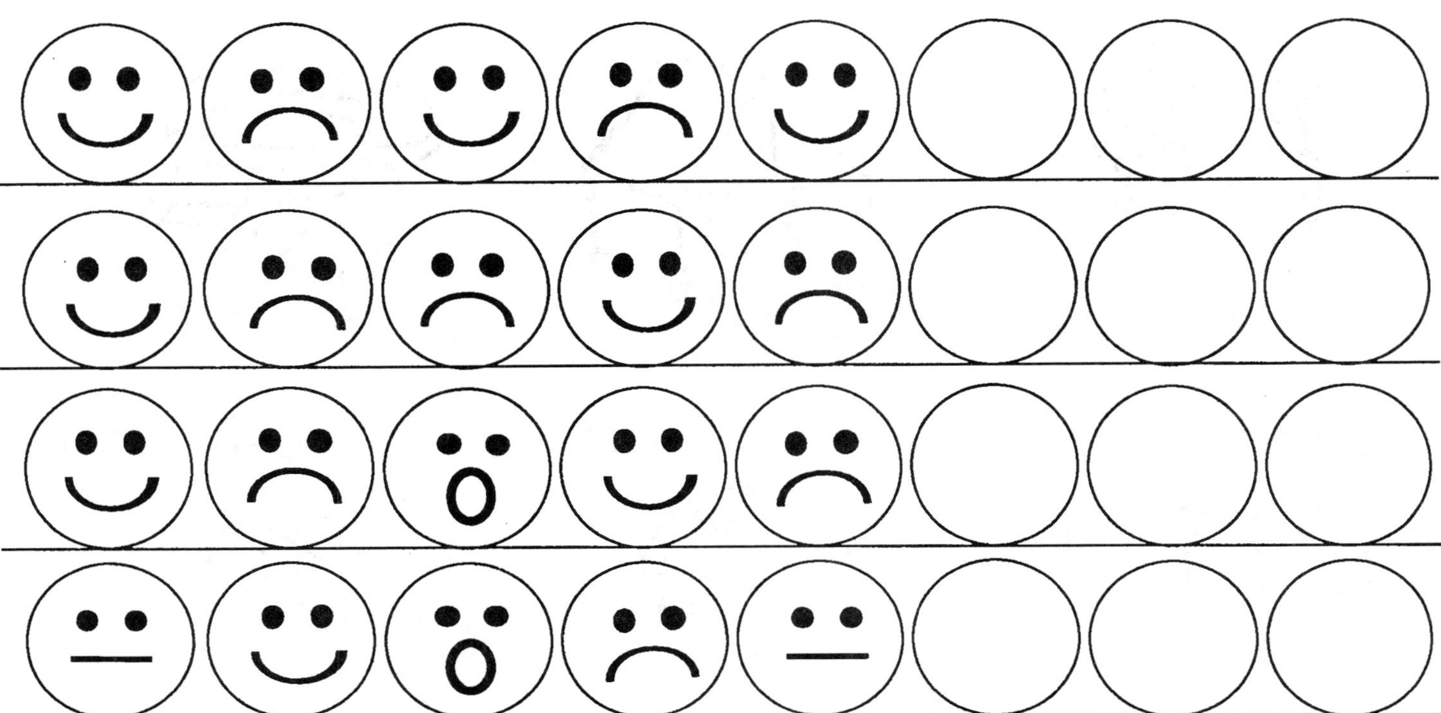

Valentine begins with the sound of (v). Color the valentine, then practice writing capital and lowercase (v's).

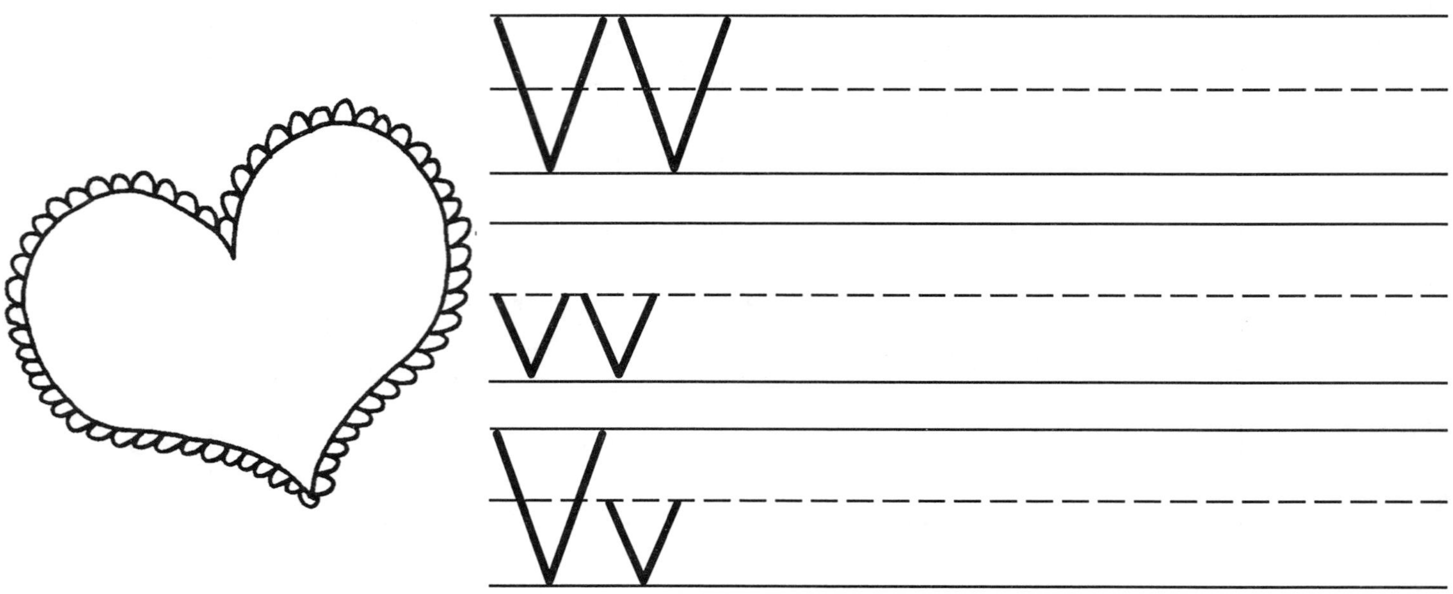

Now color all the objects below that begin with the sound of (v), like valentine.

Write the numbers 1 to 25 in the empty boxes.

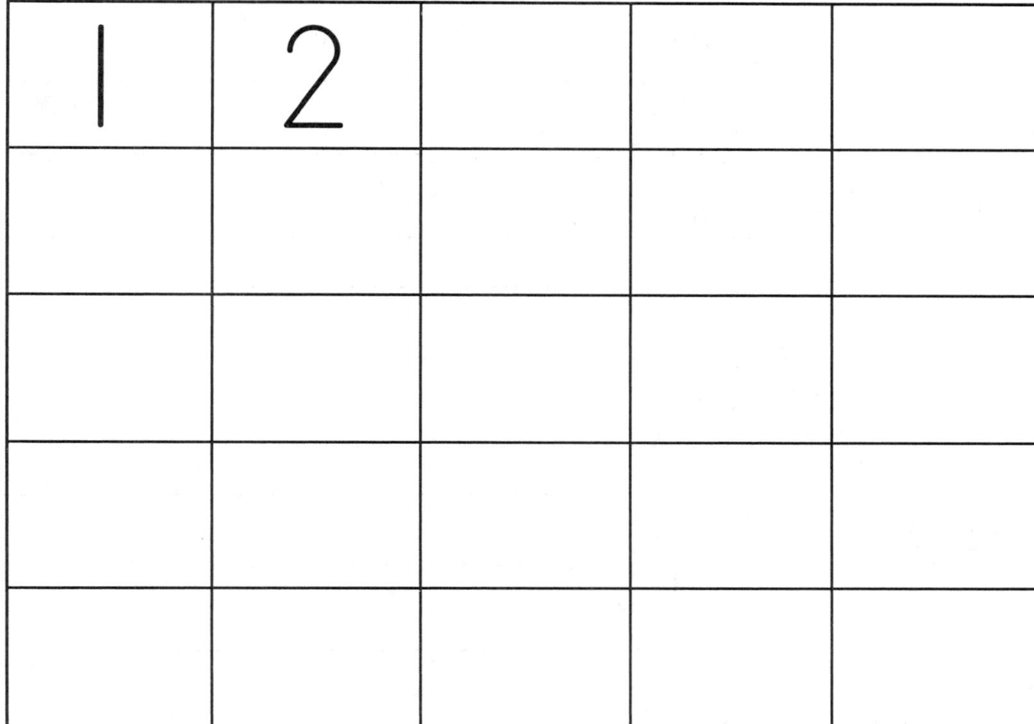

Finish drawing the other half of the pictures.

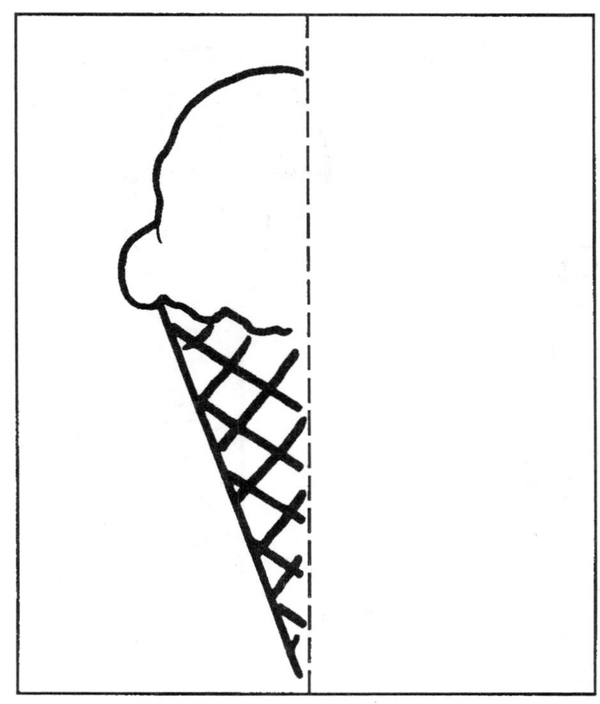

ice cream cone

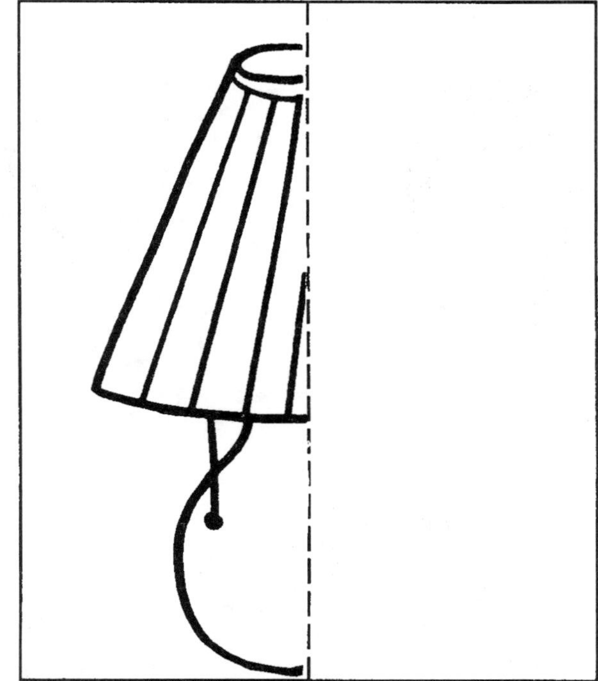

lamp

Find the objects with the beginning sound of the letter in each box. Color them.

s	
n	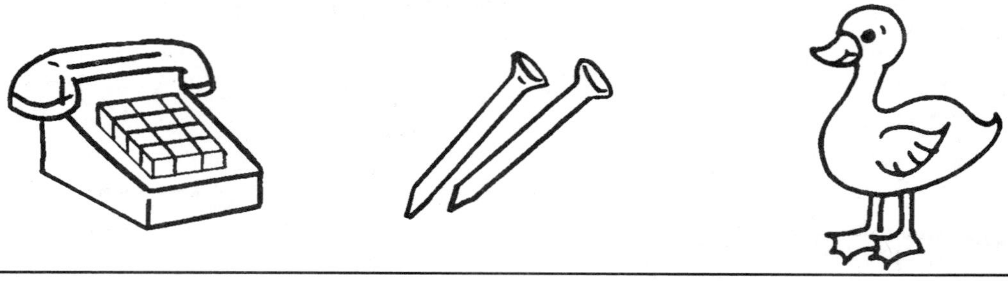
p	
t	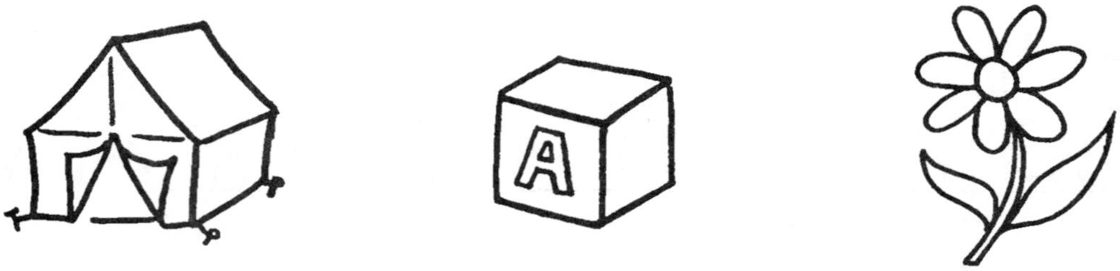
b	
m	

Find the hidden numbers from 0 to 12 and trace them in yellow. Now color the rest of the picture.

Write the lowercase letter on the blank line that follows each letter of the alphabet.

Example:

c d m n r ____ w ____

p ____ g ____ j ____ t ____

a ____ e ____ l ____ y ____

u ____ d ____ h ____ f ____

Find the objects with the beginning sound of the letter in each box. Color them.

f	
c	
d	
g	
h	
l	

Connect the dots in alphabetical order. Color the picture.

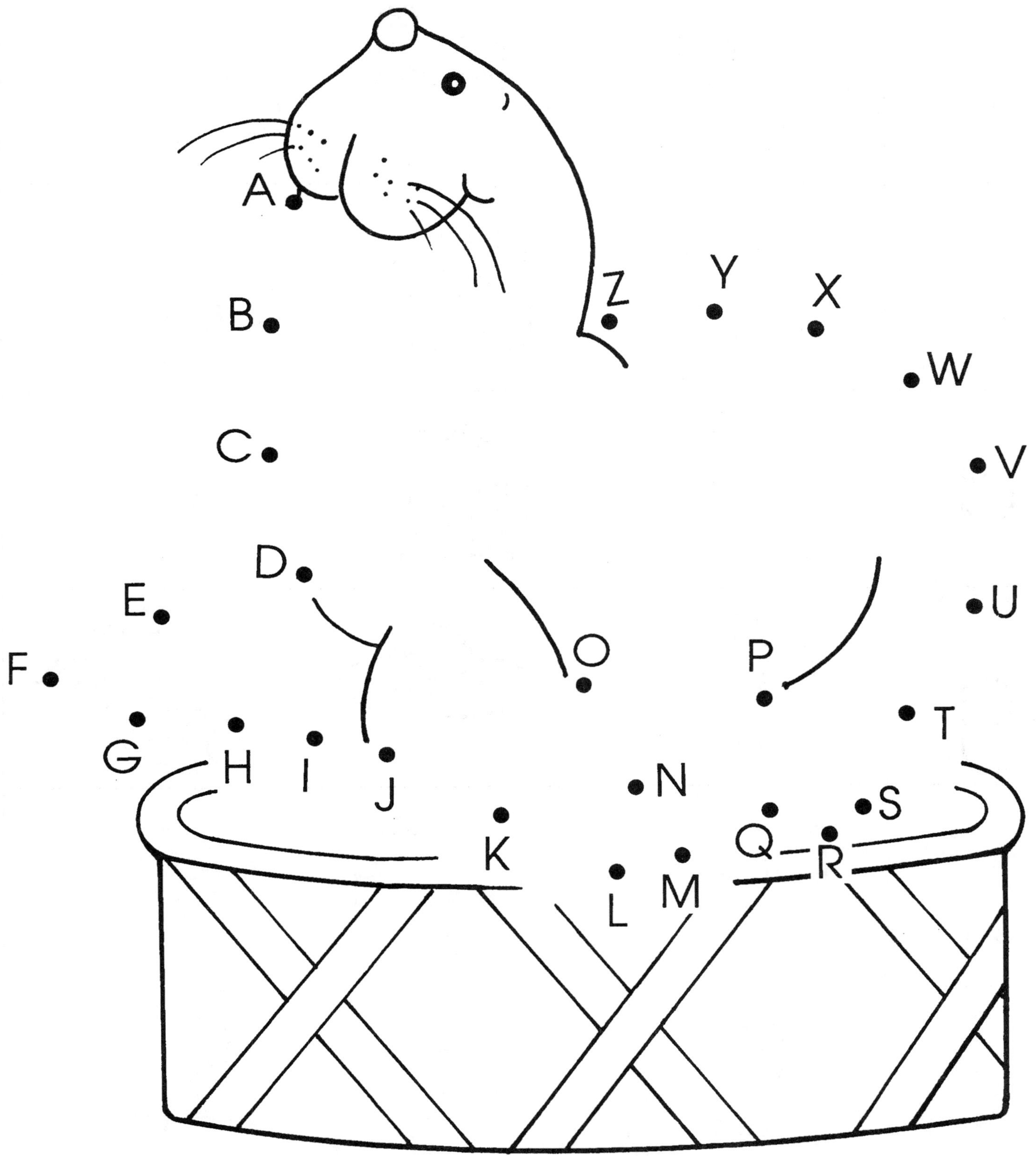

Connect the dots in alphabetical order. Color the picture.

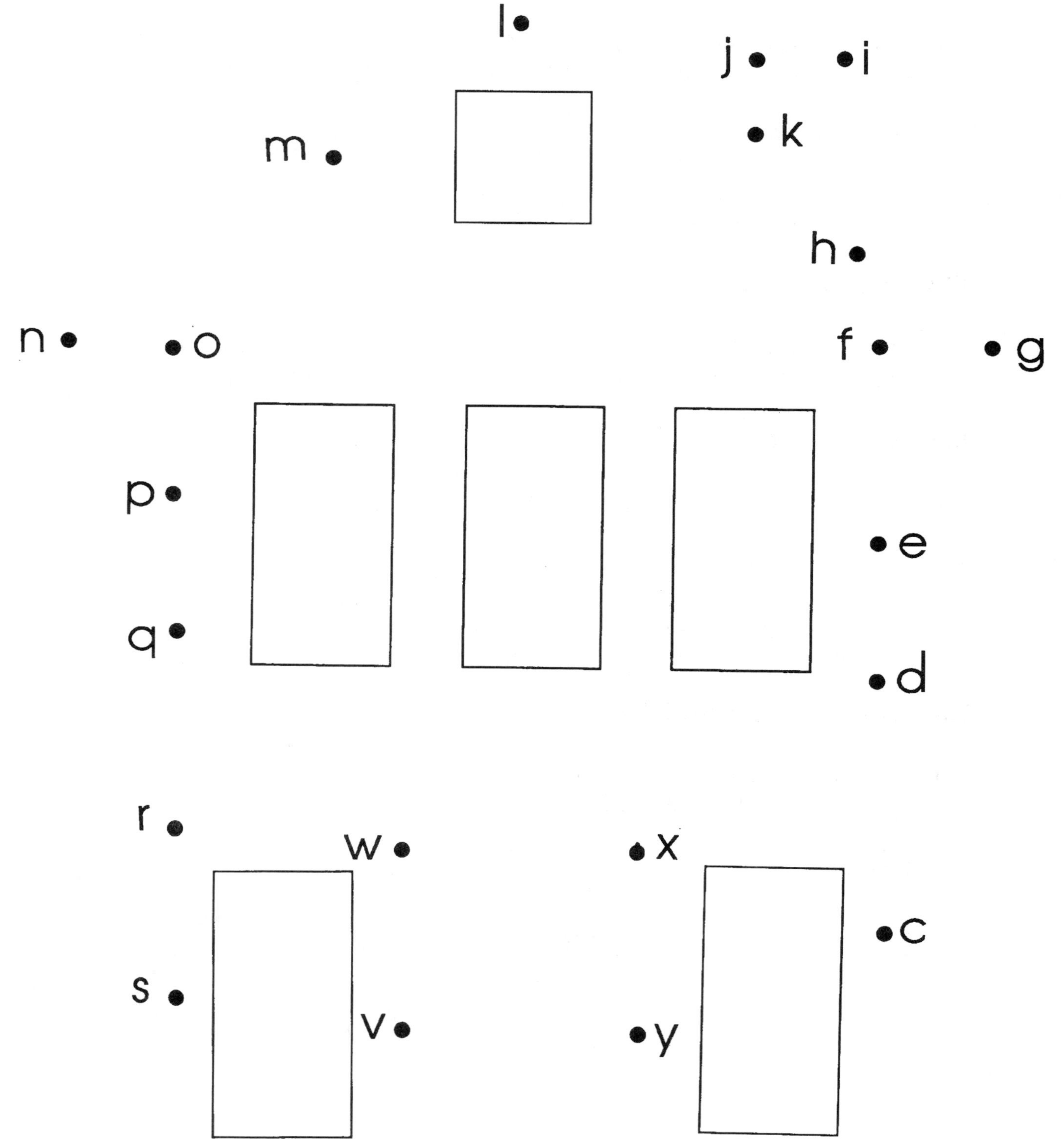

Enrichment Activities for Alphabet Cards

How much exposure your child has to the alphabet will affect how many of these activities are meaningful and/or necessary.

Letter Recognition

1. Go through the cards with your child. Separate those he/she does not know and review those he/she does know.

Alphabet Slap Game

2. Spread out the cards. Say a letter and have your child slap the card. Continue until all or most of the cards are identified.

Alphabet Partners

3. Match capital letters with lowercase letters.

Alphabetical Order

4. Mix the cards up and have your child put them back in alphabetical order, from A to Z.

Reversed Alphabetical Order

5. Mix the cards up and have your child put them in alphabetical order going backward, from Z to A.

Missing Letter

6. Put the letters in alphabetical order. Have your child close his/her eyes while you remove one or more cards. Have your child open his/her eyes and identify the missing letter or letters.

7. Have your child choose the alphabet cards to spell his/her name or the names of family members.

8. Identify which letters are vowels (a, e, i, o, u) and which ones are consonants (the other letters of the alphabet). Explain that letters have letter names as well as letter sounds. Have your child divide the alphabet cards into these two groups.

Alphabet Flash Cards to cut out and practice with.

A	B	C
D	E	F
G	H	I
J	K	L

M	N	O
P	Q	R
S	T	U
V	W	X

Y	Z	a
b	c	d
e	f	g
h	i	j

k	l	m
n	o	p
q	r	s
t	u	v

w	x	y
z		

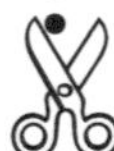

Summer Activity Contract & Calendar

Month____________________

My parents and I decided that if I complete 20 days of *Summer Bridge Activities*™ and read ______ minutes a day, my incentive/reward will be:

____

Child Signature____________________ Parent Signature____________________

Day	I have completed one day of activities (Color the Star)	I have completed ______ minutes of reading (Color the Book)	Parent Initials
1			
2			
3			
4			
5			
6			
7			
8			
9			
10			

Day	I have completed one day of activities (Color the Star)	I have completed ______ minutes of reading (Color the Book)	Parent Initials
11			
12			
13			
14			
15			
16			
17			
18			
19			
20			

Have a Fun Day...Discover Something New!

Fun Activity Ideas to Go Along with the Second Section

1. Decorate your bike. Have a neighborhood parade.
2. Catch a butterfly.
3. Get the neighborhood together and play hide-and-seek.
4. Take a tour of the local hospital.
5. Check on how your garden is doing.
6. Make snow cones with crushed ice and punch.
7. Go on a bike ride.
8. Run through the sprinklers.
9. Create a family symphony with bottles, pans, and rubber bands.
10. Collect sticks and mud. Build a bird's nest.
11. Help plan your family grocery list.
12. Go swimming with a friend.
13. Clean your bedroom and closet.
14. Go to the local zoo.
15. In the early morning, listen to the birds sing.
16. Make a cereal treat.
17. Read a story to a younger child.
18. Lie down on the grass and find shapes in the clouds.
19. Color noodles with food coloring. String them for a necklace, or glue a design on paper.
20. Organize your toys.

Finish writing the numbers on the clock. Color the (big) minute hand red. Color the (small) hour hand blue.

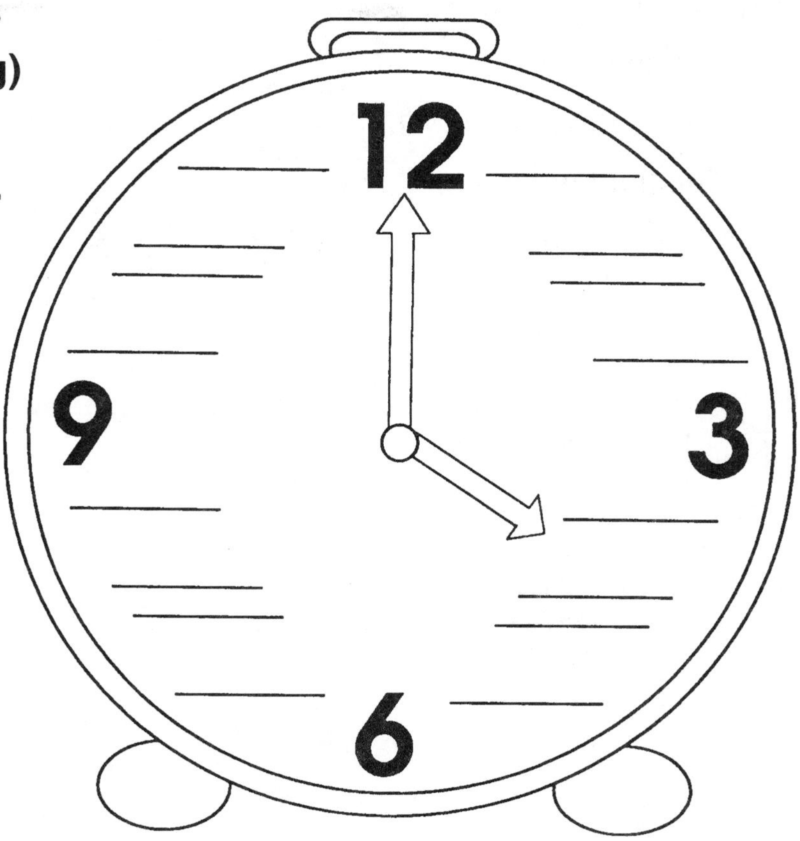

Trace and color the words and pictures with the matching crayon color.

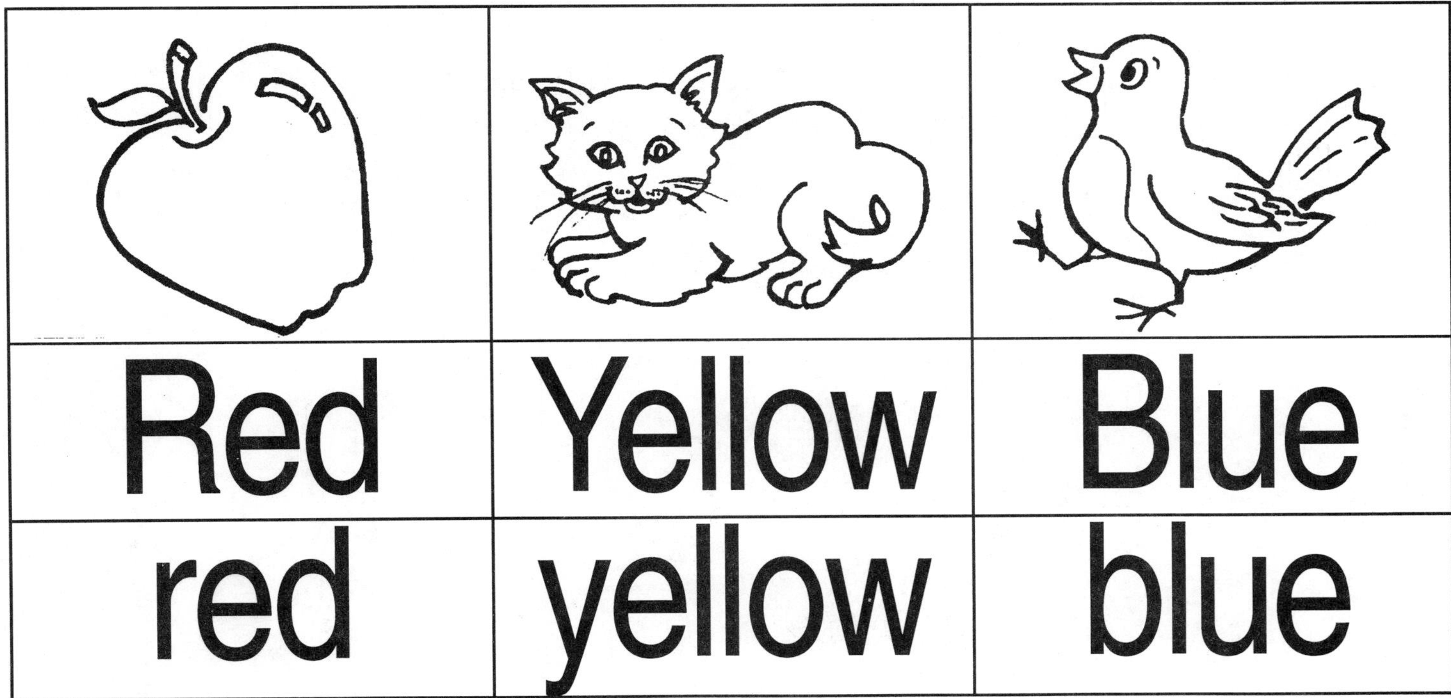

Red	Yellow	Blue
red	yellow	blue

Watermelon begins with the sound of (w). Color the watermelon, then practice writing capital and lowercase (w's).

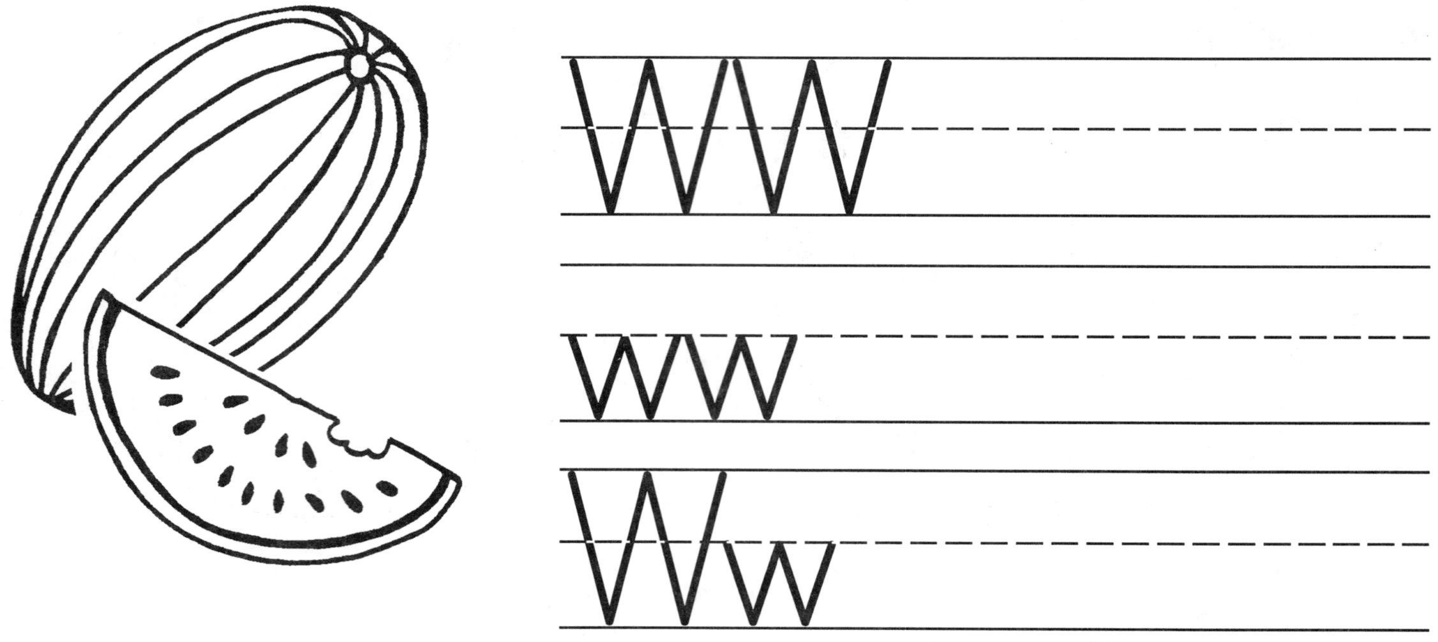

Now color all of the objects below that begin with the sound of (w), like watermelon.

Trace the numbers on the clock. Draw minute and hour hands so the clocks show the correct time. Color the minute hand red. Color the hour hand blue.

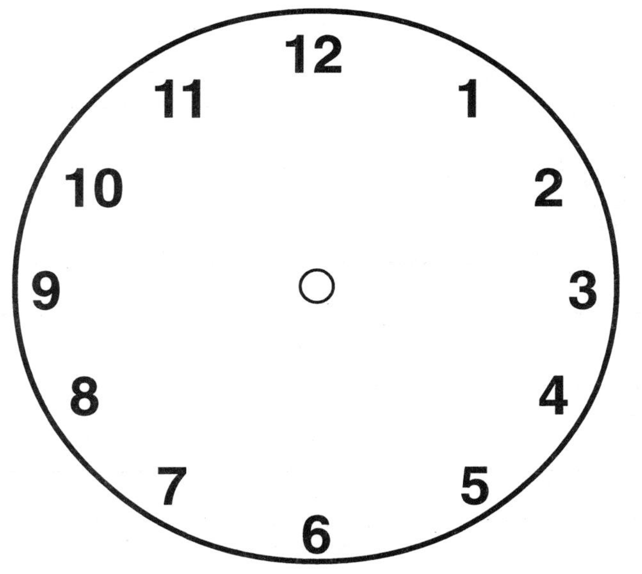

Time to wake up.

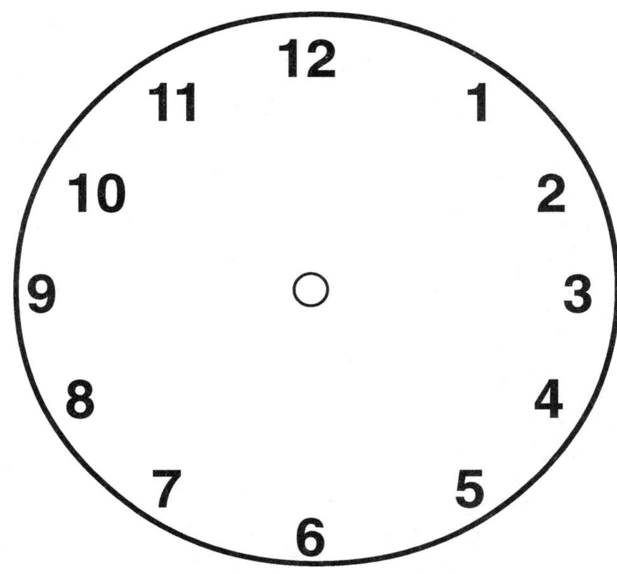

Time to go to bed.

Trace and color the words and pictures with matching crayon color.

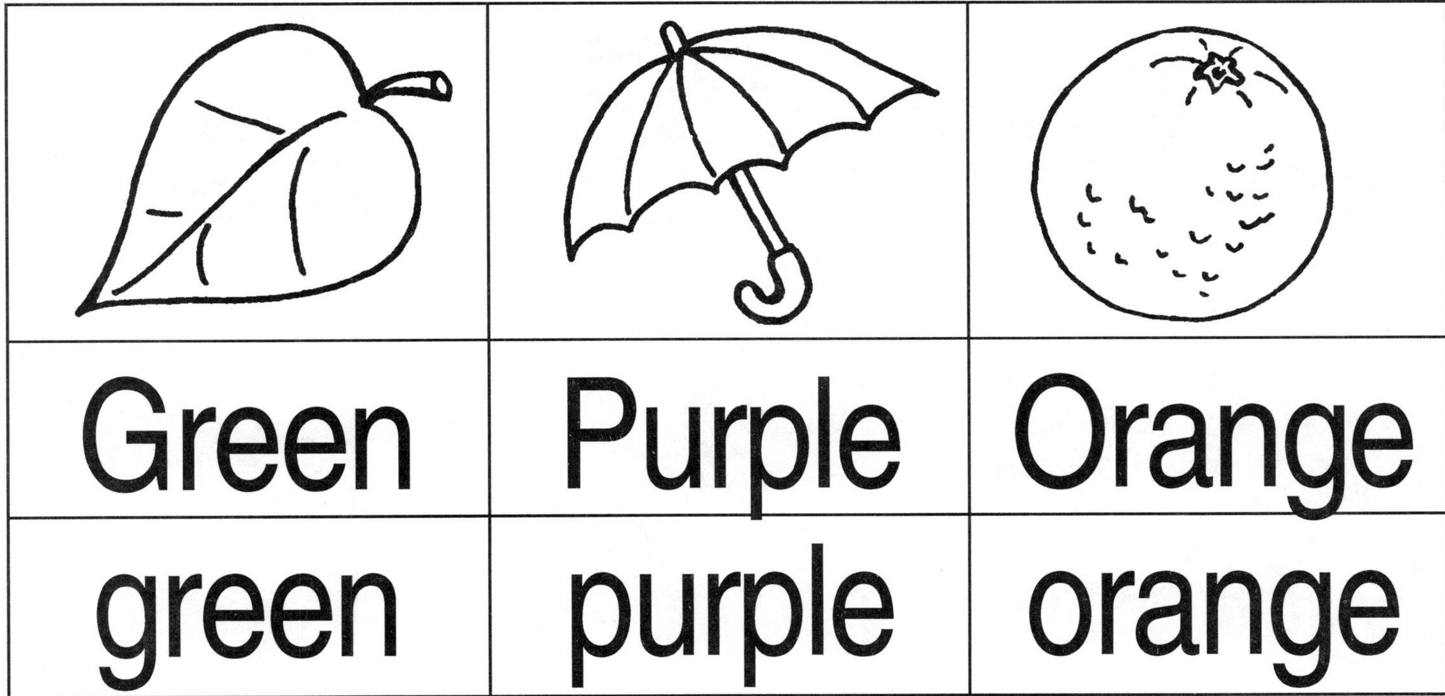

X-ray begins with the sound of (x). Color the x-ray picture, then practice writing capital and lowercase (x's).

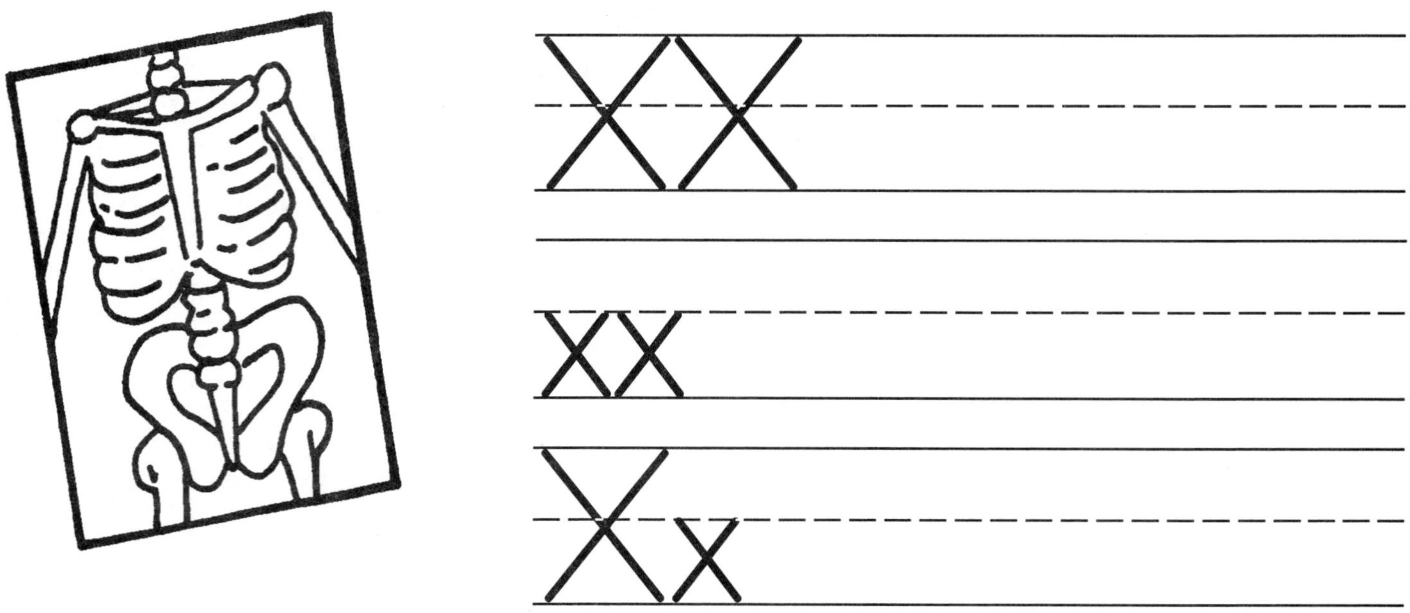

Now color all of the objects below that *end* with the sound of (x), like ox.

What time is it? Look at each clock and write the time it shows.

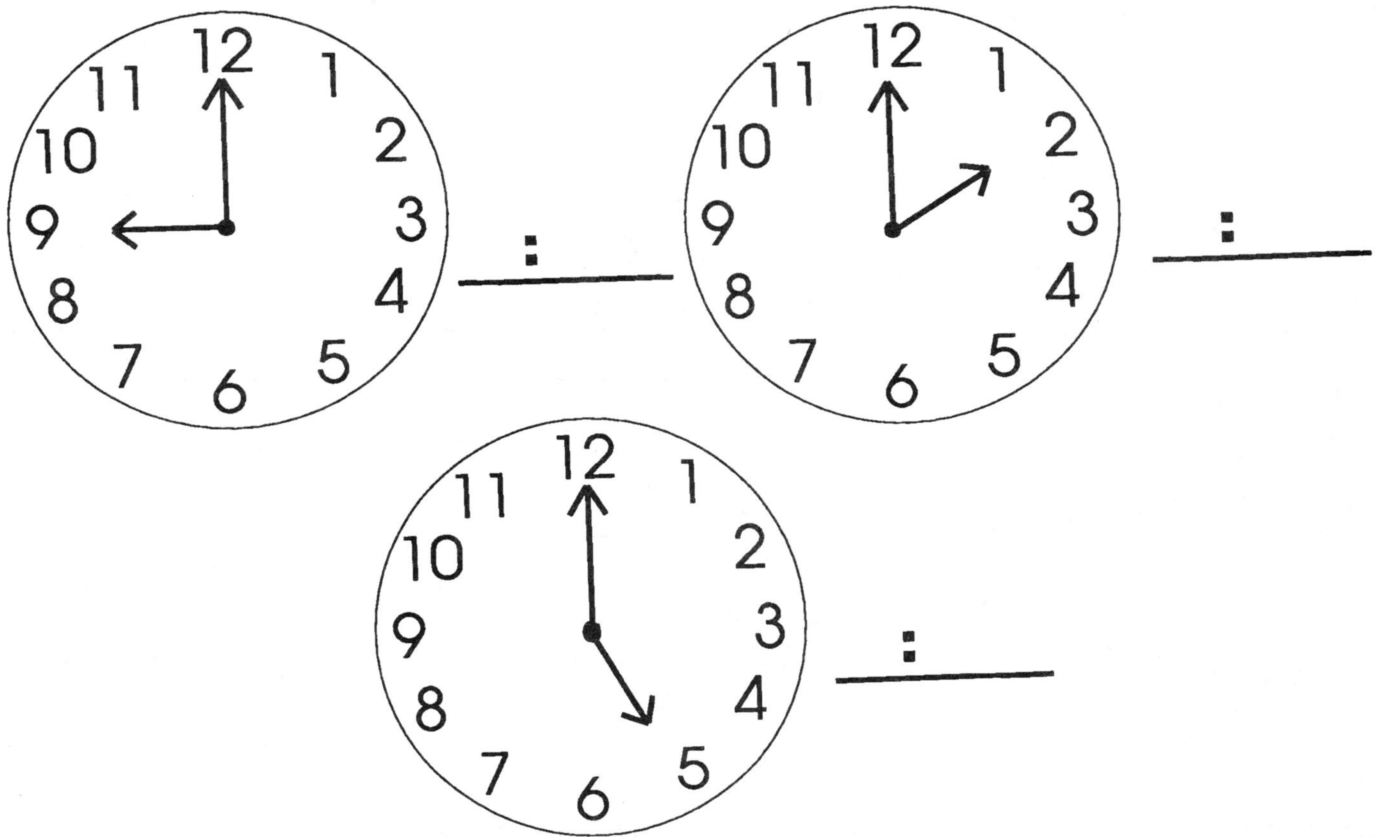

Trace and color the words and pictures with matching crayon color.

Brown	Violet	Black
brown	violet	black

Yo-yo begins with the sound of (y). Color the yo-yo, then practice writing capital and lowercase (y's).

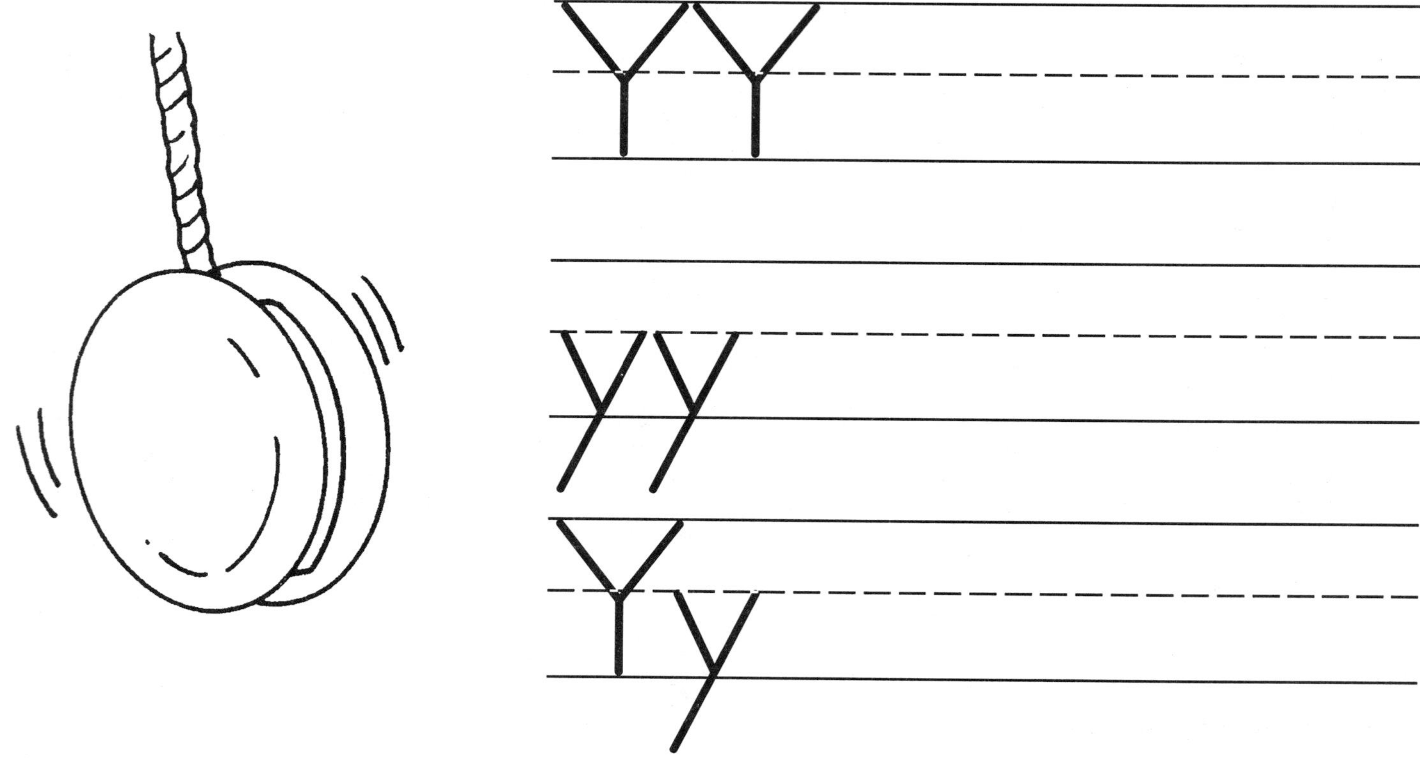

Now color all of the objects below that begin with the sound of (y), like yo-yo.

Count the dots and write the answer on the line below.

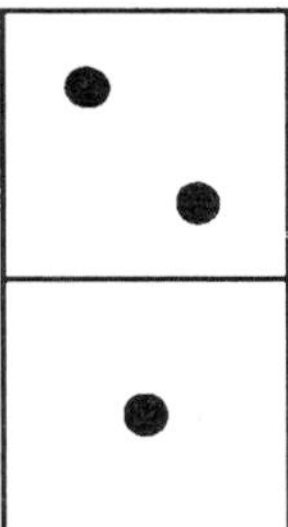 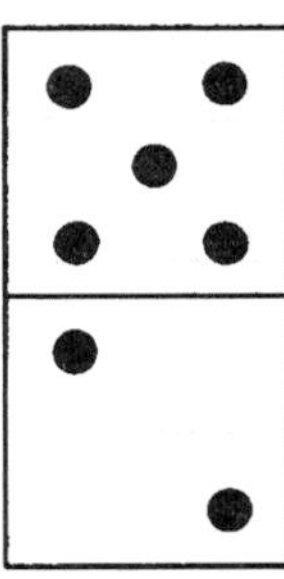 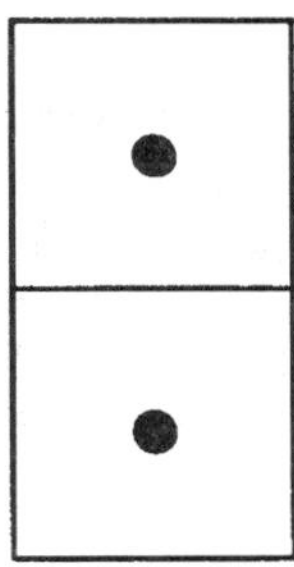 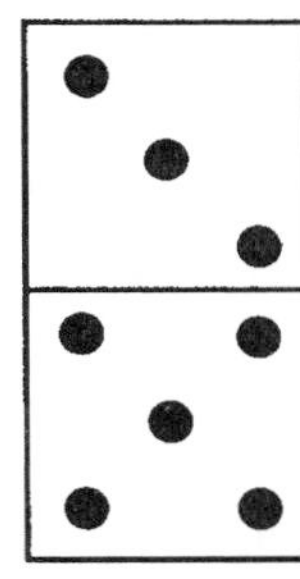 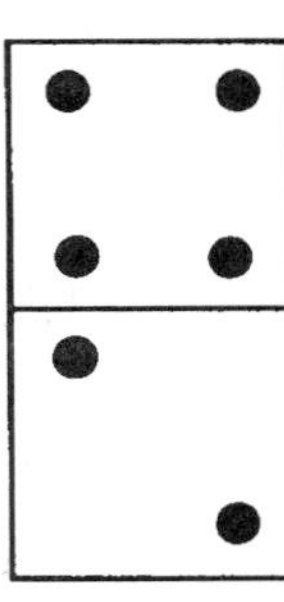

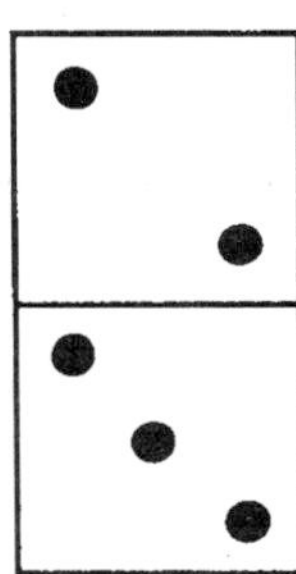 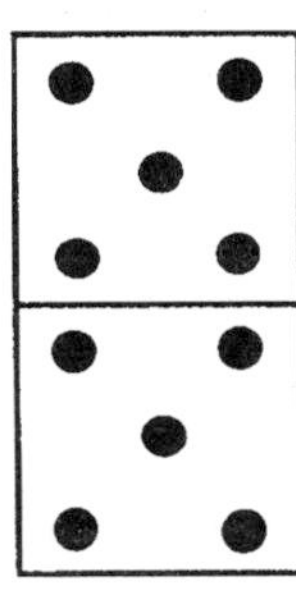 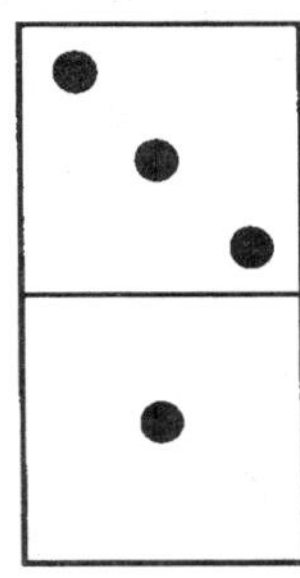 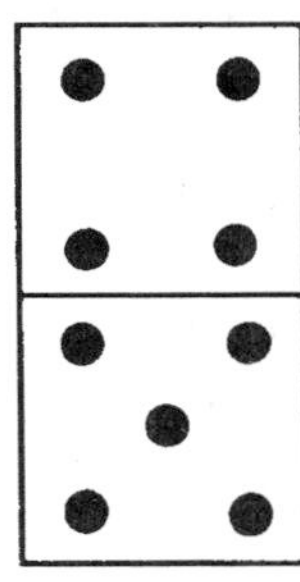 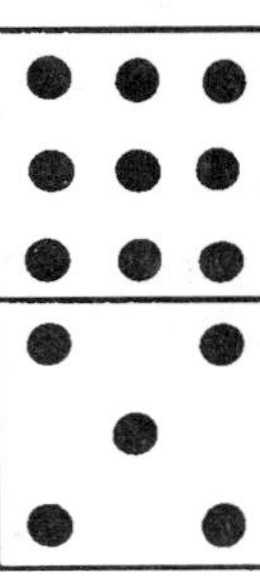

Write your first name.

Watch the pattern of these lines. Trace them, then copy the pattern on the next line.

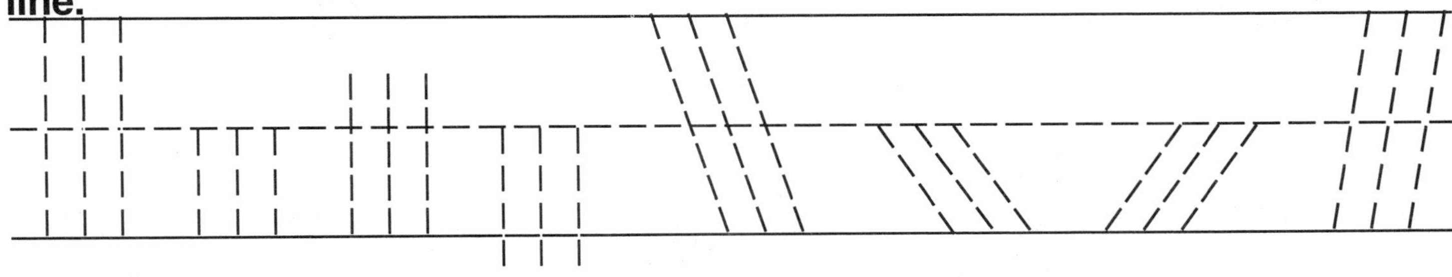

Zoo begins with the sound of (z). Color the zoo, then practice writing capital and lowercase (z's).

Now color all of the objects below that begin with the sound of (z), like zoo.

How many beans are in the pot?
Materials needed: Beans for counting. Put the amount of beans in the pot for each problem, then count to see how many you have all together!

1	2	1	3
+1	+2	+2	+1
2	3	1	2
+1	+2	+3	+3

Color the fish in the fishbowl.

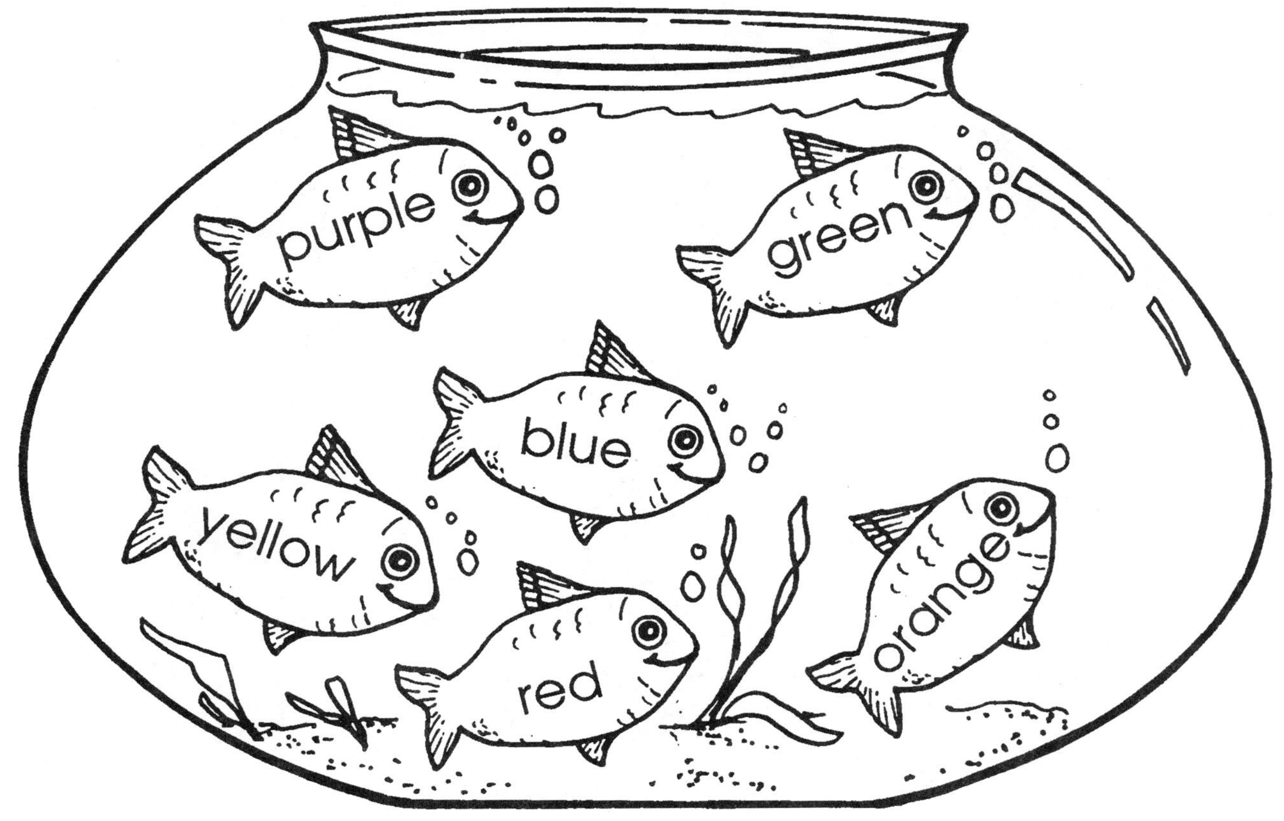

Find the objects with the beginning sound of the letter in each box. Color them.

j   	
r 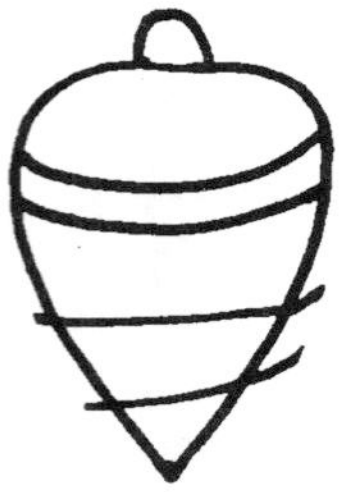  	
k   	
w   	
z   	
v   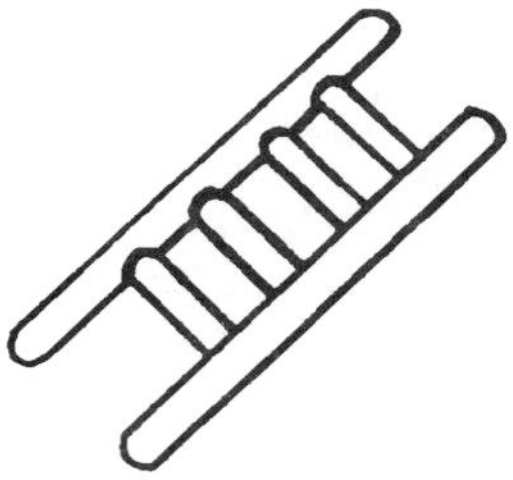	I LOVE YOU

Addition is easy when we use counters. Write your answers in the boxes.

2 
+2 

4 
+1 

5 
+0

5
+1

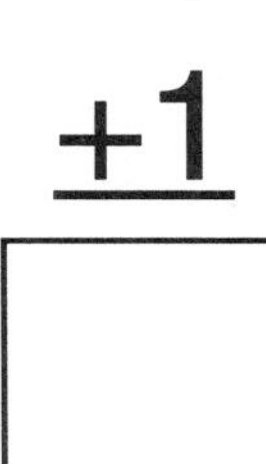

3
+2

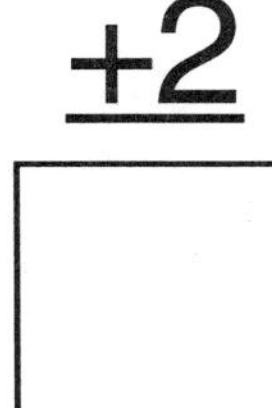

3
+1

1
+4

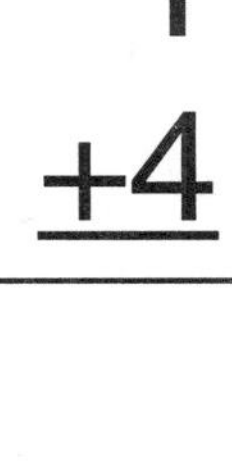

Write your first name.

Watch the pattern of these circles and lines. Trace them. Next, copy the pattern on the next line.

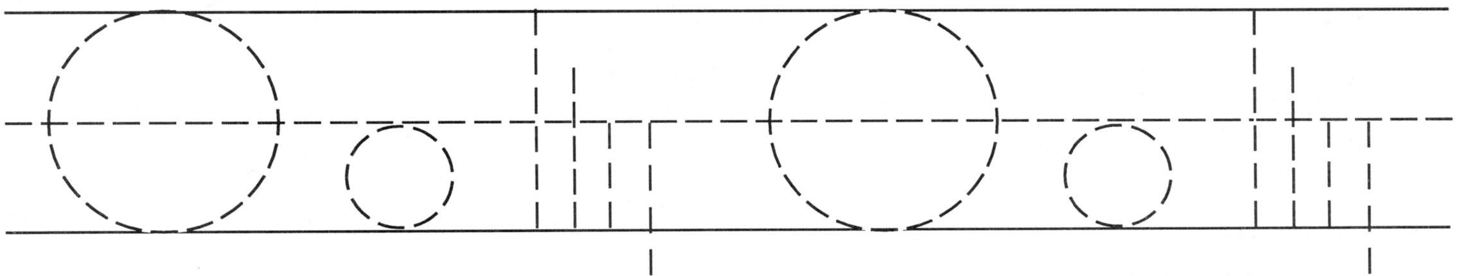

Apple begins with the sound of (a). Color the apple, then practice writing capital and lowercase (a's).

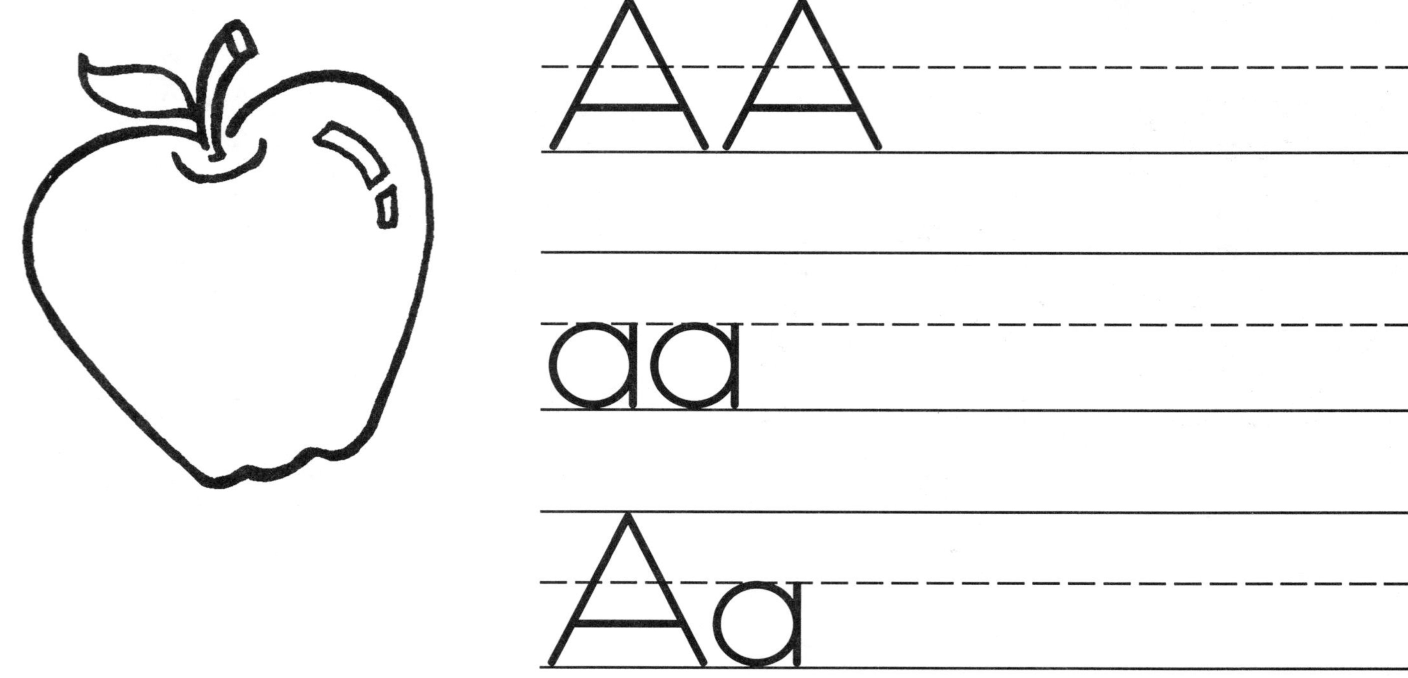

Now color all of the objects below that begin with or have the short (ă) sound, like apple.

More or less?

1. Color the bowl with fewer fish in it.

Most or least?

2. Color the pan with the most cookies in it.

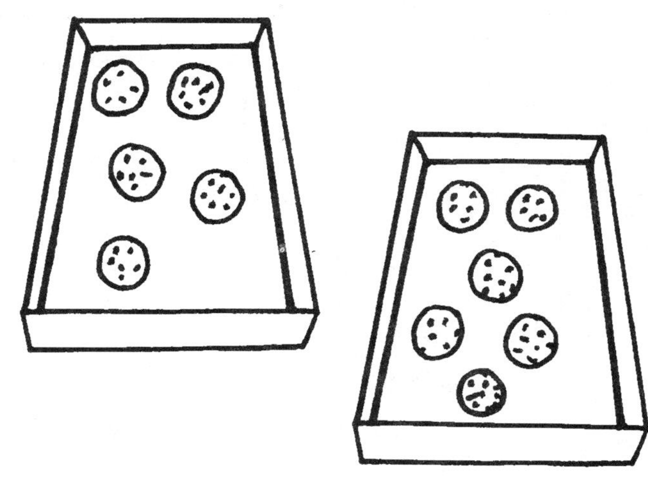

Take the mouse to his cheese.

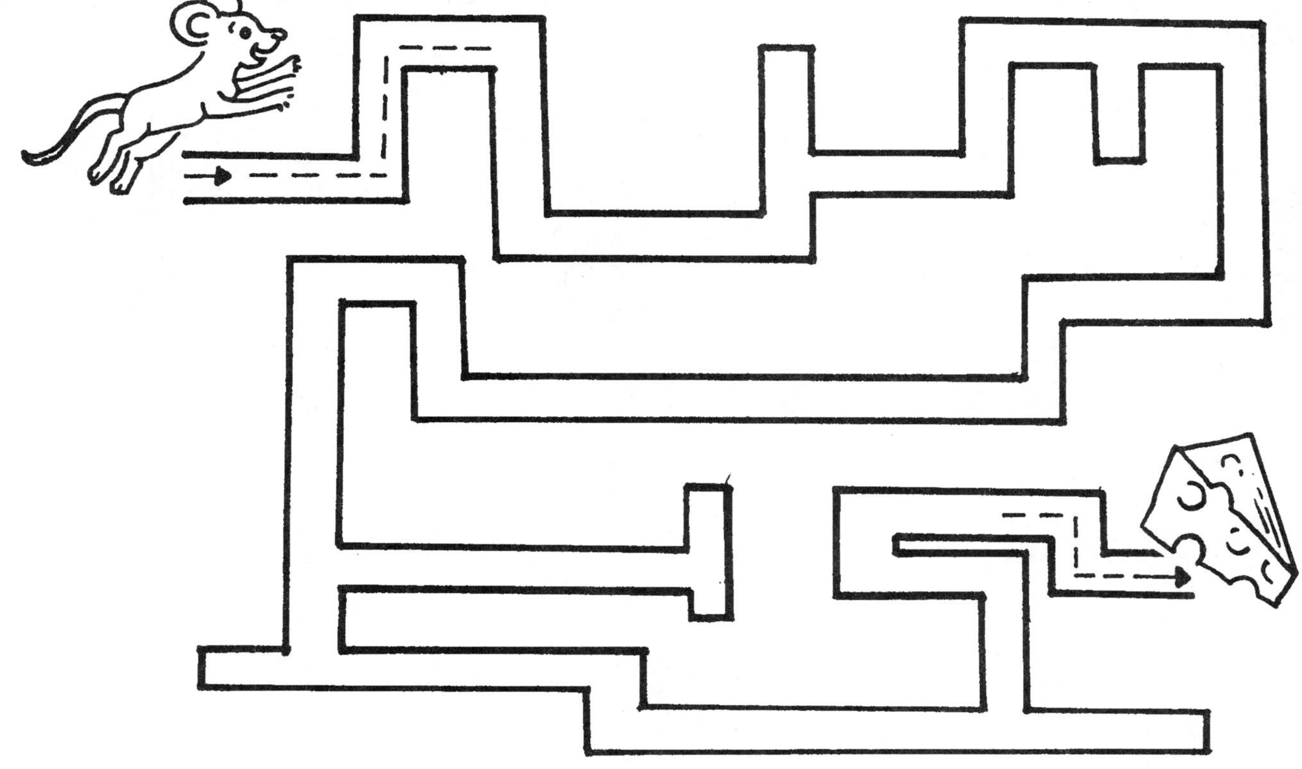

Say the name of each object and write in the missing short (ă) sound.

Example:

a nt

f___n

c___t

m___p

v___n

r___t

We can read words with the short (ă) sound.

Reading the words means putting the sounds together!

man	ant
sad	ran
bag	can
had	tag

Equal or unequal parts?

1. Color the box divided into equal parts.

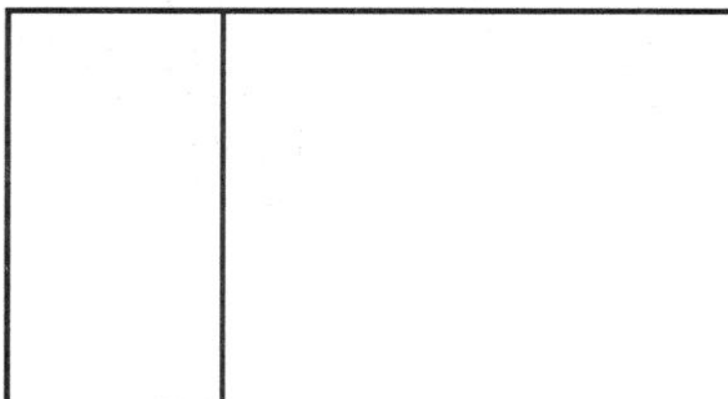
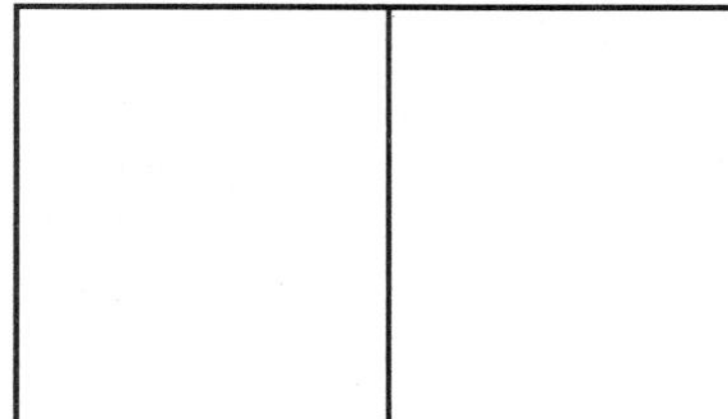

2. Color the apple divided into equal parts.

Practice writing round, lowercase letters. Be sure to start at the right place and move your pencil in the right direction.

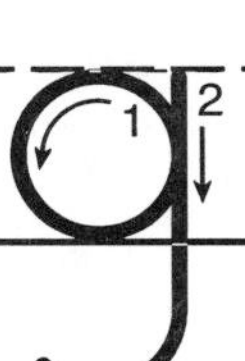

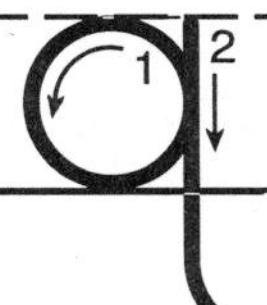

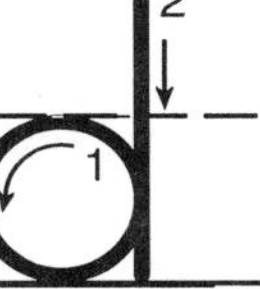

Say the name of each object. Write the letter sounds you hear to spell each word. **Example:**

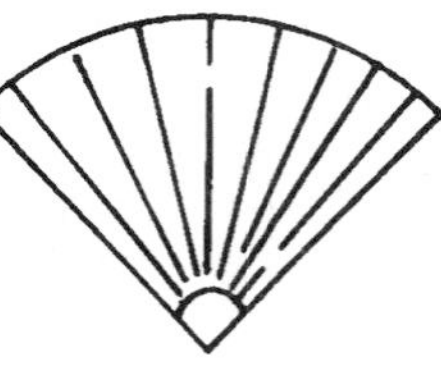

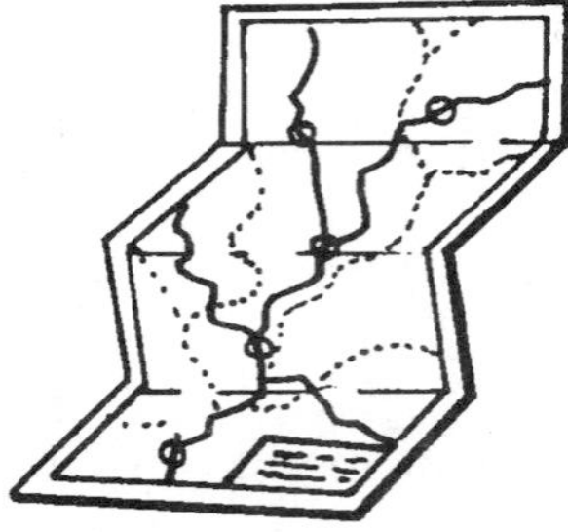

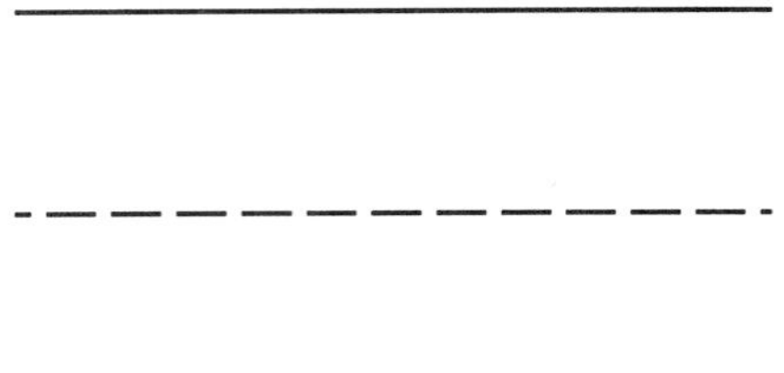

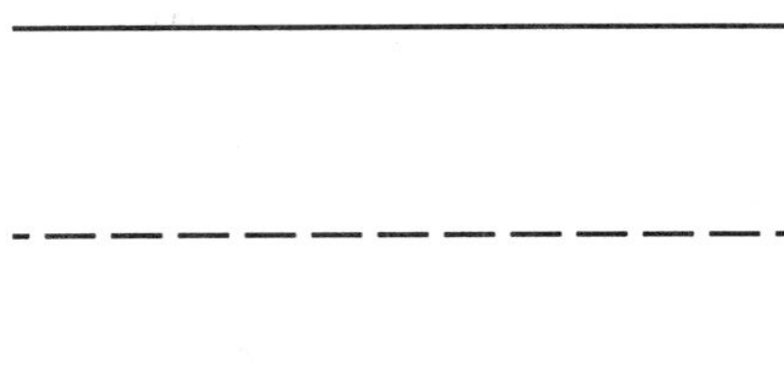

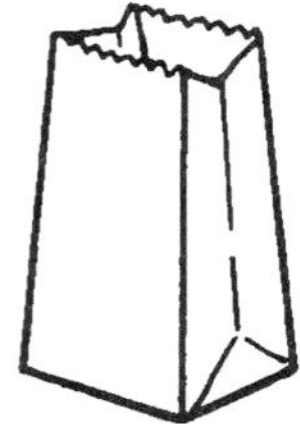

Now sound out and read these short (ă) sentences. Practice reading them fast. "The" is a sight word. Sight words cannot be sounded out.

1. The cat ran and ran.
2. The sad rat sat and sat.
3. Sam has a map. Max has a hat.
4. The fat man has a map.

More practice with addition.

5	3	1	2	2	0	4	3
+0	+2	+4	+2	+3	+5	+1	+1

2	4	3	5	0	3	1	5
+3	+0	+3	+1	+3	+2	+1	+4

Balloons! Color them all the right color to make them bright.

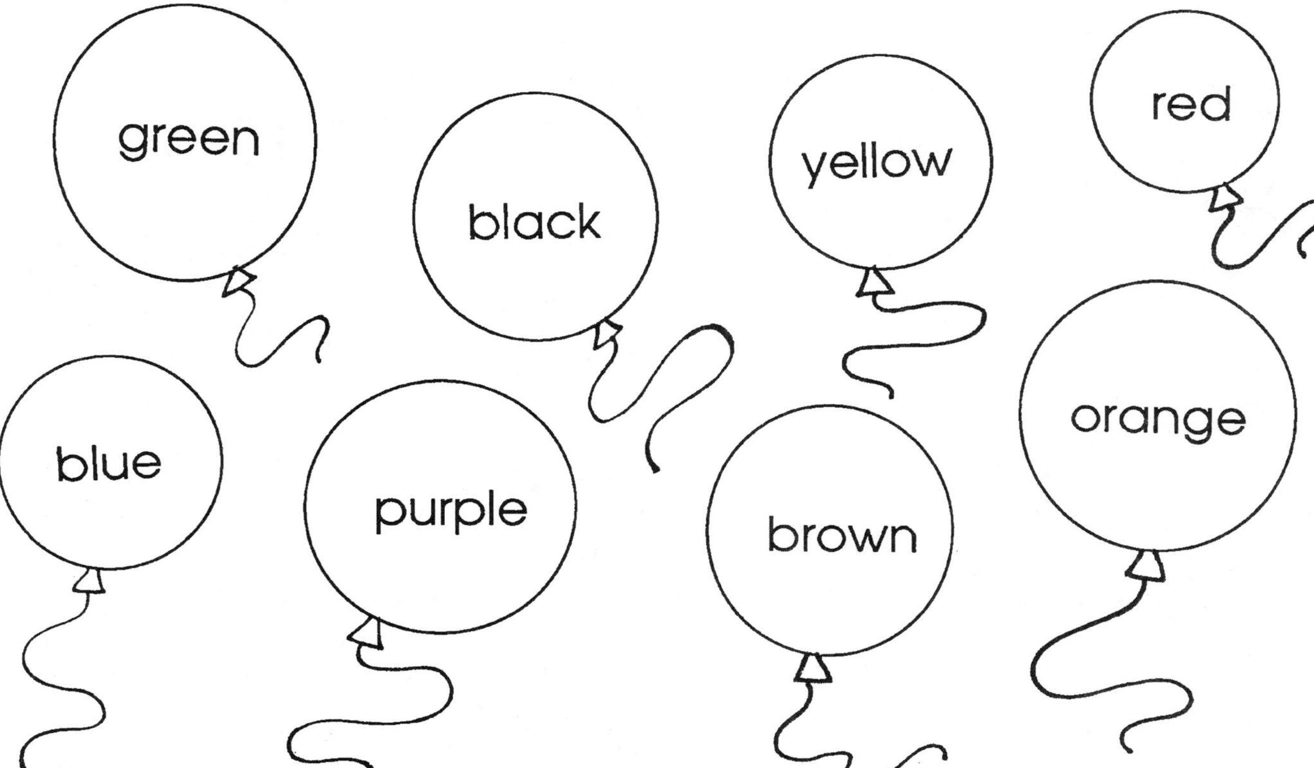

Igloo begins with the short (ĭ) sound. Color the igloo, then practice writing capital and lowercase (i's).

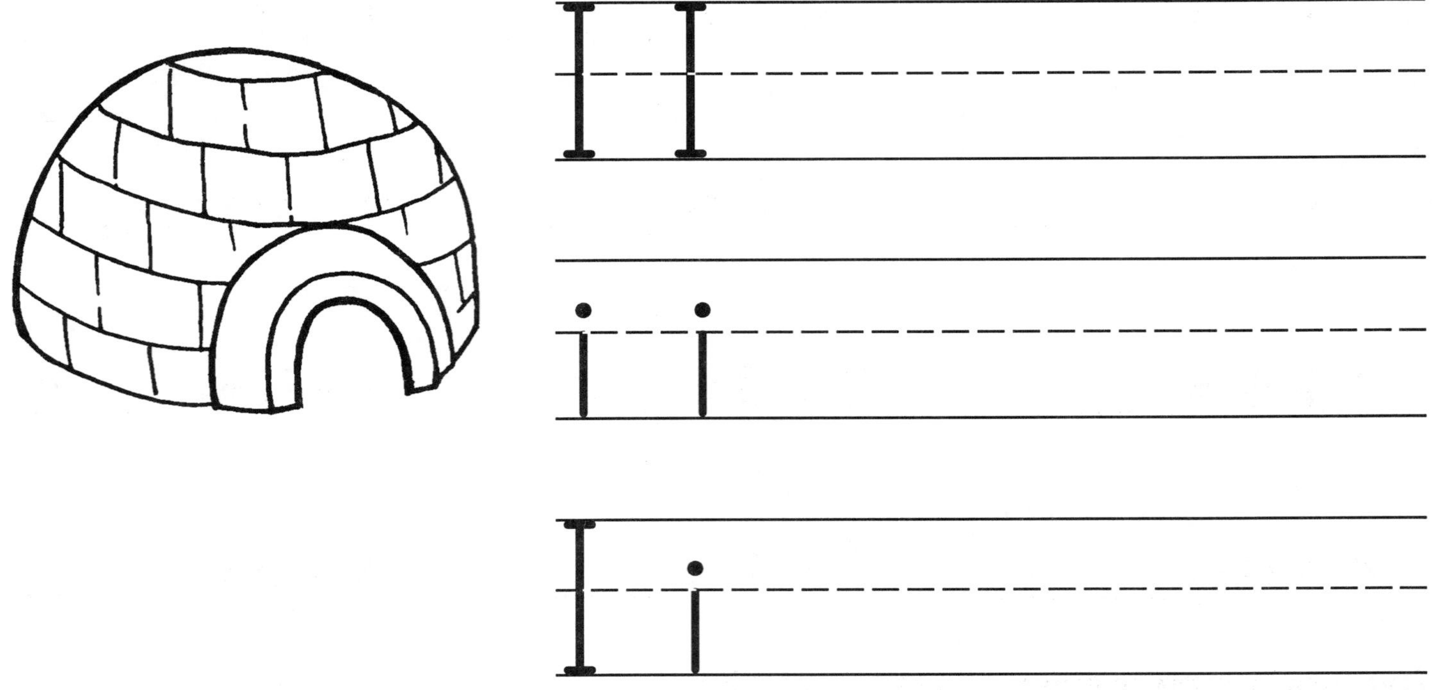

Now color all of the objects below that begin with or have the short (ĭ) sound, like igloo.

Addition from 1 to 5.

$3 + 1 =$ ______	$4 + 1 =$ ______	$1 + 2 =$ ______
$2 + 2 =$ ______	$1 + 3 =$ ______	$5 + 0 =$ ______
$1 + 4 =$ ______	$2 + 3 =$ ______	$1 + 1 =$ ______
$4 + 0 =$ ______	$2 + 1 =$ ______	$3 + 2 =$ ______

Can you name these shapes? Color them.

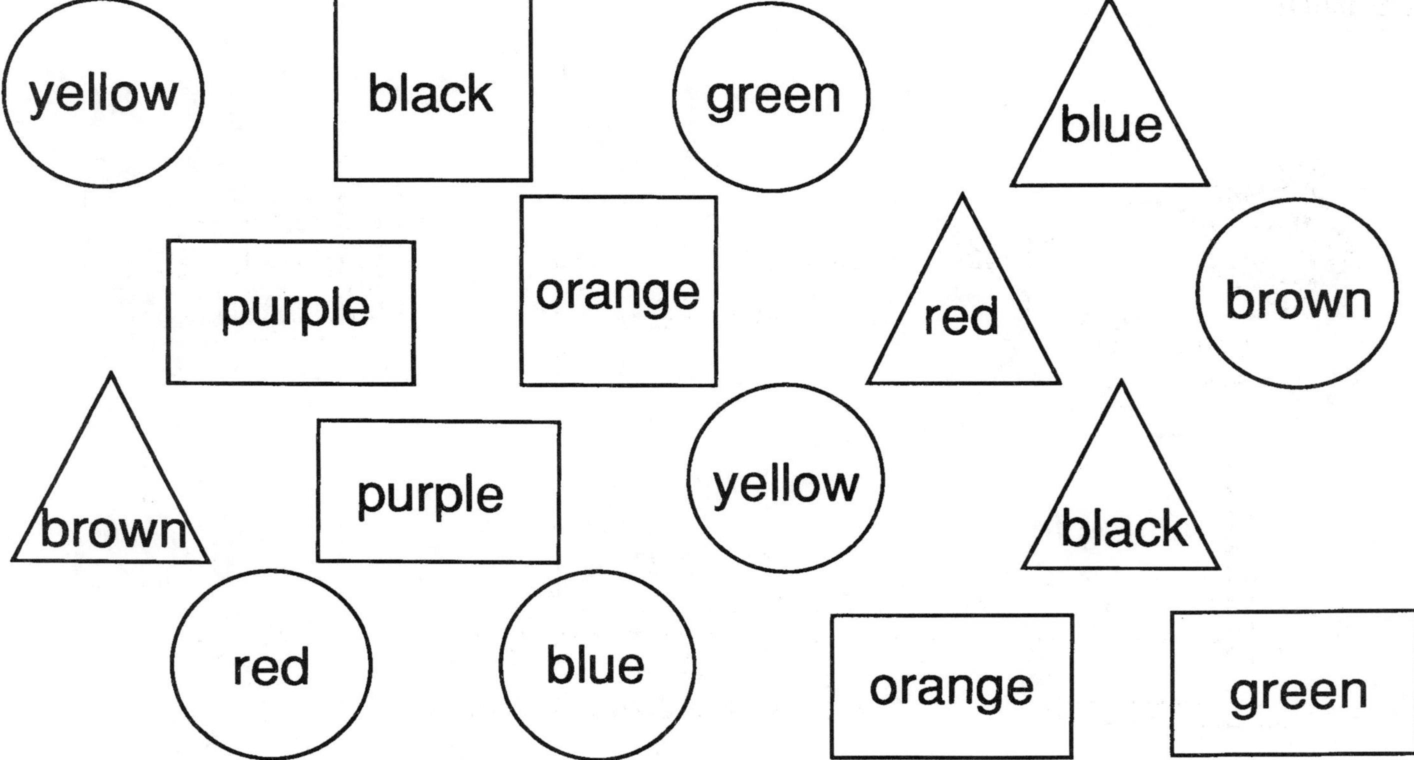

Say the name of each object and write in the missing letter.

Example:

w_i_g

l___d

m___lk

k___ng

sh___p

s___x

We can read words with the short (ĭ) sound.

Swimming in a pool of words.

him	did
in	sit
hid	win
it	is

Longest or shortest? Largest or smallest?

1. Color the longest fork.

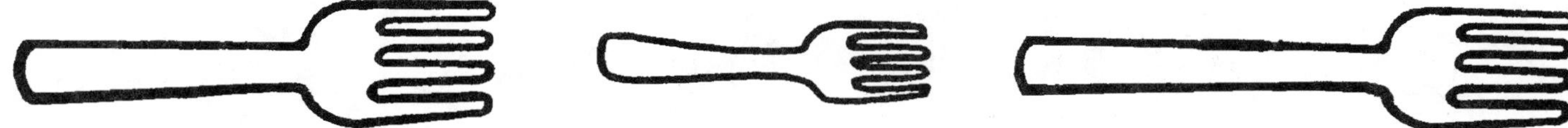

2. Color the shortest rolling pin.

3. Color the largest pie yellow and the smallest pie brown.

Let's try some letters again for added practice! These are all circle letters. Don't let (p) and (b) fool you—the circles go in different directions!

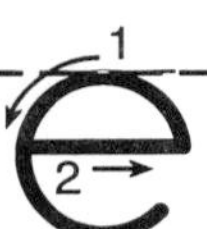

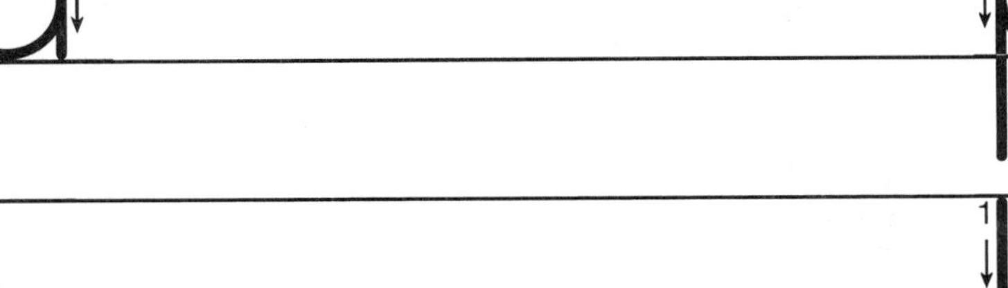

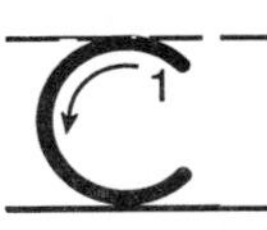

Say the name of each object. Write the letter sounds you hear to spell each word.

Now sound out and read these short (ă) sentences. Practice reading them fast. "The" is a sight word. Sight words cannot be sounded out.

1. Jim hid <u>the</u> lid in a bag.

2. Will <u>the</u> <u>lid</u> fit <u>the</u> tin can?

3. <u>The</u> big fat cat did a flip.

4. Tim will pass <u>the</u> big pig to Jill.

5. Kim will sit on <u>the</u> box.

Tallest or shortest? Lightest or heaviest?

1. Color the tallest building.

2. Color the heaviest animal.

Lines and curves make up these letters. See if you can follow the arrows.

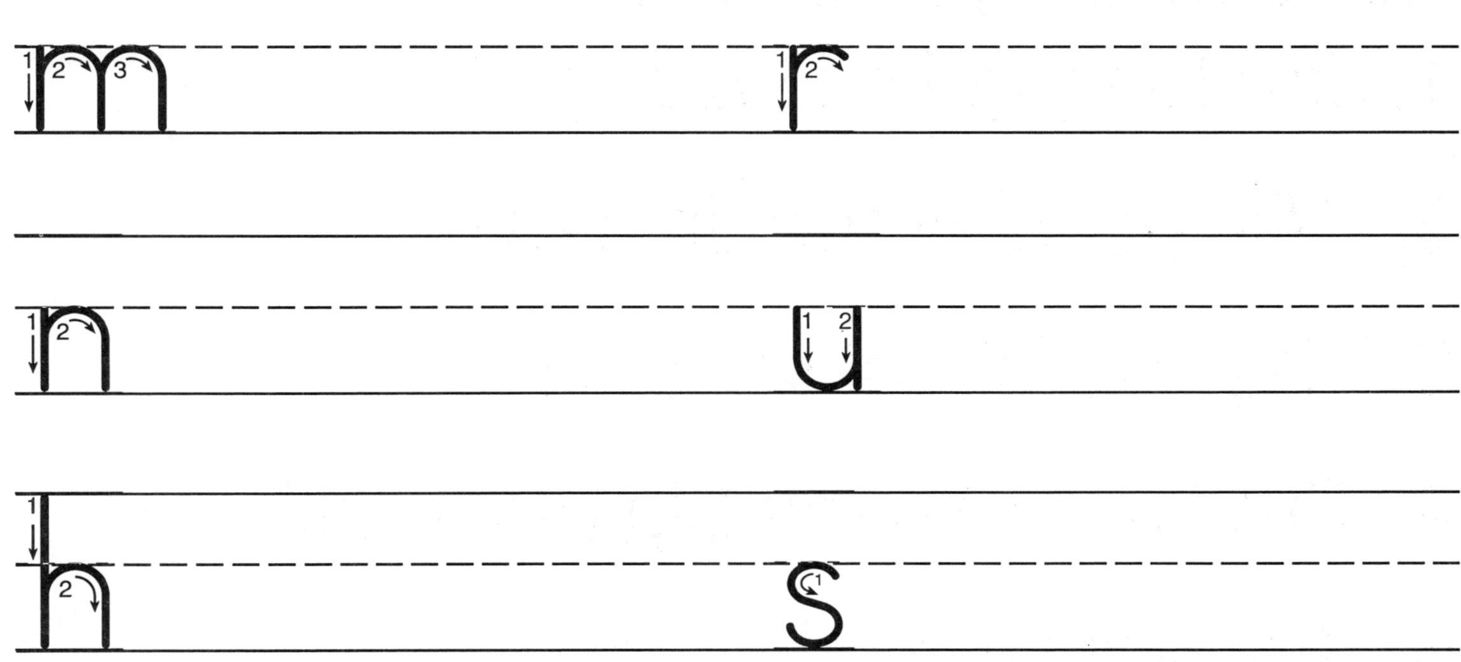

Umbrella begins with the short (ŭ) letter sound. Color the umbrella, then practice writing capital and lowercase (u's).

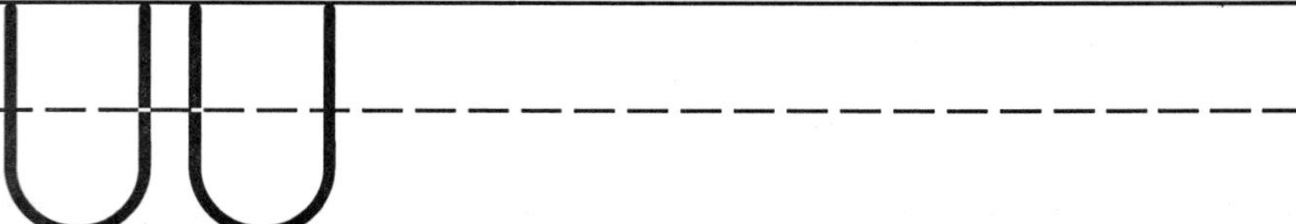

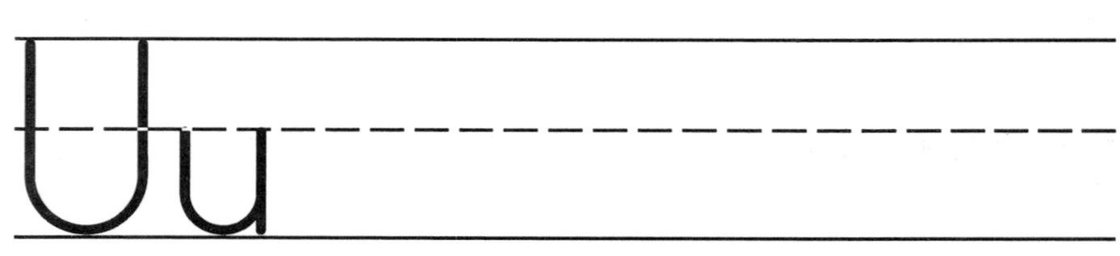

Now color all of the objects below that begin with or have the short (ŭ) sound, like umbrella.

For each problem, put the number of beans in the pot that equal the top number, and take away the beans equaling the bottom number.

2	3	4	5
-1	-2	-1	-2
3	2	4	5
-2	-2	-3	-3

Make a rainbow by tracing and coloring the suggested colors.

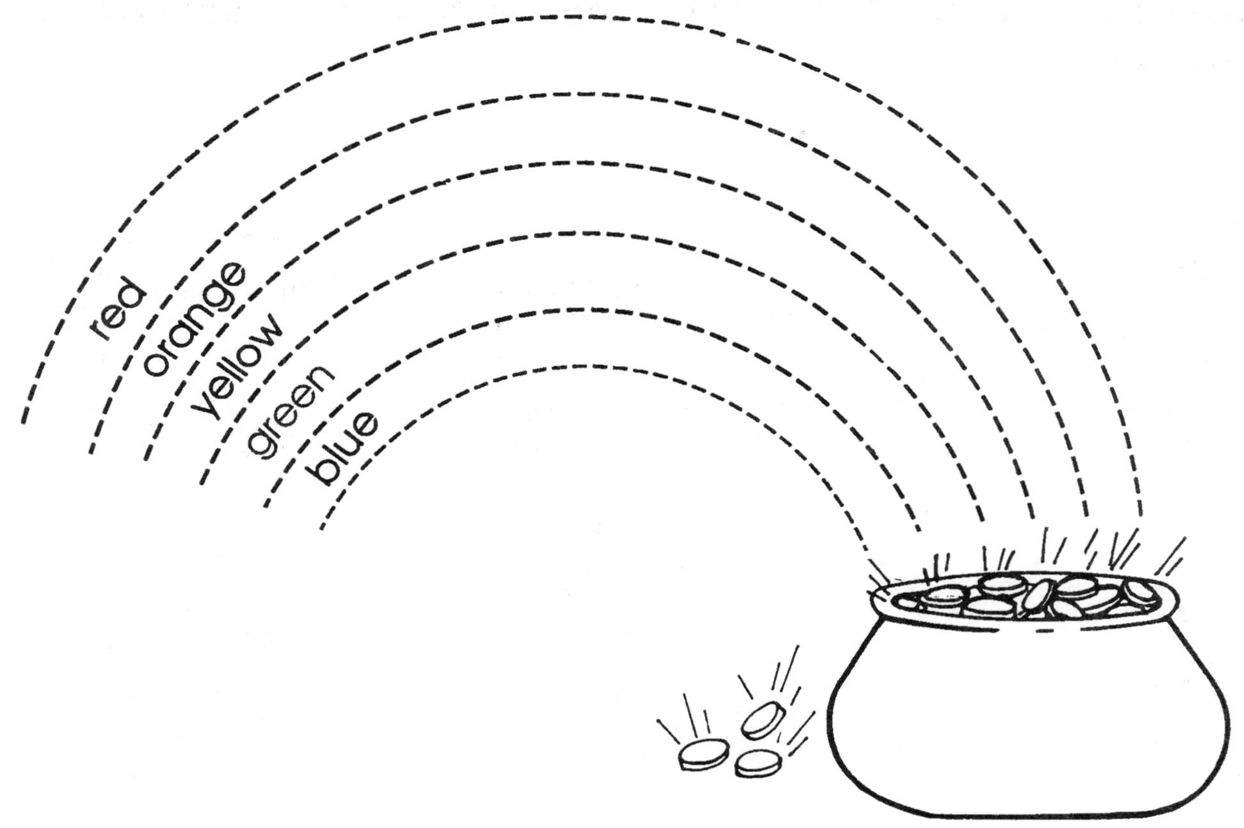

Say the name of each object and write in the missing letter.

Example:

b u g

pl__g

d__ck

br__sh

t__b

c__t

We can read words with the short (ŭ) sound.

mud	dug
cut	up
fun	mug
us	hut

You're not all wet when you work on these words!

Subtraction is easy when you use counters.

2 
-1

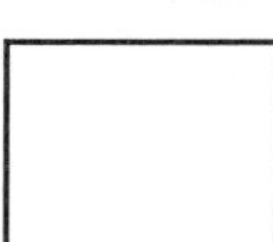

4 
-2

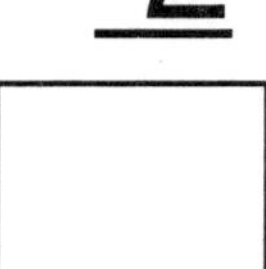

5 
-3

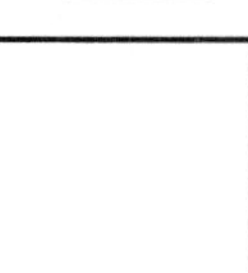

5	3	4	2
-2	-2	-3	-2

Ice cream cones come in lots of flavors. Color these ice cream cones.

Say the name of each picture. Write down the letter sounds you hear to spell the word.

Example:

sun

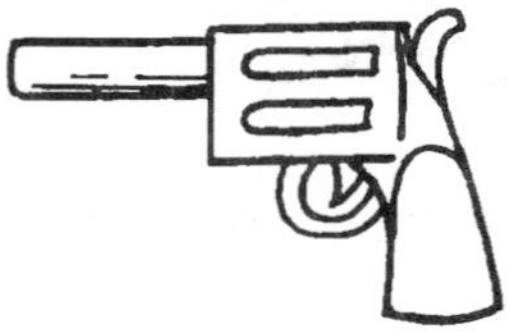

Now sound out these short vowel sentences. Practice reading them fast. "The" is a sight word, so you can't sound it out.

1. Can a bug hum in a jug?
2. It is fun in the tub.
3. The man can hug the pup.
4. Ann has mud in the mug, yuck.

Help the dog find his bone by following the path in number order from 0 to 12. Color the pictures.

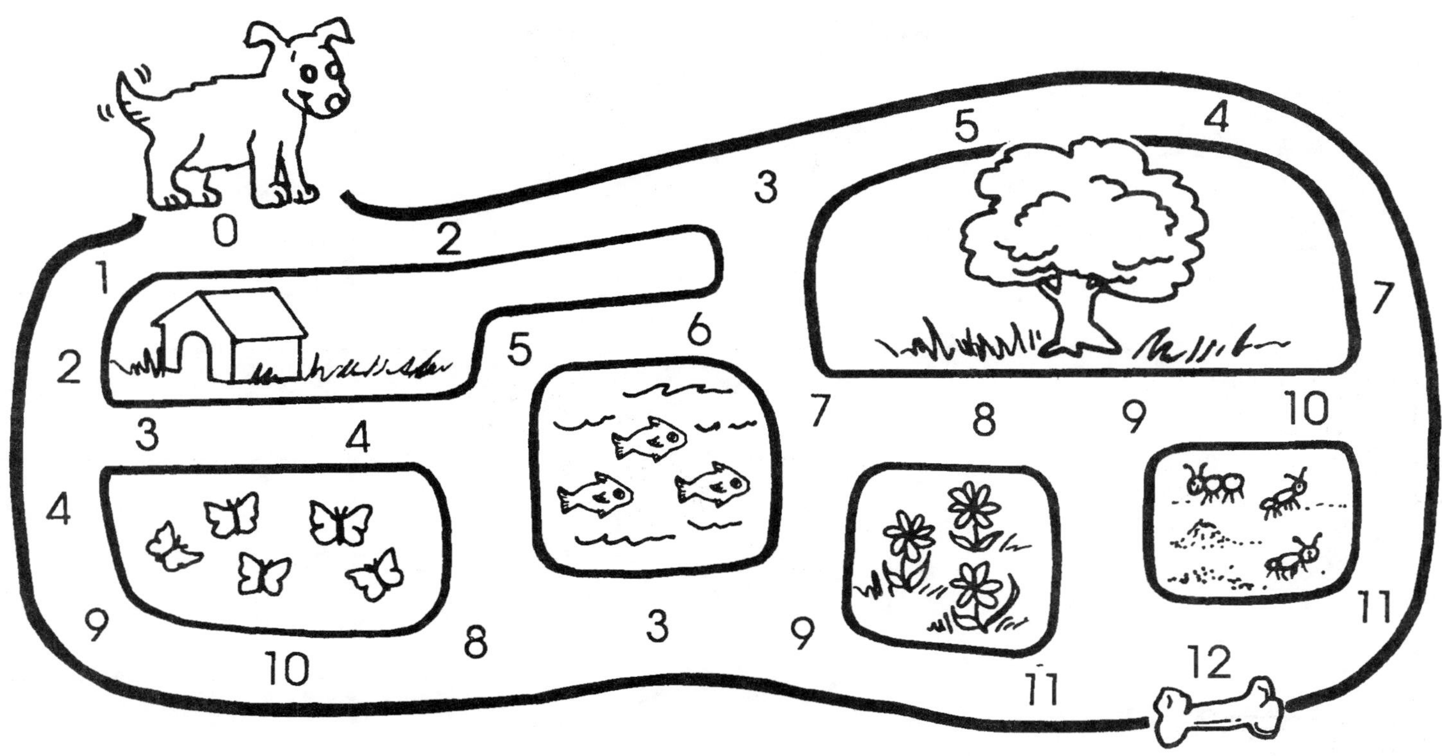

Practice writing slanted lowercase letters. Try to keep your letters within the lines.

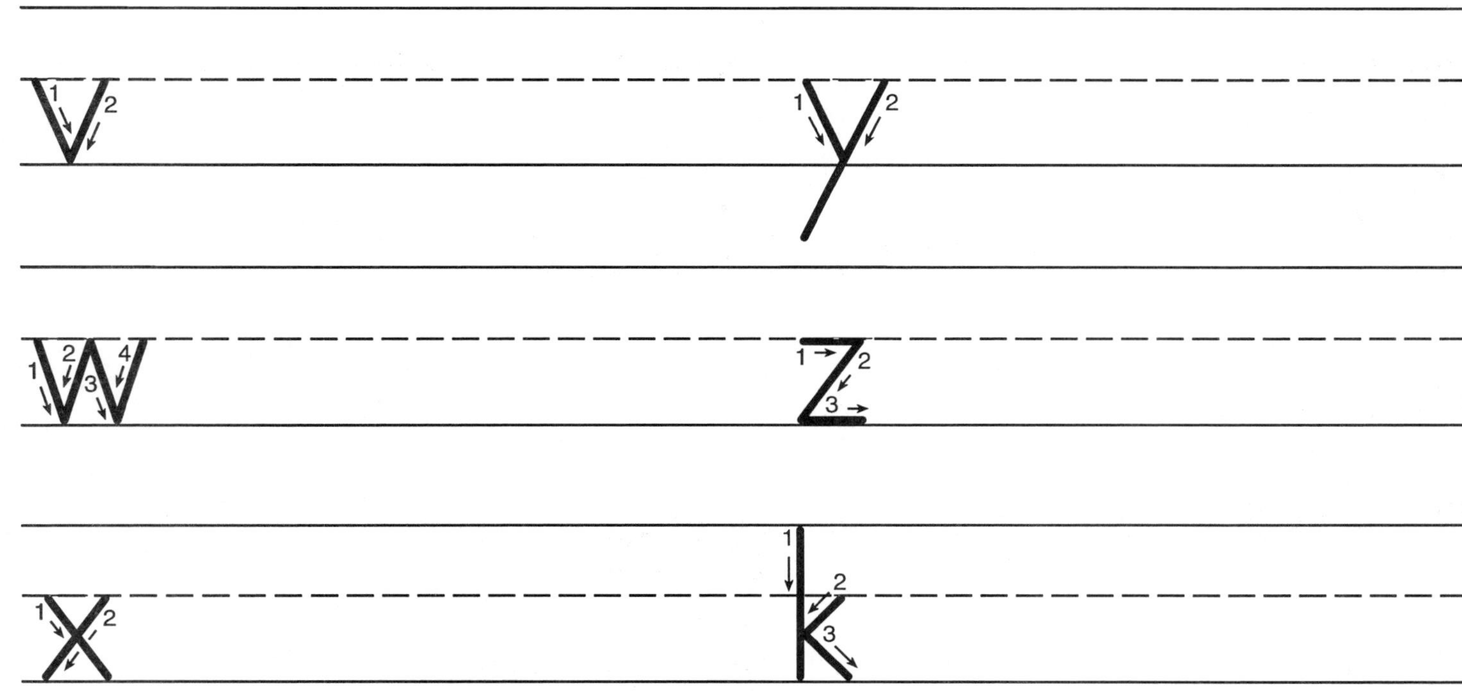

Octopus begins with the short (ŏ) sound. Color the octopus, then practice writing capital and lowercase (o's).

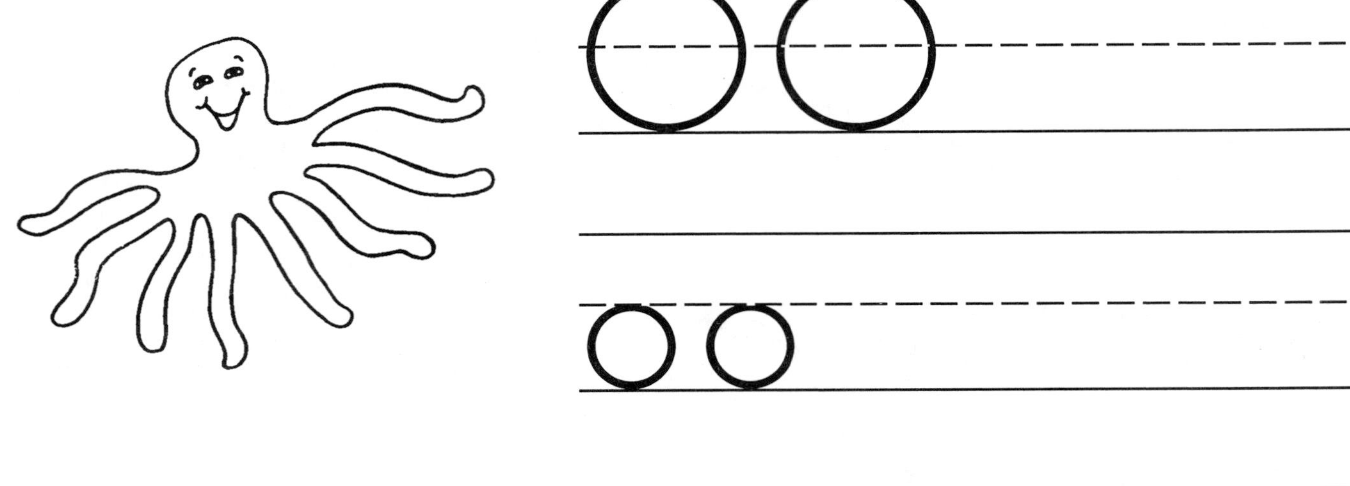

Now color all of the objects below that begin with or have the short (ŏ) sound, like octopus.

Subtraction from 1 to 5.

3 - 1 = ______ 4 - 1 = ______ 2 - 1 = ______

2 - 2 = ______ 3 - 2 = ______ 5 - 4 = ______

4 - 3 = ______ 3 - 3 = ______ 4 - 2 = ______

5 - 3 = ______ 4 - 0 = ______ 5 - 2 = ______

Straight letters are fun to make. Just be sure they stand straight and tall within the lines.

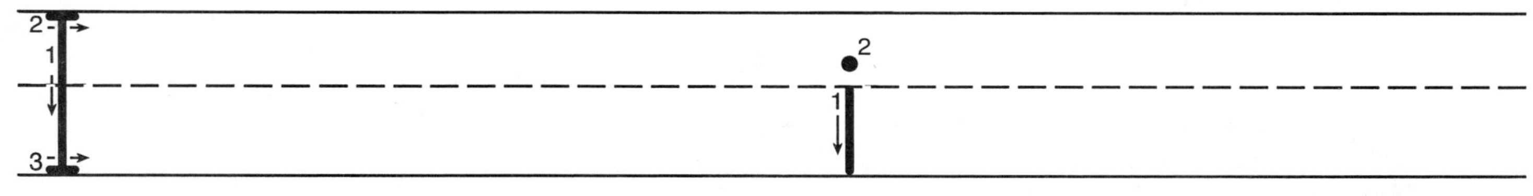

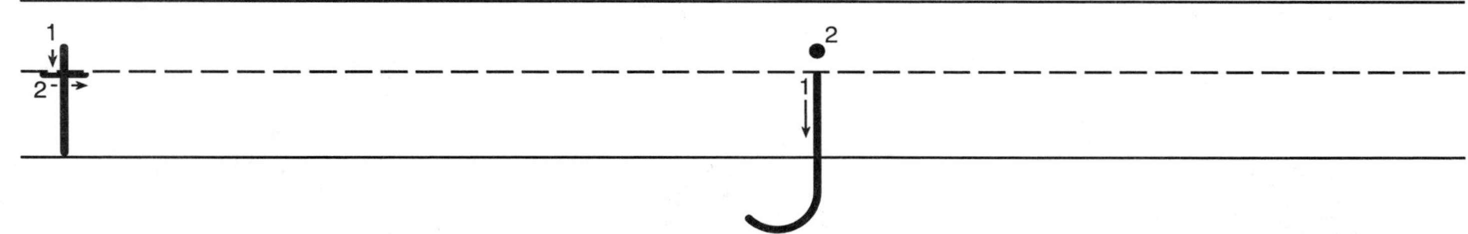

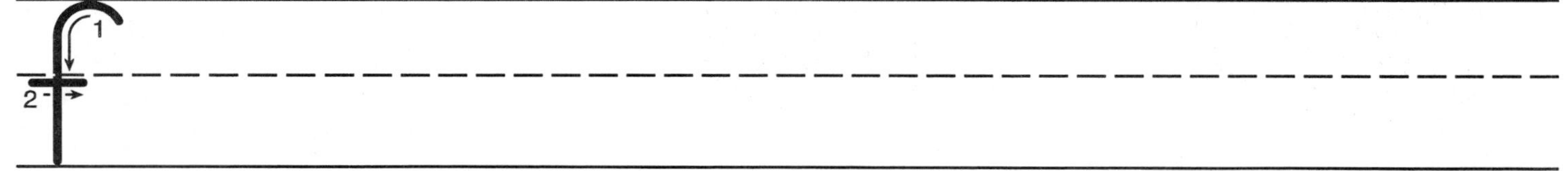

Say the name of each object and write in the missing short (ŏ) sound.

Example:

We can read words with the short (ŏ) sound.

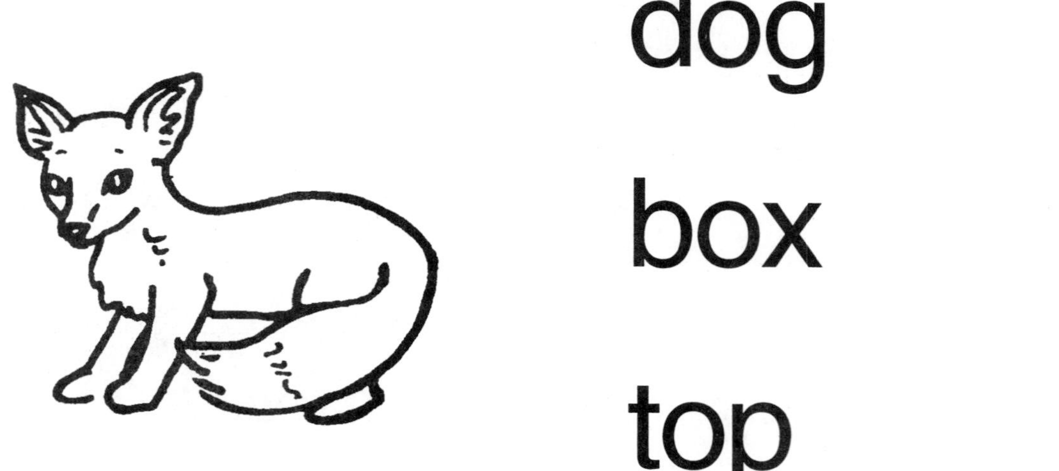

These words won't "out fox" you!

dog	hot
box	pop
top	fog
got	rob

More practice with subtraction.

5	3	1	4	2	3	5	4
-1	-2	-1	-2	-1	-1	-5	-3

3	5	2	4	3	5	4	5
-3	-2	-2	-1	-2	-4	-4	-3

Finish the second drawing in each box so it looks just like the first one.

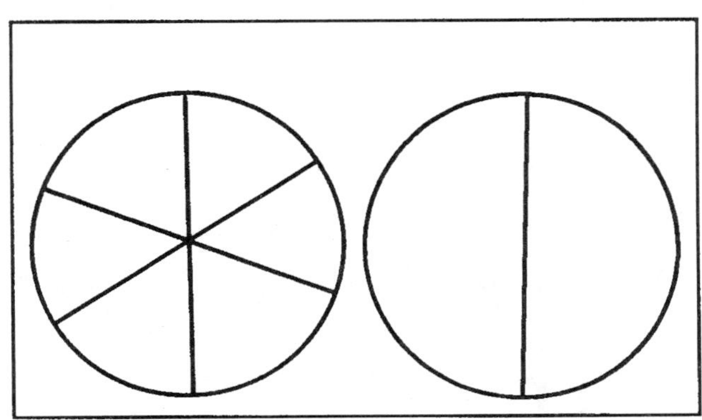

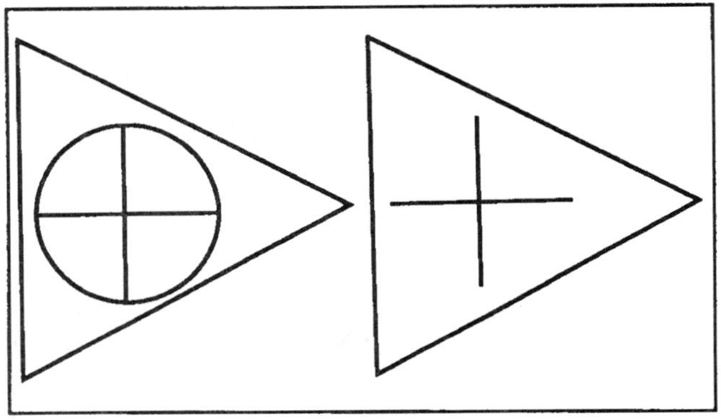

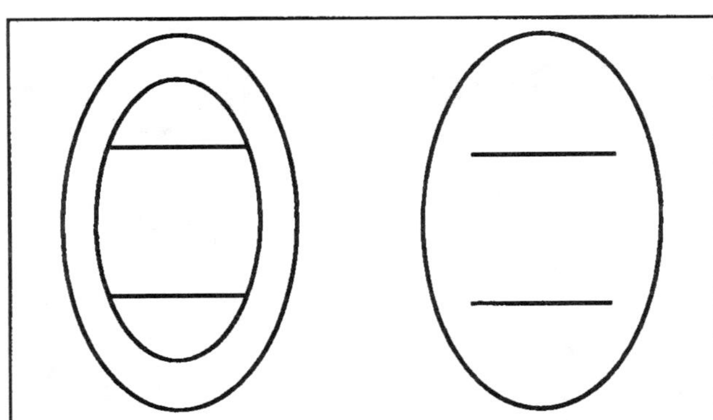

Say the name of each object. Write down the letter sounds you hear to spell the word.

Example:

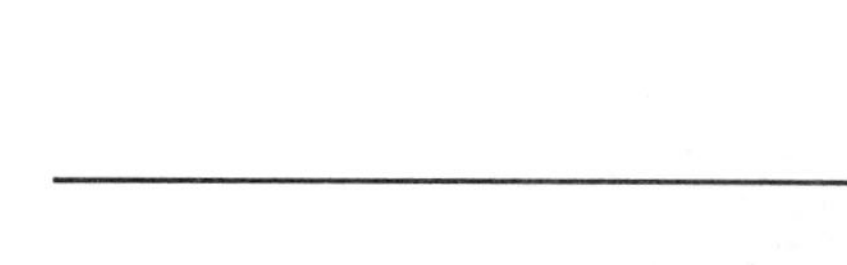

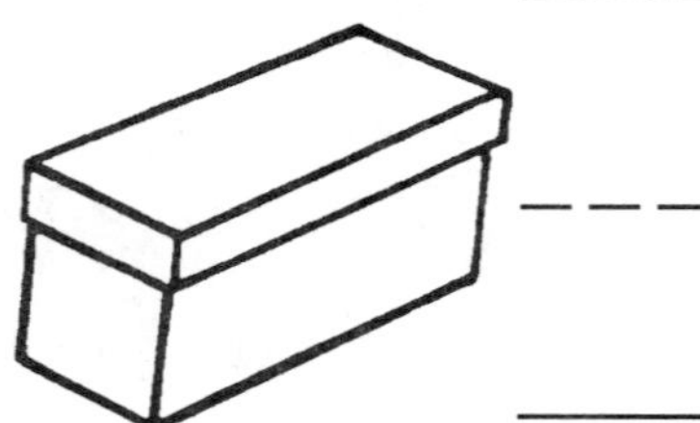

Now sound out these short vowel sentences. Practice reading the sentences fast. Remember, "the" is a sight word and cannot be sounded out.

1. The frog can jump on top of the box.
2. The fox, dog, and rat run in the hot sun.
3. The hog sat on a rock.
4. Bob sat in the fog all day long.

Circle the numbers that are exactly like the number in the first box of each row.

12	21	12	15	12	51	12	21	12
96	96	69	69	86	96	66	96	96
54	55	54	45	43	54	45	54	52
71	71	17	71	11	71	71	17	71
35	53	55	35	35	33	35	53	35
23	28	23	32	23	35	23	23	32
69	69	96	96	96	69	69	66	69

Make your own color chart.

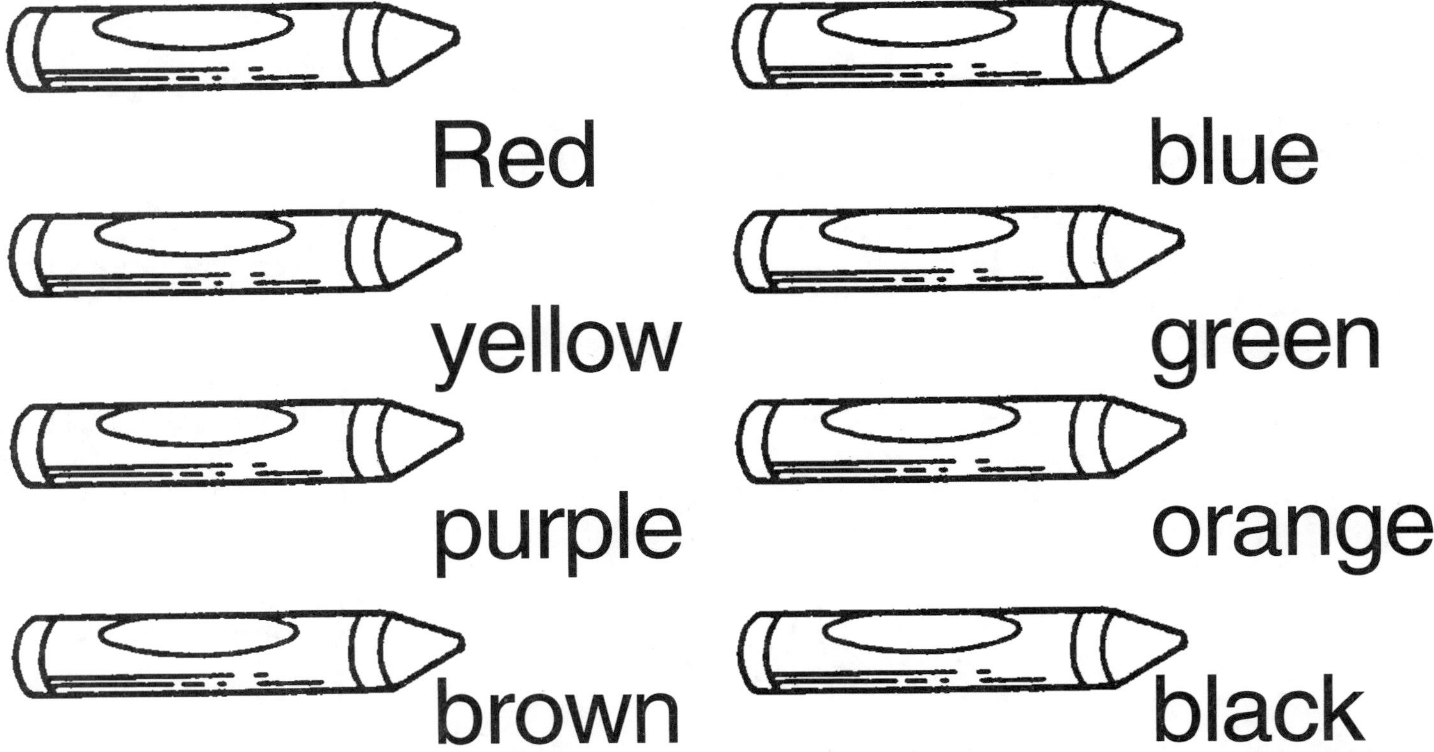

Egg begins with the short (ĕ) sound. Color the egg, then practice writing capital and lowercase (e's).

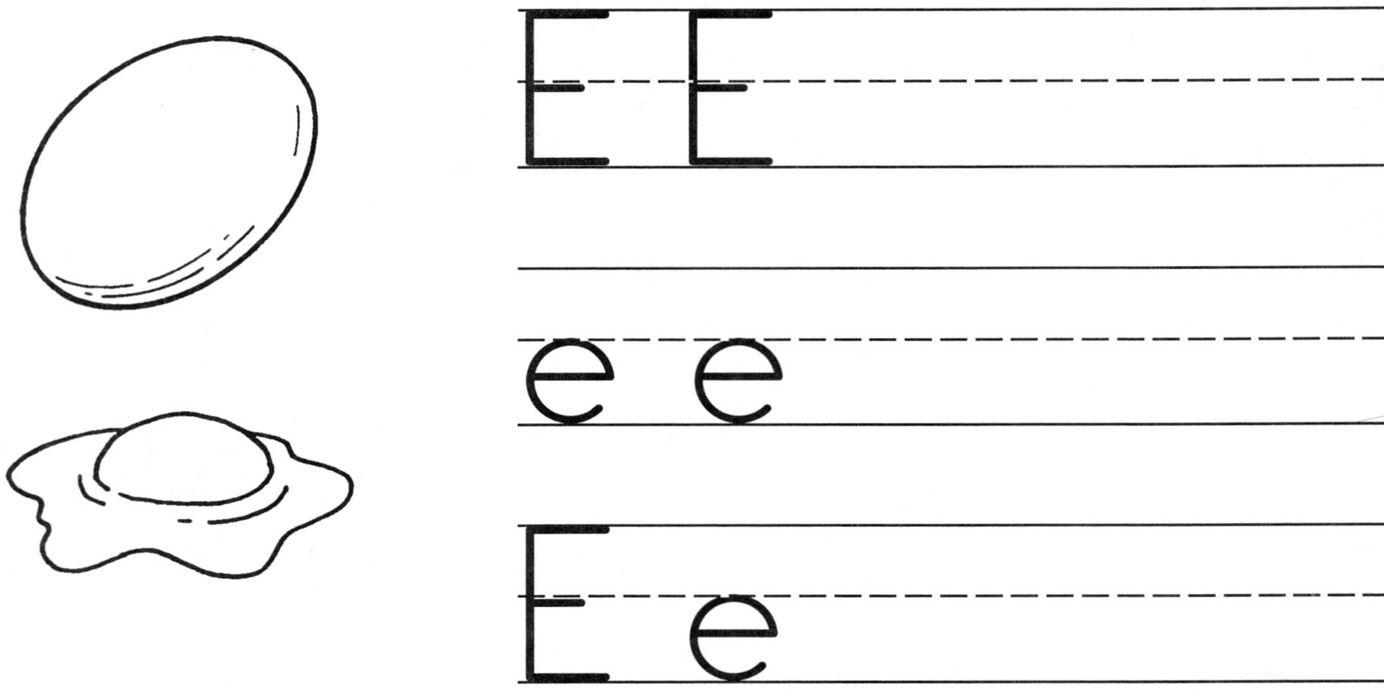

Now color all of the objects below that begin with or have the short (ĕ) sound, like egg.

This ruler measures inches. We use a ruler to measure things.

1 2 3 4 5 6 7

How many inches do you think these lines are?

Example: 4 inches

______

______

______

Practice writing your name on these lines. All three lines are different sizes!

Say the name of each object and write in the missing letter.

Example:

b**e**ll

t___nt

p___n

v___st

___gg

n___st

We can read words with the short (ĕ) sound.

Catch these words!

pet	den
men	web
ten	jet
bed	hen

Measuring with a ruler is lots of fun. Make your own lines showing the correct inches.

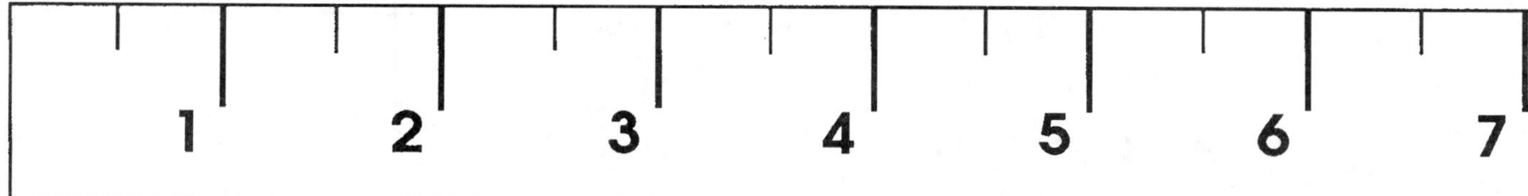

____________________ 3 inches

____________________ 5 inches

____________________ 6 inches

____________________ 4 inches

Draw and color at least three things in your bedroom. Have an adult help you label them.

Say the name of each picture. Write down the letter sounds you hear to spell the word.

Example:

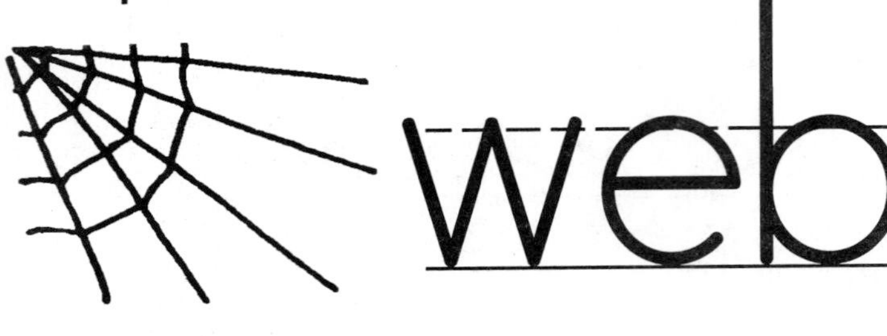

Now sound out these short vowel sentences. Practice reading them fast.

1. The T.V. set is off and Jed is in his bed.
2. Peg has the mumps.
3. Ben sends Peg a gift. It is a puppet in a box.

Connect the dots in alphabetical order.

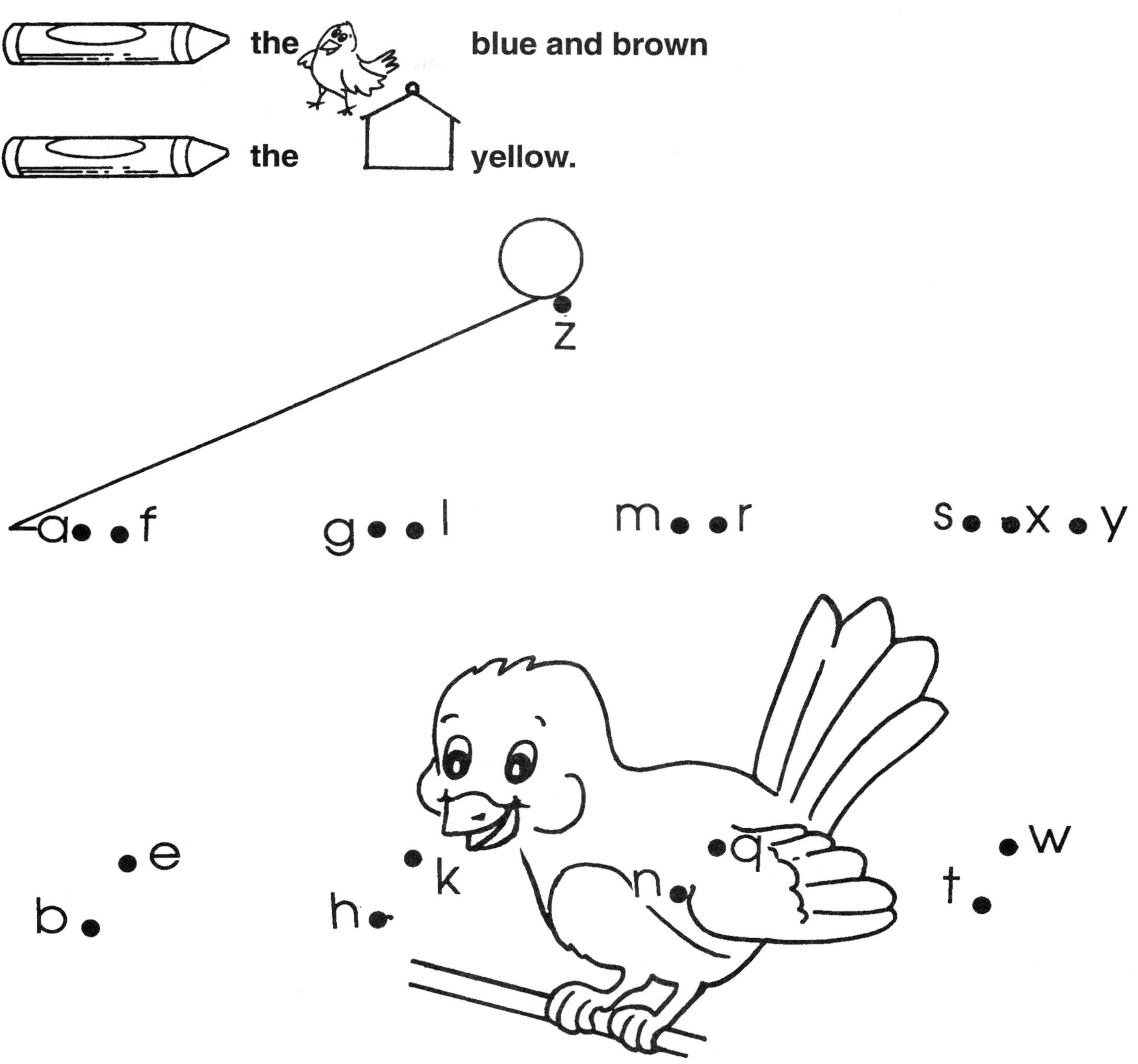

Connect the numbered dots and color.

Enrichment Activities for Number Cards 1 to 100

If your child does not recognize all the numbers from 1 to 100, start with the ones he/she knows and gradually work through the other numbers. Use only those activities you feel your child needs.

Number Recognition

1. Go through cards in order, having your child count them orally.

Number Recognition

2. Mix up the cards and have your child identify them.
3. Randomly select 5 or 6 cards and have your child identify them.
4. Randomly select 5 or 6 cards and have your child identify which number is less, or least.
5. Randomly select 5 or 6 cards and have your child put them in order from the greatest to the least, or vice versa.
6. Group all the numbers after putting them in order into groups of ten. Teach your child to count to 100 by 10's.
7. Arrange all the numbers into groups of five and count to 100 by 5's.
8. Counting by twos is usually more difficult for young children—group concrete objects such as socks, shoes, or mittens into groups of two. Have your child count them by ones, then show him/her how to count by twos, going no further than ten or twenty to begin with. Label the pairs with the number cards.

9. Put the cards 1 through 20 in order, then turn all the odd numbers over and have your child identify out loud, in order, those that are left. Some people call this "skip counting."

Missing Numbers

10. Place all the cards in order on the floor or table. Turn over cards randomly while your child closes his/ her eyes. Have him/her open his/her eyes and identify those numbers that are missing or not showing. Use the same method with tens and fives.

11. Put all the cards in order and turn over all the numbers except 10's. Then have your child count by 10's. This also could be done for the 5's and 2's.

What Comes Next?

12. Mix up the cards. Turn one over, then have your child identify it and tell you what number would come next. You could put a different slant on the game by asking, "What number would be one more than this number?"

13. What number comes before or means "one less than"? Use the same method used in activity #12.

14. Have your child draw a number card out of the stack. Identify the number. Starting with that number, have your child count forward or backward.

15. Have your child draw two cards from the stack. Have him/her identify the one that is less or least. Start with that card and keep counting until you get to the other number (the greater number) card he/she picked out.

Number Cards. 1–100 to cut and practice

1	2	3	4	5
6	7	8	9	10
11	12	13	14	15
16	17	18	19	20
21	22	23	24	25

26	27	28	29	30
31	32	33	34	35
36	37	38	39	40
41	42	43	44	45
46	47	48	49	50

51	52	53	54	55
56	57	58	59	60
61	62	63	64	65
66	67	68	69	70
71	72	73	74	75

76	77	78	79	80
81	82	83	84	85
86	87	88	89	90
91	92	93	94	95
96	97	98	99	100

Summer Activity Contract & Calendar

Month____________________

My parents and I decided that if I complete 20 days of *Summer Bridge Activities*™ and read ______ minutes a day, my incentive/reward will be:

____

Child Signature____________________ Parent Signature____________________

Day	I have completed one day of activities (Color the Star)	I have completed ______ minutes of reading (Color the Book)	Parent Initials
1	☆	📖	
2	☆	📖	
3	☆	📖	
4	☆	📖	
5	☆	📖	
6	☆	📖	
7	☆	📖	
8	☆	📖	
9	☆	📖	
10	☆	📖	

Day	I have completed one day of activities (Color the Star)	I have completed ______ minutes of reading (Color the Book)	Parent Initials
11	☆	📖	
12	☆	📖	
13	☆	📖	
14	☆	📖	
15	☆	📖	
16	☆	📖	
17	☆	📖	
18	☆	📖	
19	☆	📖	
20	☆	📖	

Have a Fun Day...Discover Something New!

Fun Activity Ideas to Go Along with the Third Section

1. Play hopscotch, marbles, or jump rope.
2. Visit a fire station.
3. Take a walk around your neighborhood and name all of the trees and flowers you can.
4. Make up a song.
5. Make a hut out of blankets.
6. Put a note in a helium balloon and let it go.
7. Write about your favorite vacation memories. Start a journal.
8. Make 3-D nature art. Glue leaves, twigs, dirt, grass, and rocks on paper.
9. Find an ant colony. Spill some food and see what happens.
10. Play charades.
11. Make up a story by drawing pictures.
12. Do something to help the environment. Clean up an area by your house.
13. Weed a row in the garden. Mom will love it!
14. Take a trip to a park.
15. Learn about different road signs.
16. Make a map of your neighborhood.
17. Have a back-to-school party.
18. Call a friend.
19. Cut pictures out of old magazines and write a story.
20. Take some photos with a camera and have them developed.

When we count pennies, we count by one's. If you can, use a real penny to cover each picture as you count.

 ¢

 ¢

_____________¢

Circle the design that is exactly the same as the design in first box of each row.

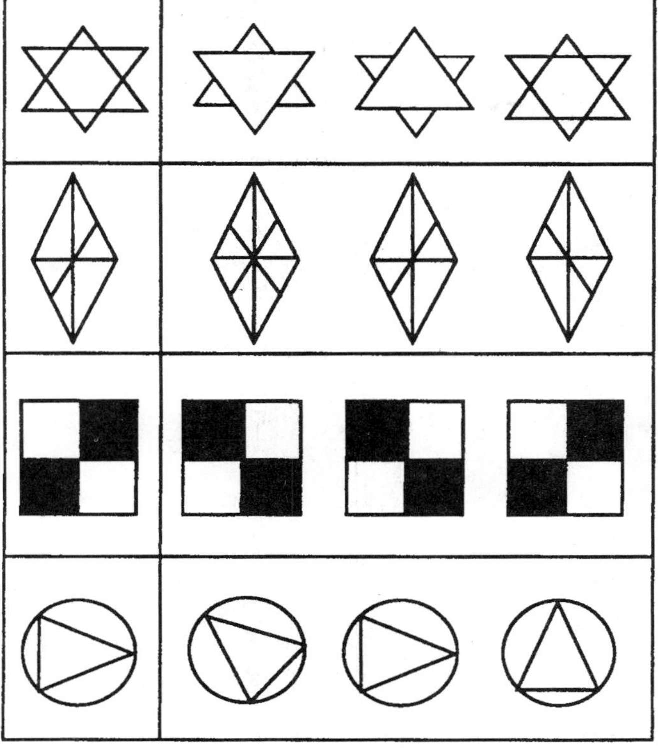

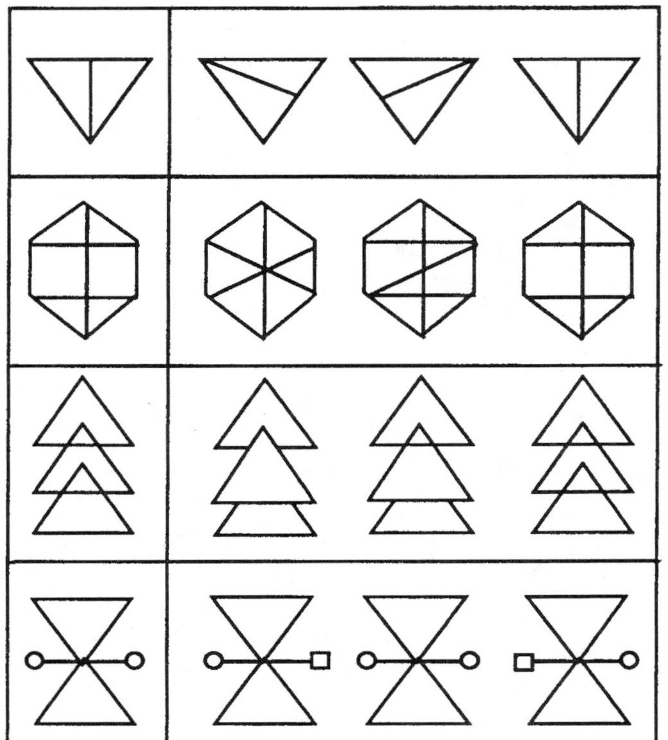

Say the picture word. Circle the short vowel sound that you hear (ă,ĕ,ĭ,ŏ,ŭ).

Example:			
a e (i)	u o a	i e u	a i u
i e u	a u i	e o i	a e u
o a u	e a i	e o i	a o u
u e a	o e i	i e u	e i o
a e u	i e o	o u a	e o u

Counting by 5's can be fun when you use your fingers.

Examples:

Count out loud: 5—10—15—20—25—30—35—40—45—50
55—60—65—70—75—80—85—90—95—100

Use a differently colored crayon to trace the path from shape to matching shape.

Say the name of each picture. Write the short vowel letter sound you hear.

Example:

When we count nickels, we count by 5's. If you can, cover each picture with a real nickel as you count.

    ____________¢

       ____________¢

    ____________¢

Crossword puzzle: Fill in the squares with the picture word.

Example:

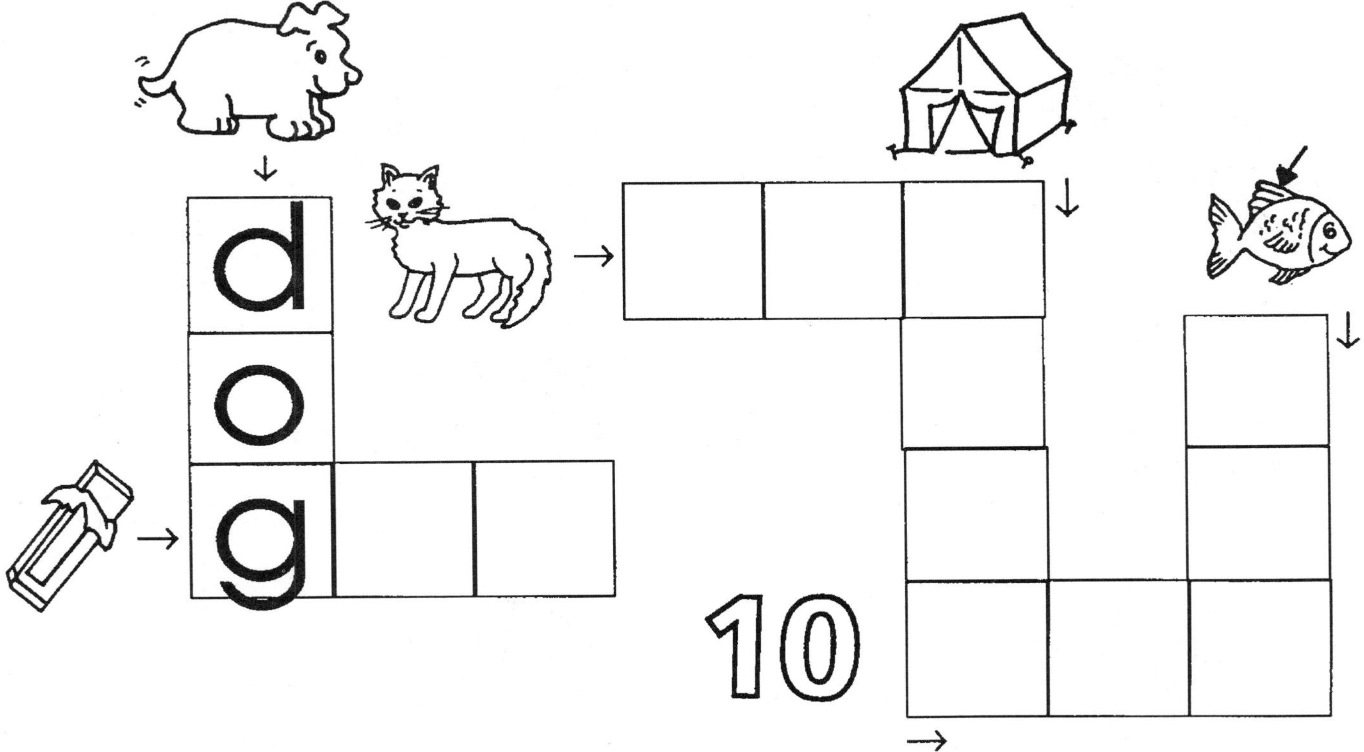

Say the name of each object and spell it out with the letter sounds that you hear. Use the short vowels (ă,ĕ,ĭ,ŏ,ŭ).

Example:

Practice writing to 100 by 10's.

Example:

10
20
30
40
50
60
70
80
90
100

10	60
20	70
30	80
40	90
50	100

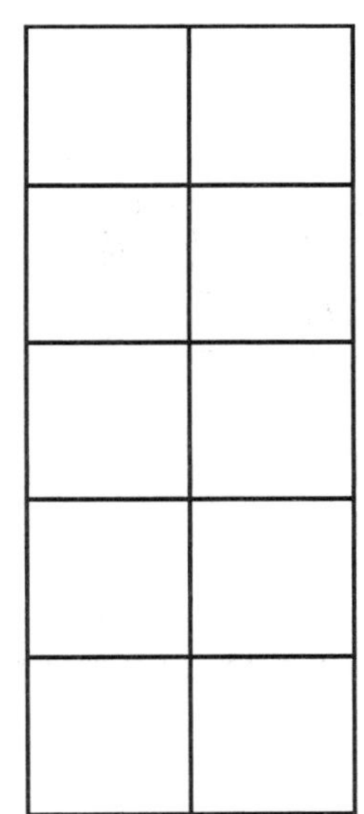

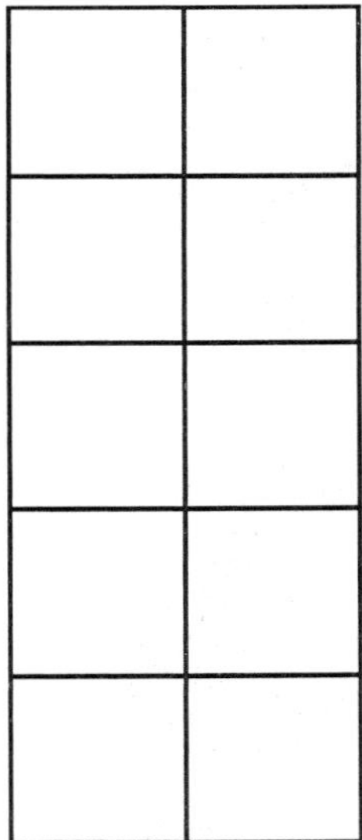

Word search: Find the words and circle them.

sun

men

pin

sad

hen

up

w	p	i	n	u
s	a	d	c	o
l	f	s	u	n
h	e	n	p	m
t	m	e	n	b

Say the picture word. Write the beginning letter sound you hear.

Example:

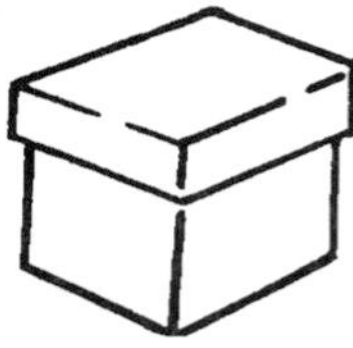

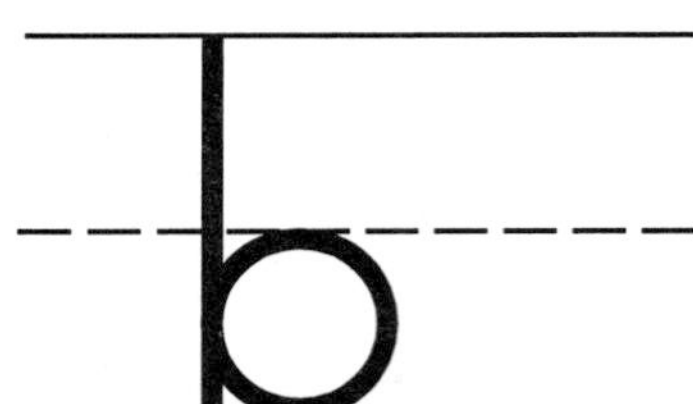

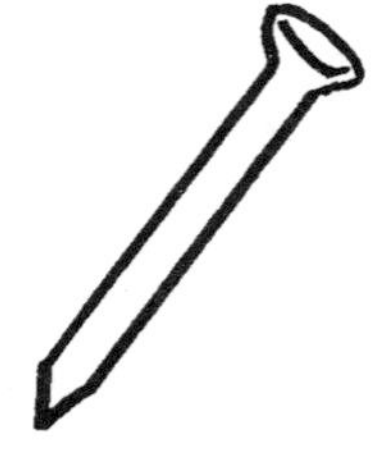

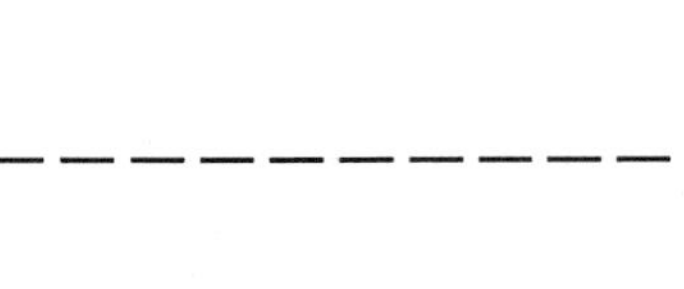

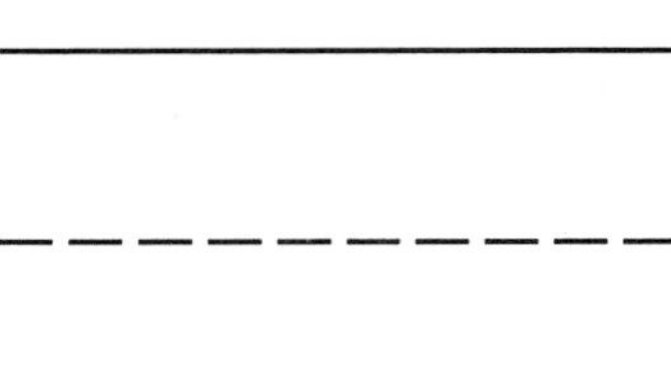

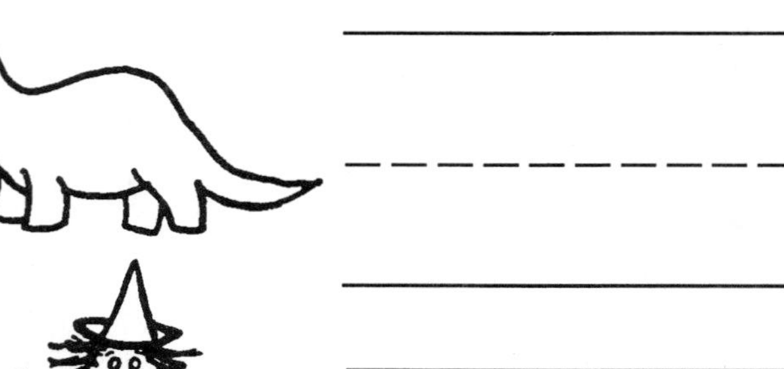

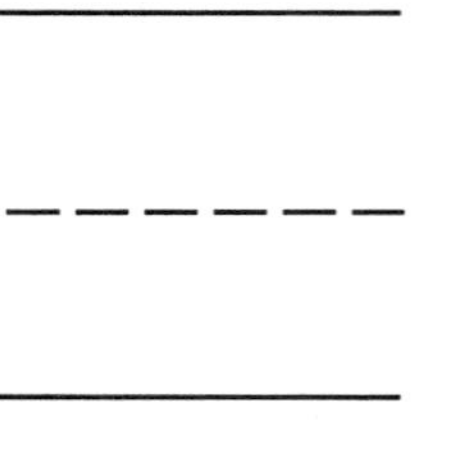

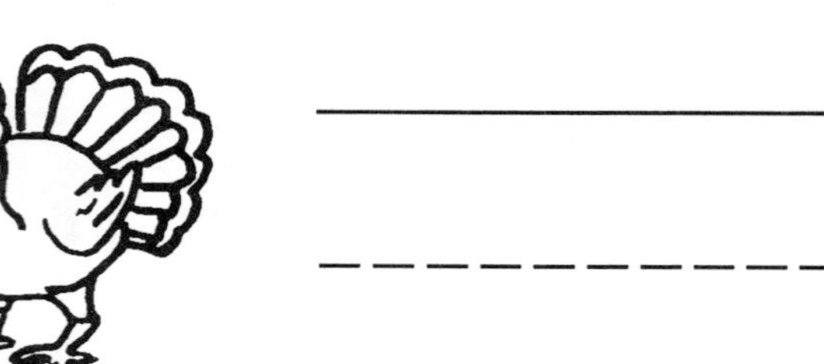

When we count dimes, we count by 10's. If you can, cover each picture with a real dime as you count.

__________¢

__________¢

__________¢

Make shapes exactly like the first one in each row. The dots will help you.

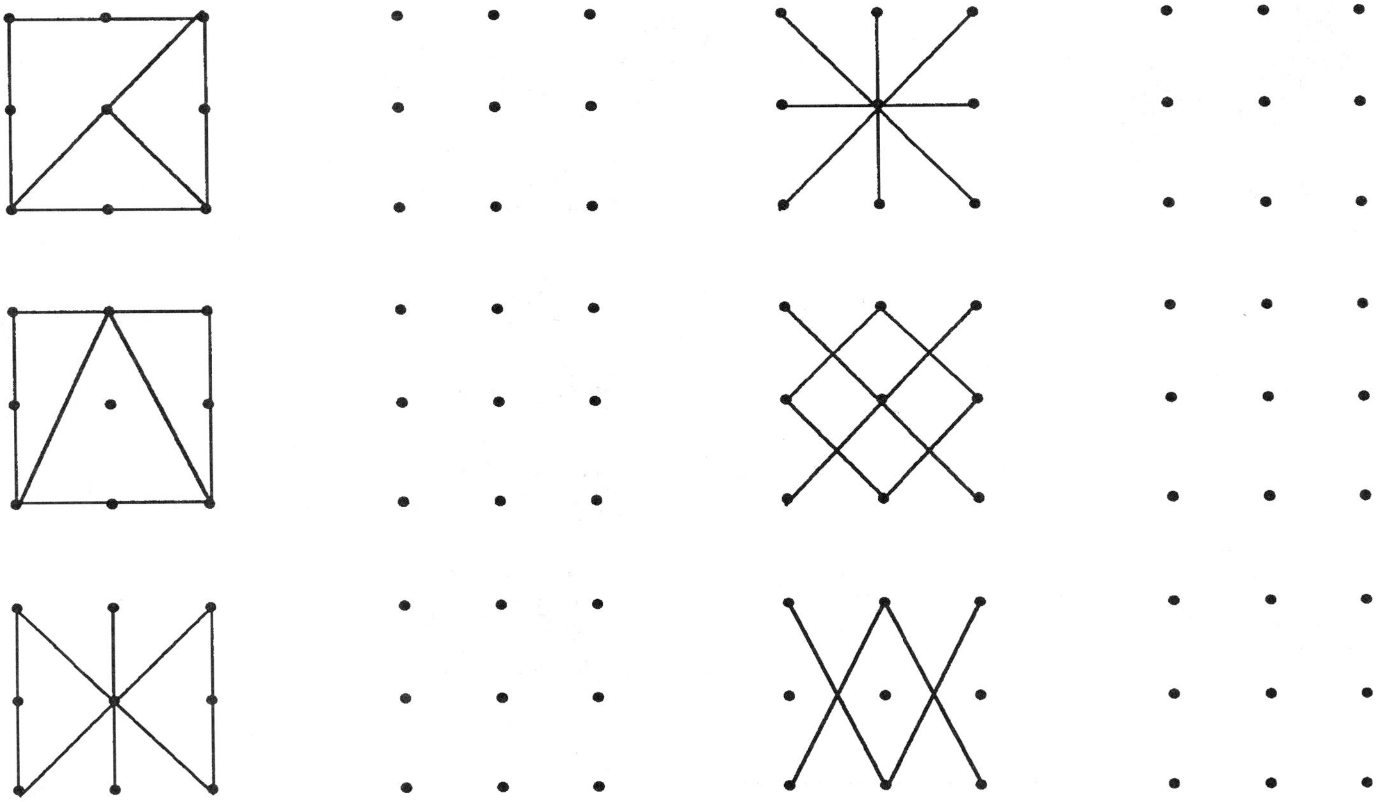

Say the picture word. Write the beginning letter sound you hear.

Example:

m

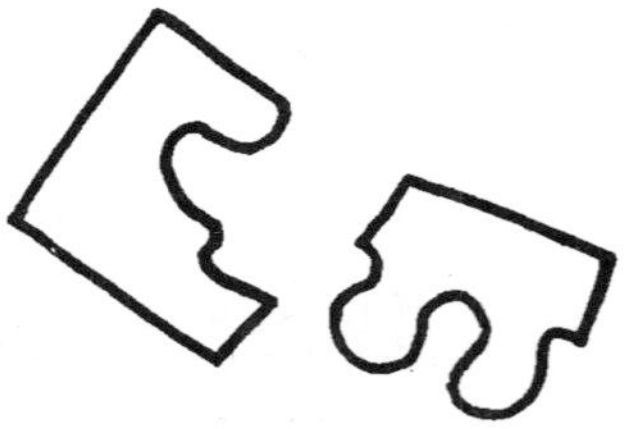

Count the money in these hands and write the correct amount.

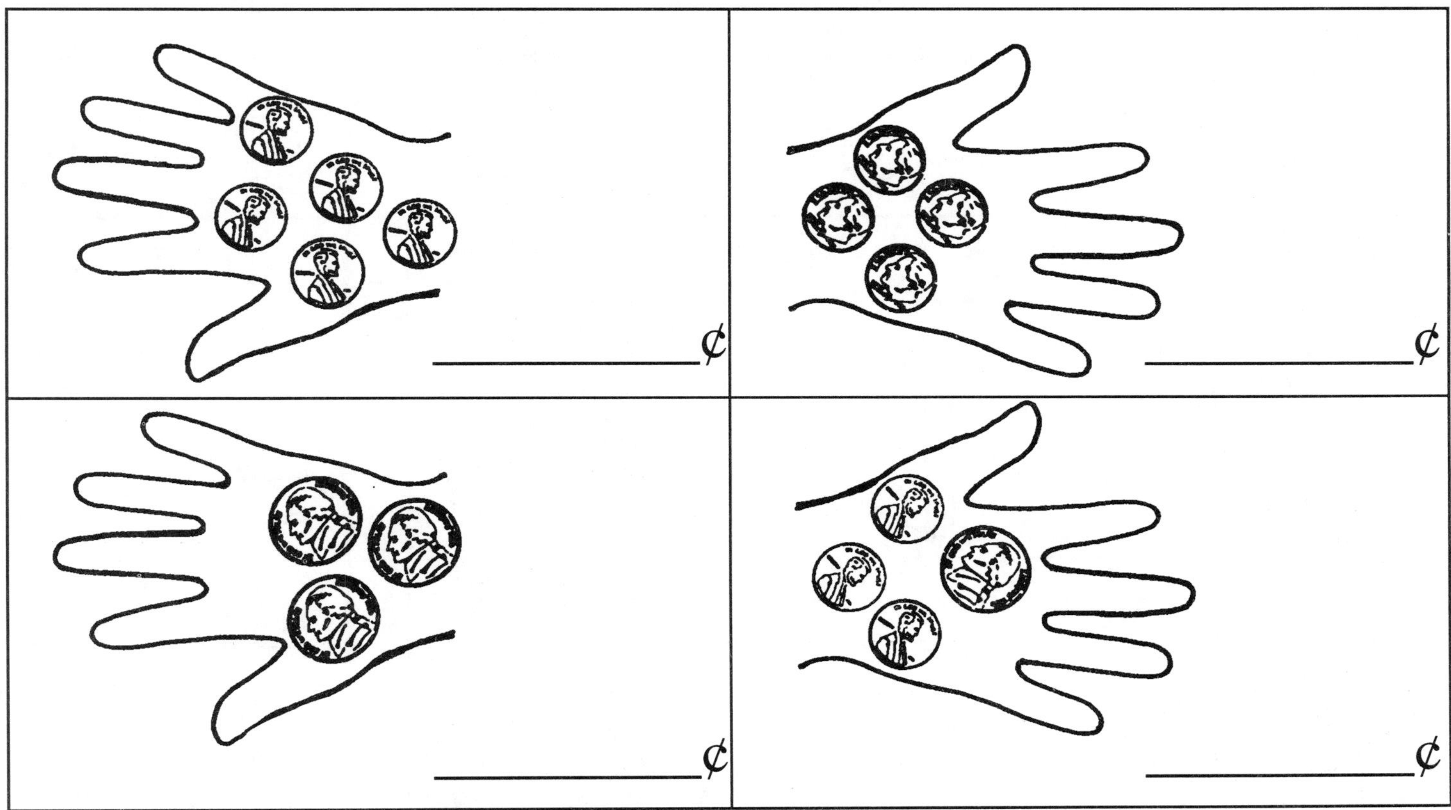

Draw and color pictures of your favorite:

food	friend
toy	color

Say the picture word. Circle the ending letter sound you hear.

Example: 			
w b (t)	c s g	z v p	k n m
g c d	j k w	r z l	d p c
k f x	t l n	h r b	f t l
c d p	h j g	n m h	t j h
r h n	t m c	j r s	b p d

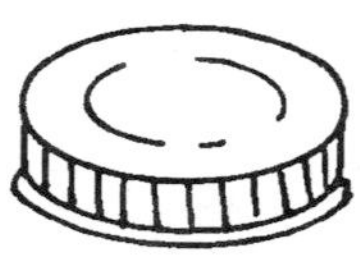

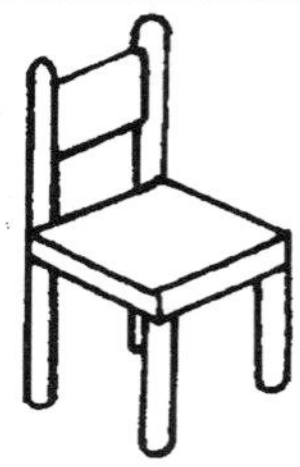

Count the wheels on the train by 2's.

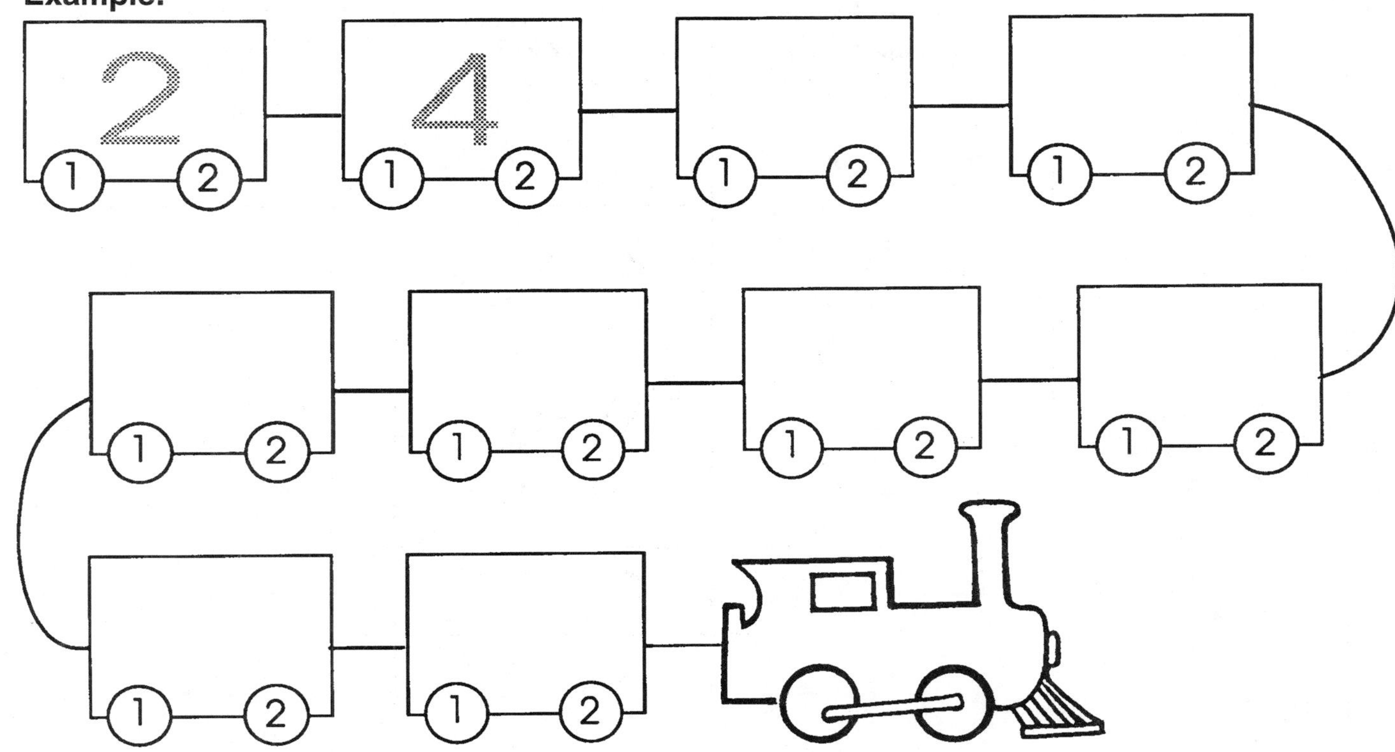

Complete this crossword puzzle.

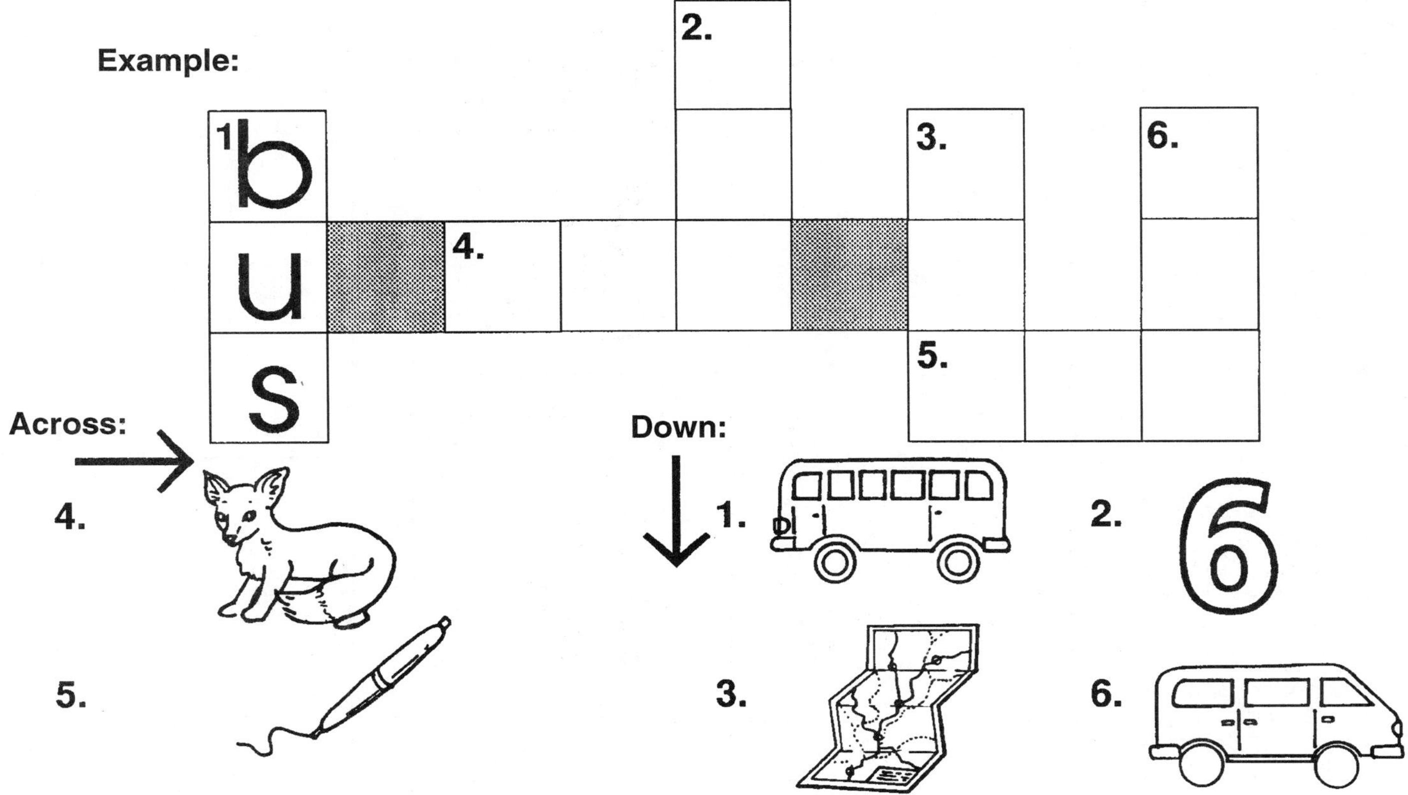

Say the picture word. Write the ending letter sound

Example:

g

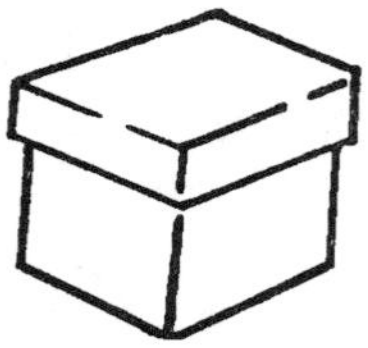

Addition to 10.

6 + 2 = ___	5 + 1 = ___	4 + 3 = ___
1 + 7 = ___	2 + 8 = ___	9 + 0 = ___
3 + 5 = ___	4 + 6 = ___	7 + 2 = ___
8 + 1 = ___	1 + 9 = ___	6 + 3 = ___
5 + 4 = ___	6 +1 = ___	3 + 7 = ___
0 + 8 = ___	3 + 4 = ___	2 + 5 = ___

Search for the number words from 1 to 10.

1. one
2. two
3. three
4. four
5. five
6. six
7. seven
8. eight
9. nine
10. ten

m	a	z	t	s	i	x
t	e	n	w	x	o	p
y	i	f	o	u	r	o
f	g	s	e	v	e	n
i	h	l	n	i	n	e
v	t	h	r	e	e	b
e	c	d	e	f	g	h

Say the name of each object. Write the beginning and ending letter sounds you hear.

Example: d ___ k

Addition to 10.

5	4	9	2	3	8	6
+3	+5	+1	+7	+4	+2	+3

9	1	4	5	6	3	2
+0	+8	+5	+2	+2	+5	+4

Trace the first design, then make one exactly like it.

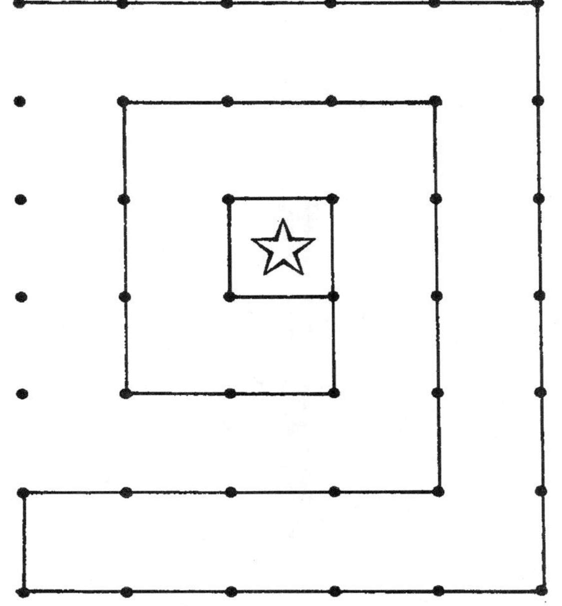

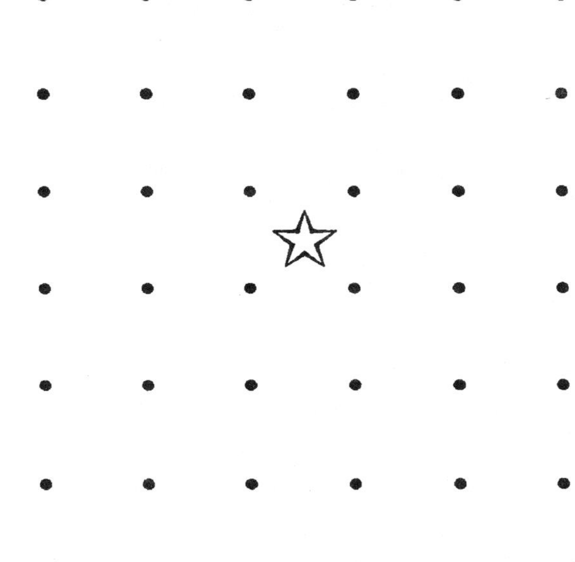

Long (ā) vowel.
Apron begins with the long (ā) vowel sound. Gate and tail have the long (ā) sound, also.

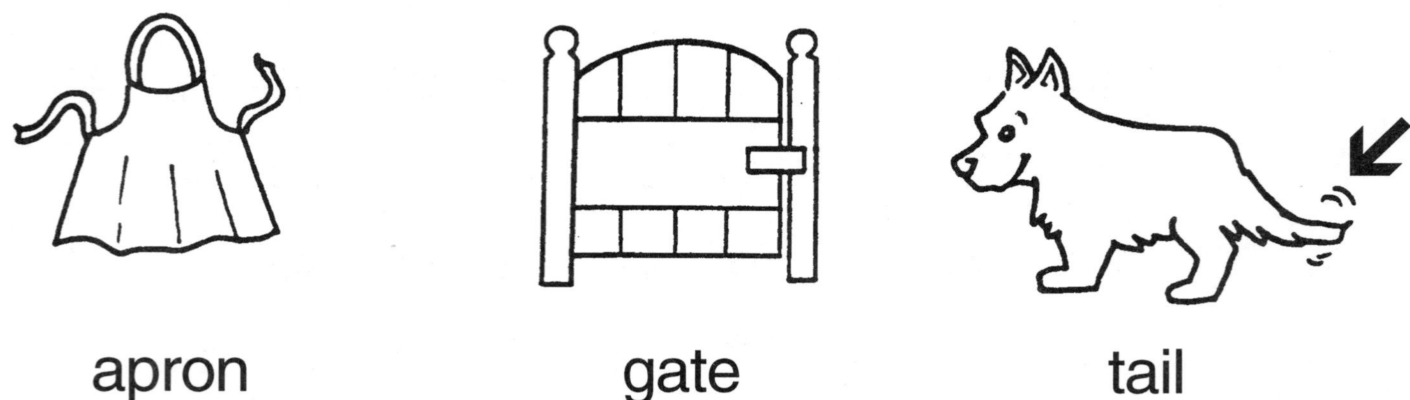

apron gate tail

Say the name of each object and write in the missing letter. Color the pictures.

Example:

acorn

_pe

r_ke

v_se

tr_in

ch_in

l_ke

c_ke

Touch each number and say it out loud with an adult in your family.

0	1	2	3	4	5	6	7	8	9	10	11
12	13	14	15	16	17	18	19	20	21	22	23
24	25	26	27	28	29	30	31	32	33	34	35
36	37	38	39	40	41	42	43	44	45	46	47
48	49	50	51	52	53	54	55	56	57	58	59
60	61	62	63	64	65	66	67	68	69	70	71
72	73	74	75	76	77	78	79	80	81	82	83
84	85	86	87	88	89	90	91	92	93	94	95
96	97	98	99	100							

Color the object red in each box you think would make the most noise.
Color the object green in each box you think would make the least noise.

Practice sounding out and reading these long (ā) words.

bake	cane	cage	tape
skate	lane	page	cape
apron	gate	snail	chain
ape	ate	pail	train

Say the name of each picture. Write down the letter sounds you hear to spell the word.

__ __ __ e

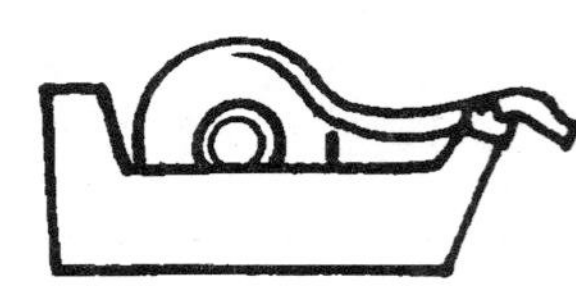

__ __ __ e

__ __ __ __ e

__ __ i __

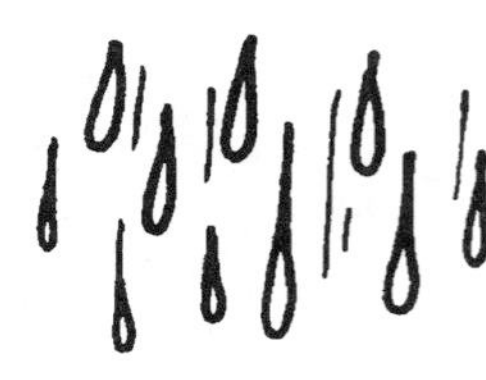

__ __ i __

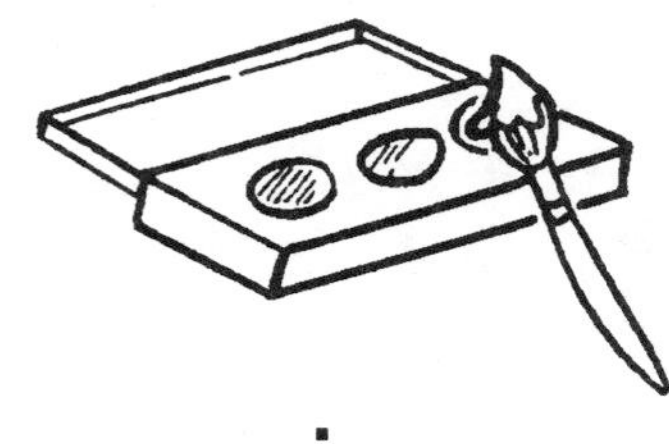

__ __ i __ __

Sound out these long vowel sentences. Practice reading them fast.

1. I can make a big cake.
2. The fat snail is in a red pail.
3. Gail can skate with her cape.

Write the numbers 1 to 50 in the empty boxes.

1	2								
									50

Read the word in each row and color the two pictures that rhyme with it.

cat   	
fan   	
top 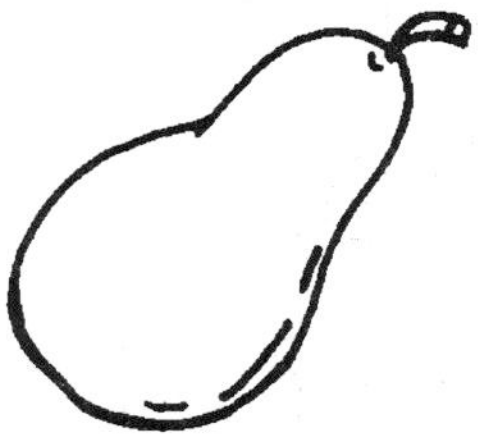  	

Eel begins with the long (ē) sound. Sheep and beads have the long (ē) sound, also.

eel sheep beads

Say the name of each object and write in the missing letter or letters. Color the pictures.

Example:

b<u>ee</u>

j_ _p

b_ans

s_al

p_as

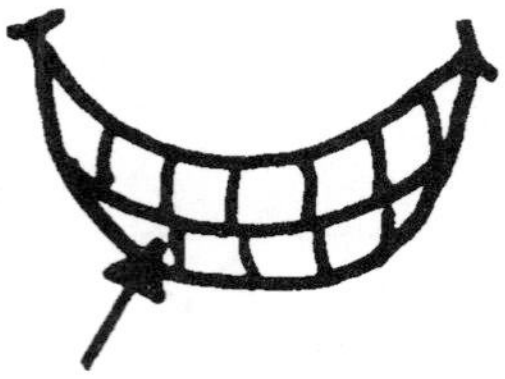

t_ _th

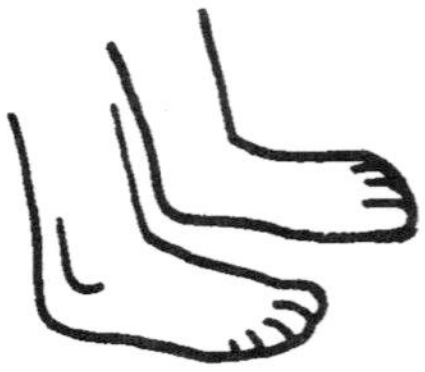

f_ _t

l_af

Subtraction to 10.

5 - 2 = ___ 9 - 3 = ___ 10 - 1 = ___

7 - 4 = ___ 6 - 2 = ___ 8 - 5 = ___

9 - 5 = ___ 10 - 2 = ___ 7 - 3 = ___

8 - 4 = ___ 5 - 5 = ___ 6 - 3 = ___

10 - 0 = ___ 6 - 4 = ___ 5 - 3 = ___

9 - 4 = ___ 8 - 7 = ___ 7 - 2 = ___

Match the rhyming pictures.

Example:

Practice sounding out and reading these long (ē) words.

eel	tree	feet	freeze
feel	seed	sweet	breeze
peas	beads	beak	beach
beans	meal	jeans	steam

Say the name of each picture. Spell it out with the letter sounds you hear.

___ ___ ___ ___

3

___ ___ ___ ___ ___

___ ___ ___ ___

___ ___ a ___ ___

___ ___ a ___

___ ___ a ___

Sound out and read these sentences. Practice reading them fast.

1. The big tree has lots of green leaves.
2. Take a nap, Jean, and go to sleep.
3. The queen has a string of beads.

Subtraction to 10.

7	8	9	6	5	8	9
-3	-5	-1	-2	-4	-3	-5

6	8	5	7	9	8	9
-3	-7	-2	-5	-4	-6	-3

Draw and color something real.	Draw and color something make-believe.

Ice cream begins with the long ($\bar{\text{i}}$) sound. Bike and pie have the long ($\bar{\text{i}}$) sound, also.

ice cream   bike   pie

Say the name of each object and write in the missing letter.

Example:

ice   sm_le

d_ve    d_me

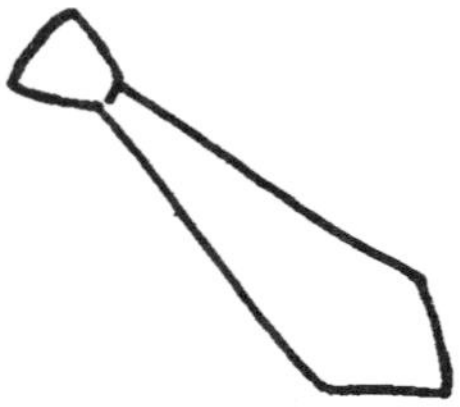

t_e    tr_ ke

h_ve    p_pe

Write numbers 26 to 75 in the empty boxes.

26	27								
									75

Trace over the first design, then make one exactly like it.

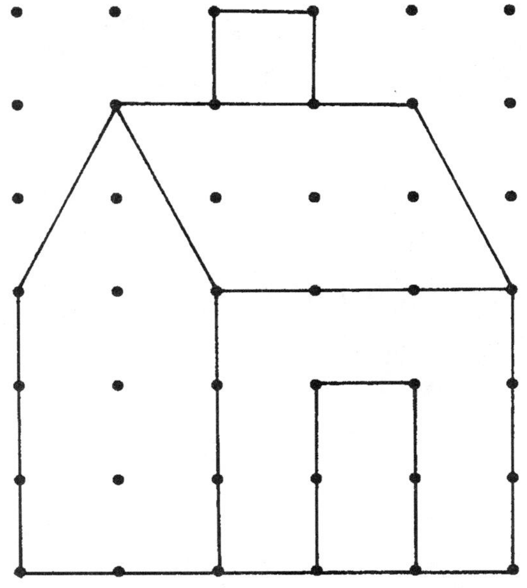

Practice sounding out and reading these long (ī) words.

pie	wide	ripe	like
tie	side	pipe	hike
life	hire	rise	mile
wife	tire	wise	file

Say the name of each picture and write in the letter sounds you hear to spell the word.

__ __ __ e

__ __ __ e

__ __ __ __ e

__ __ __ e

__ __ __ e

__ __ __ e

Sound out and read these sentences. Practice reading them fast.

1. The bike is Tim's size to ride.
2. I can swim and run a mile.
3. Jill likes to swim and dive.
4. The sun will shine and I will paint my five kites.

Addition and subtraction. Watch the signs carefully.

7	8	9	6	5	3	2
+3	-2	-5	+2	+3	+8	+5

6	8	9	7	9	8	5
-3	-7	+1	-5	-4	-6	+4

Circle the two objects in each row that rhyme. Color those objects that do not rhyme.

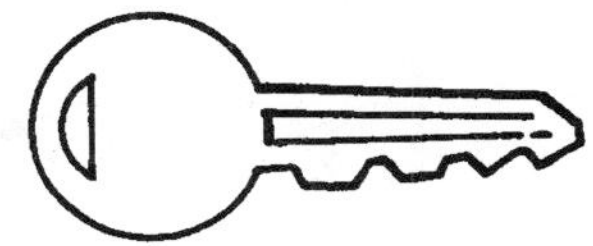
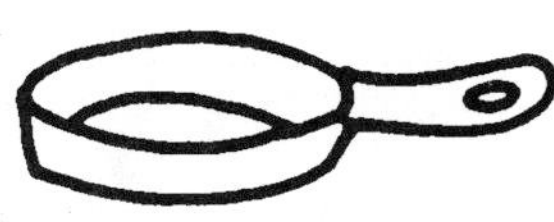

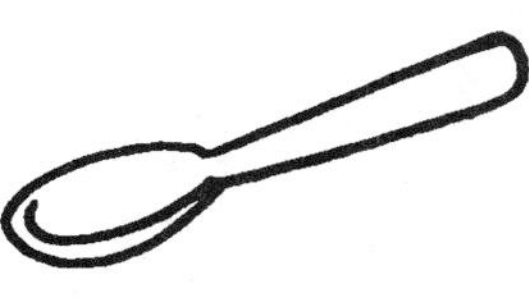

Open begins with the long (ō) sound. Boat and nose have the long (ō) sound, also.

open

boat

nose

Say the name of each object and write in the missing letter.

Addition and subtraction. Watch the signs carefully.

9 - 3 = ____ 6 + 4 = ____ 5 + 3 = ____

2 + 7 = ____ 8 - 2 = ____ 7 - 5 = ____

4 + 5 = ____ 6 - 3 = ____ 6 + 3 = ____

8 - 3 = ____ 9 - 4 = ____ 7 - 3 = ____

5 + 4 = ____ 8 - 6 = ____ 9 - 5 = ____

6 + 2 = ____ 4 - 3 = ____ 7 + 2 = ____

Say the name of the picture in each box, then draw something that rhymes with it.

Practice sounding out and reading these long (ō) words.

hose	note	joke	bone
rose	quote	poke	cone
toad	boat	roast	goat
float	toast	soap	soak

Say the name of each picture. Write in the letter sounds you hear to spell the words.

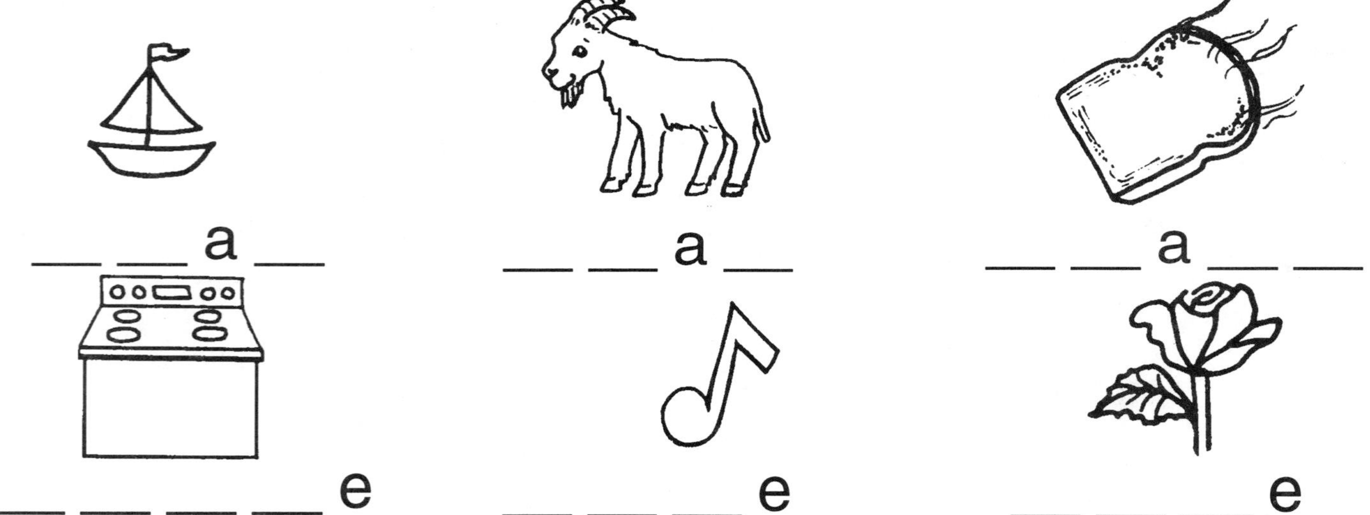

Sound out and read these sentences. Practice reading them fast.

1. The roast is on top of the stove.
2. The dog stole his bone from the store.
3. Joe drove the dog back to the store.
4. Joan wore a rose on her torn dress.

Write the numbers 51 to 100 in the empty boxes.

51	52								
									100

Draw and color the members of your family. Can you write their names by their pictures?

Unicorn begins with a long (ū) sound. Cube and music have the long (ū) sound, also. Sometimes the long (ū) sounds like (oo), as in "flute."

unicorn

cube

music

Say the name of each object and write in the missing letter.

Example:

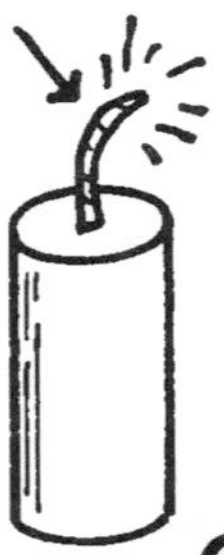

fuse

_nicorn

m_le

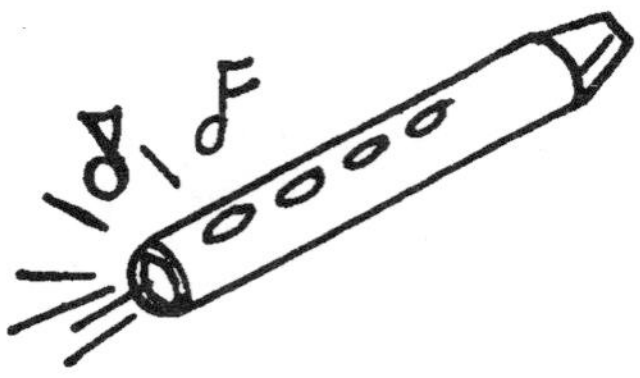

fl_te

gl_e

_niform

c_ te

t_be

What about adding or subtracting with doubles?

1	2	3	4	5	6	0
+1	+2	+3	+4	+5	+6	+0

1	2	3	4	5	6	0
-1	-2	-3	-4	-5	-6	-0

Finish drawing the other half of the pictures.

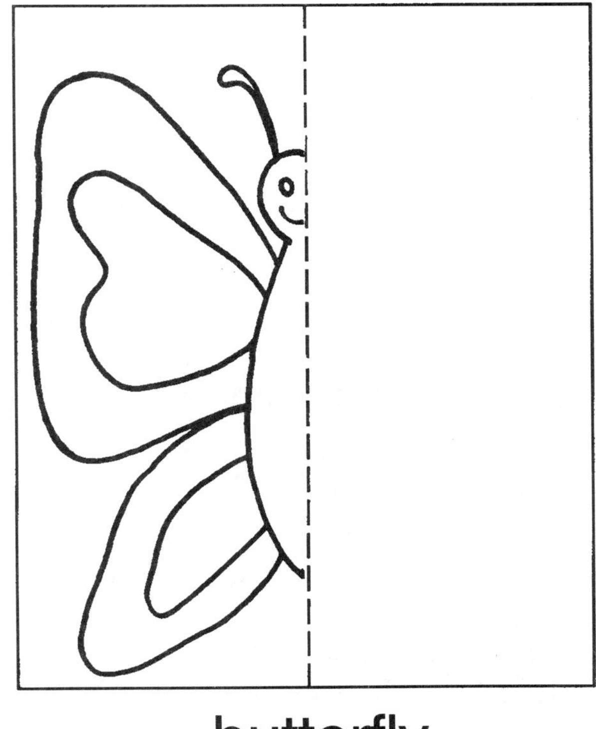
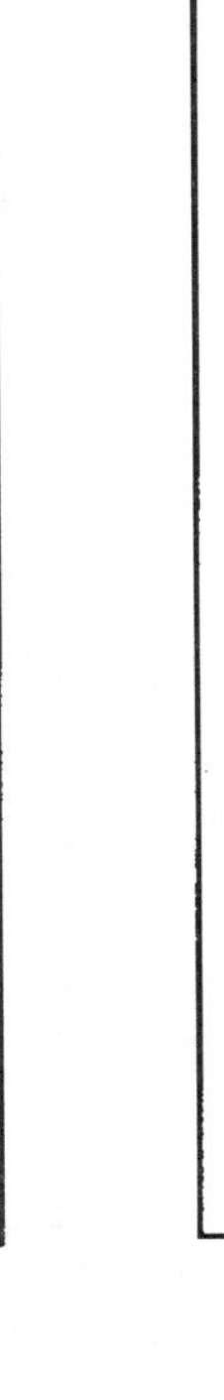

butterfly

clown

Practice sounding out and reading these long (ū) words.

cute	mule	fume	tube
cube	mute	fuse	rude
bugle	blue	true	prune
flute	clue	glue	tune

Say the name of each picture. Write down the lette sounds you hear to spell the word.

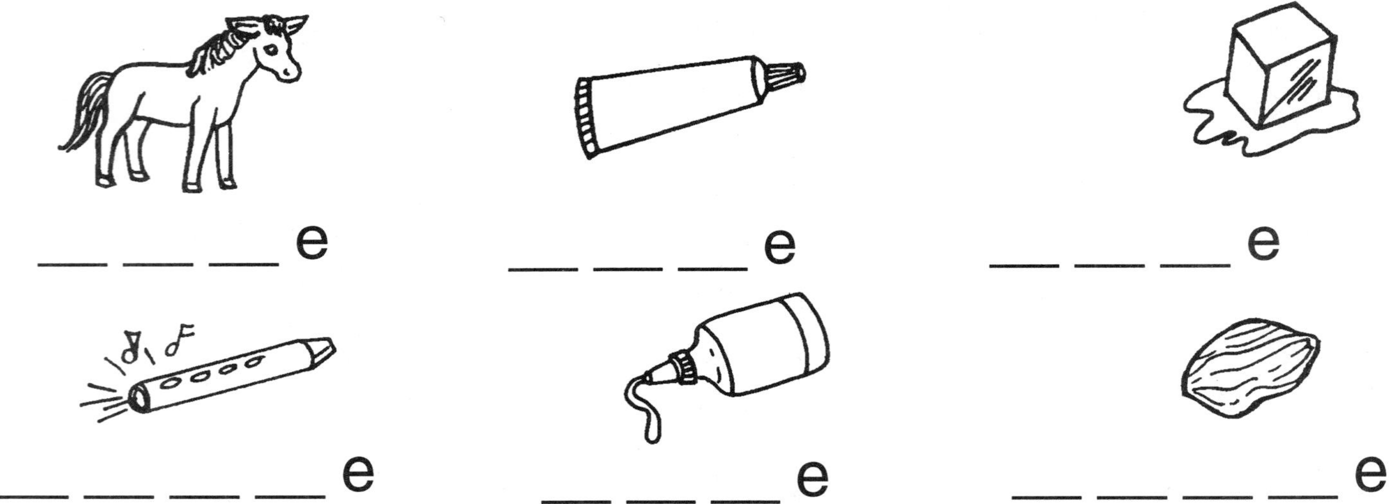

___ ___ ___e ___ ___ ___e ___ ___ ___e

___ ___ ___ ___e ___ ___ ___e ___ ___ ___ ___e

Sound out and read these sentences. Practice reading them fast.

1. The bad dude broke the rule.
2. Cute June likes music on the flute.
3. The mule ate blue prunes.
4. It is true, I can rescue the unicorn.

Circle the number that means the most in each box.

Example:

(26) or 15	70 or 71	25 or 15
59 or 60	9 or 11	87 or 69

Circle the number that means the least in each box.

Example:

63 or (36)	45 or 38	12 or 21
30 or 50	90 or 93	28 or 42

Using the letters in the box, see how many words you can make with these word endings.

r s t c b m p n

Example:

_p_an	____at	____in
____an	____at	____in
____an	____at	____ug
____an	____at	____ug
____ut	____et	____op
____ut	____et	____op

"Placement" words are important. They tell us where objects are.
***On*, *in*, *by*, and *under* are "placement words" or prepositions.**

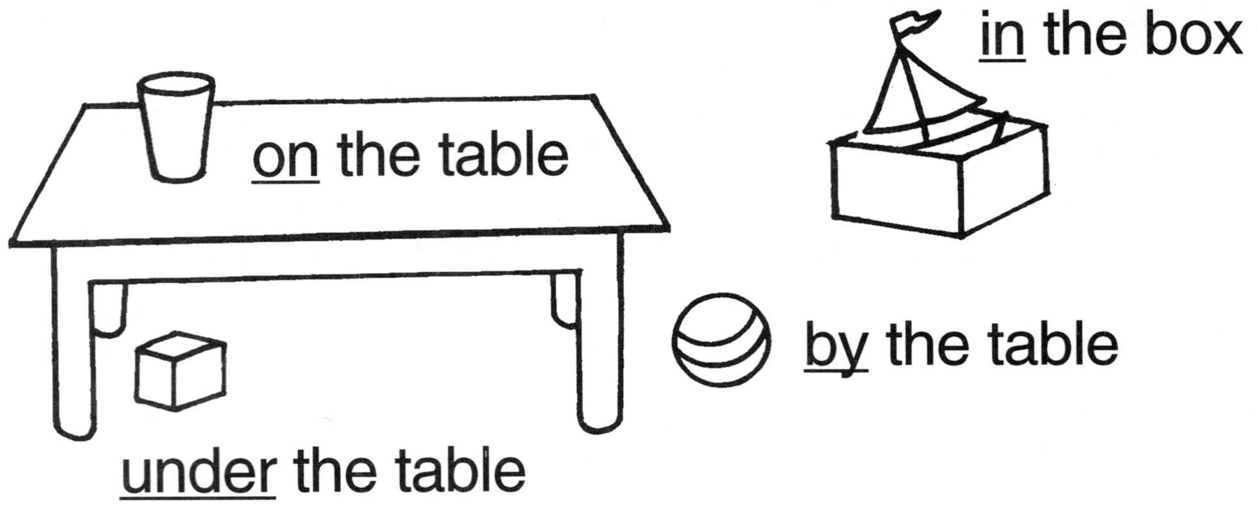

Write the correct preposition in each box.

Can you think of other prepositions? Ask Mom or Dad for ideas!

Write in the missing numbers from 1 to 100.

0 1 2 __ 4 5 __ __ __ 9 10 11

12 13 __ __ 16 __ __ __ 20 21 __ __

24 __ 26 __ __ 29 __ 31 __ __ 34 __

36 __ __ __ 40 __ __ __ __ 45 46 __

__ __ __ 51 __ __ 54 __ __ 57 58 __

60 __ __ __ 64 __ 66 __ __ 69 __ 71

__ 73 __ __ 76 77 __ __ __ 81 82 83

__ __ __ __ __ 89 __ __ __ __ __ __

__ __ __ __ 100

Make your own design by connecting the dots.

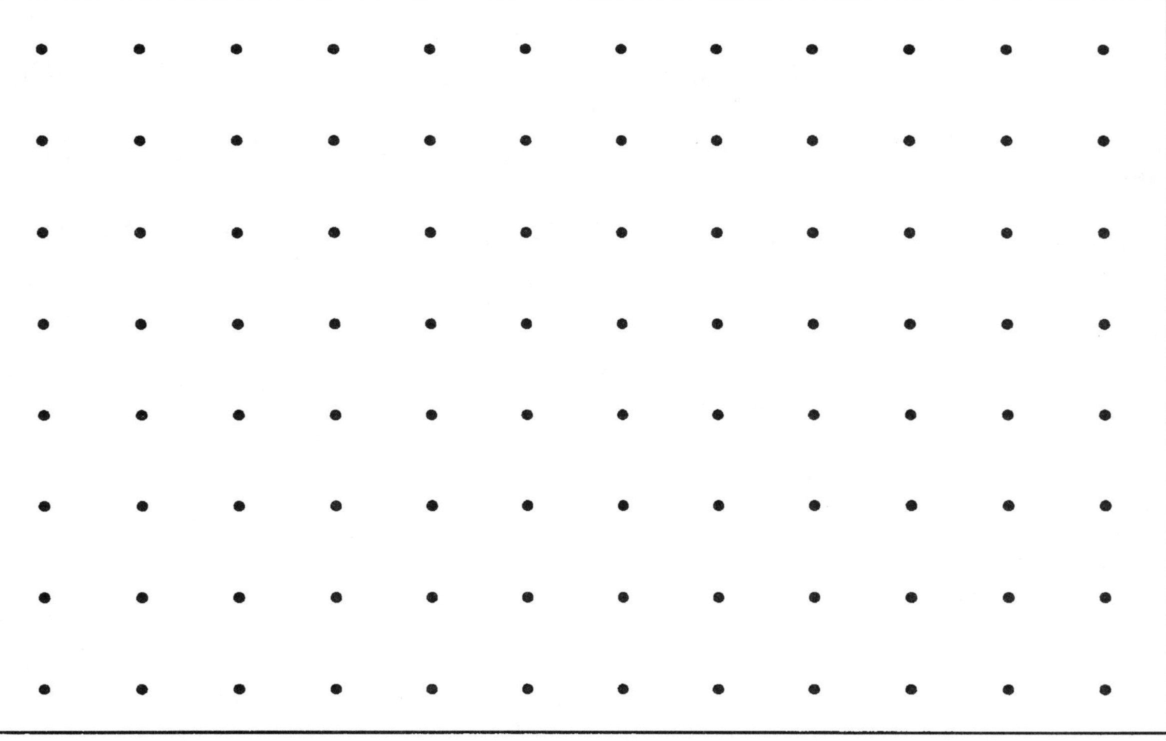

These are different kinds of homes. Follow the directions below.

nest	dog house
house	barn

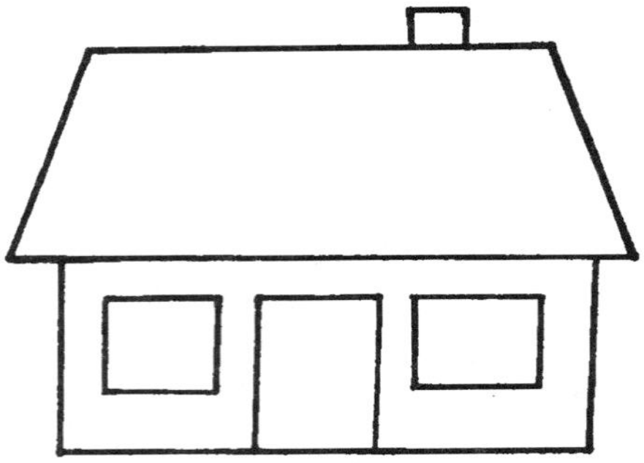

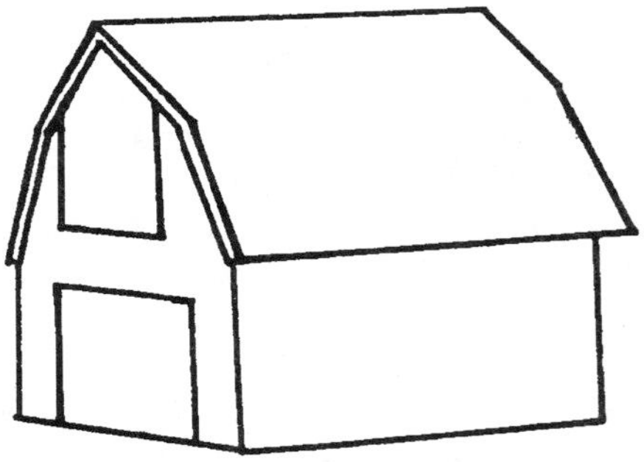

Color:

the house yellow

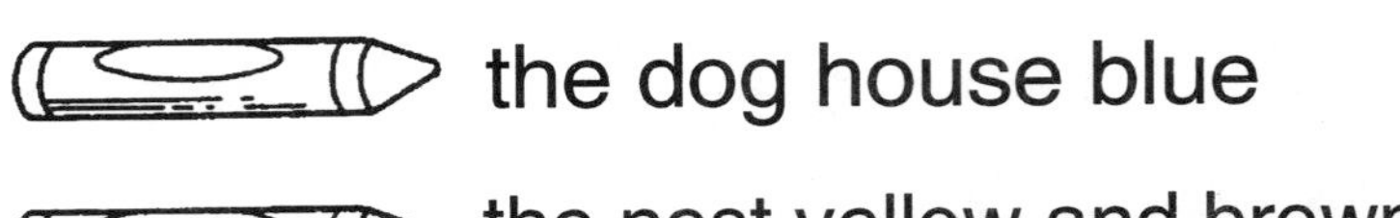

the dog house blue

the barn red

the nest yellow and brown

Draw a person or animal to go with each house. Now draw and color another kind of house.

Connect the dots in alphabetical order. Color the picture.

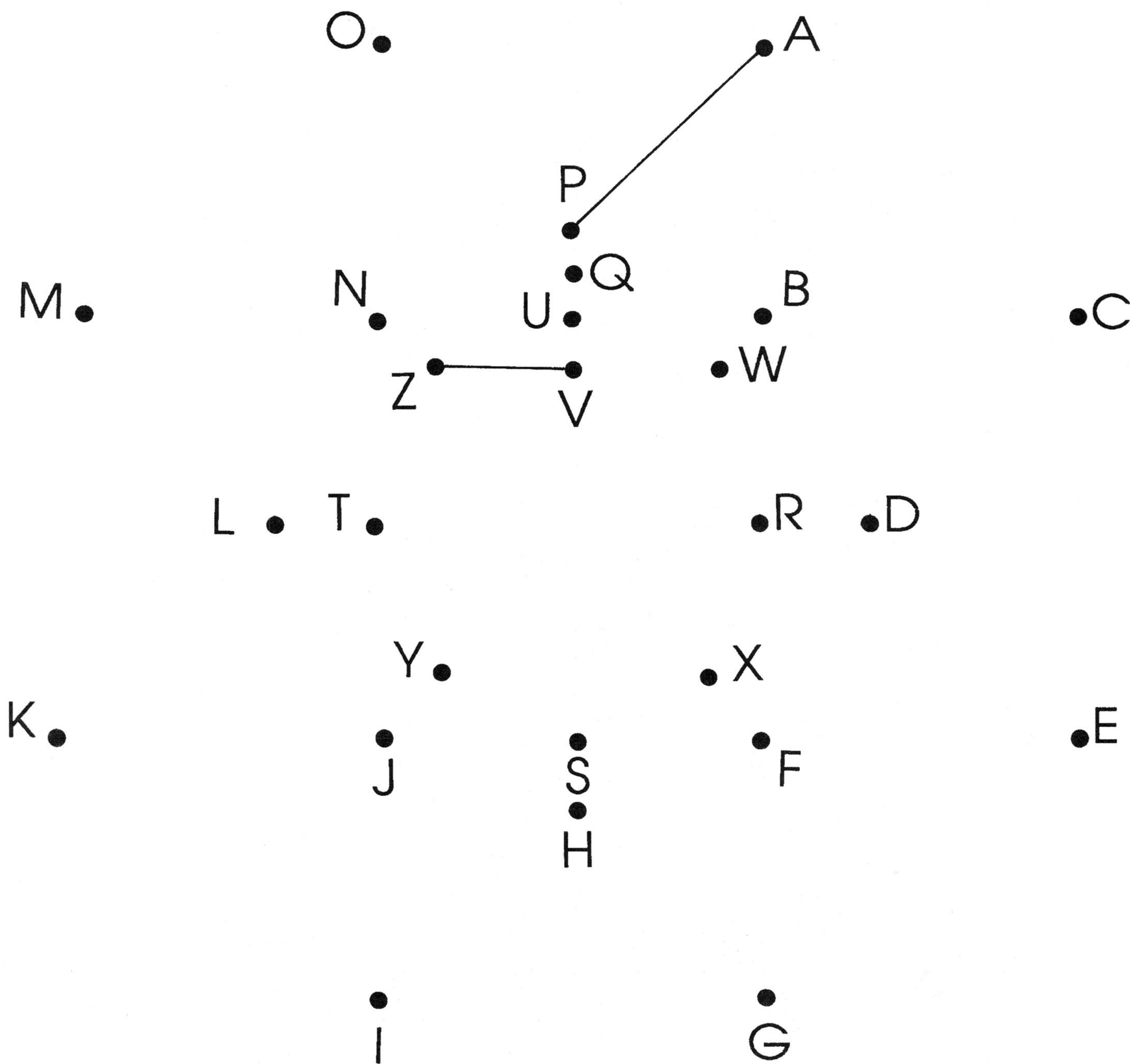

Connect the dots, 1 to 100, and color the picture.

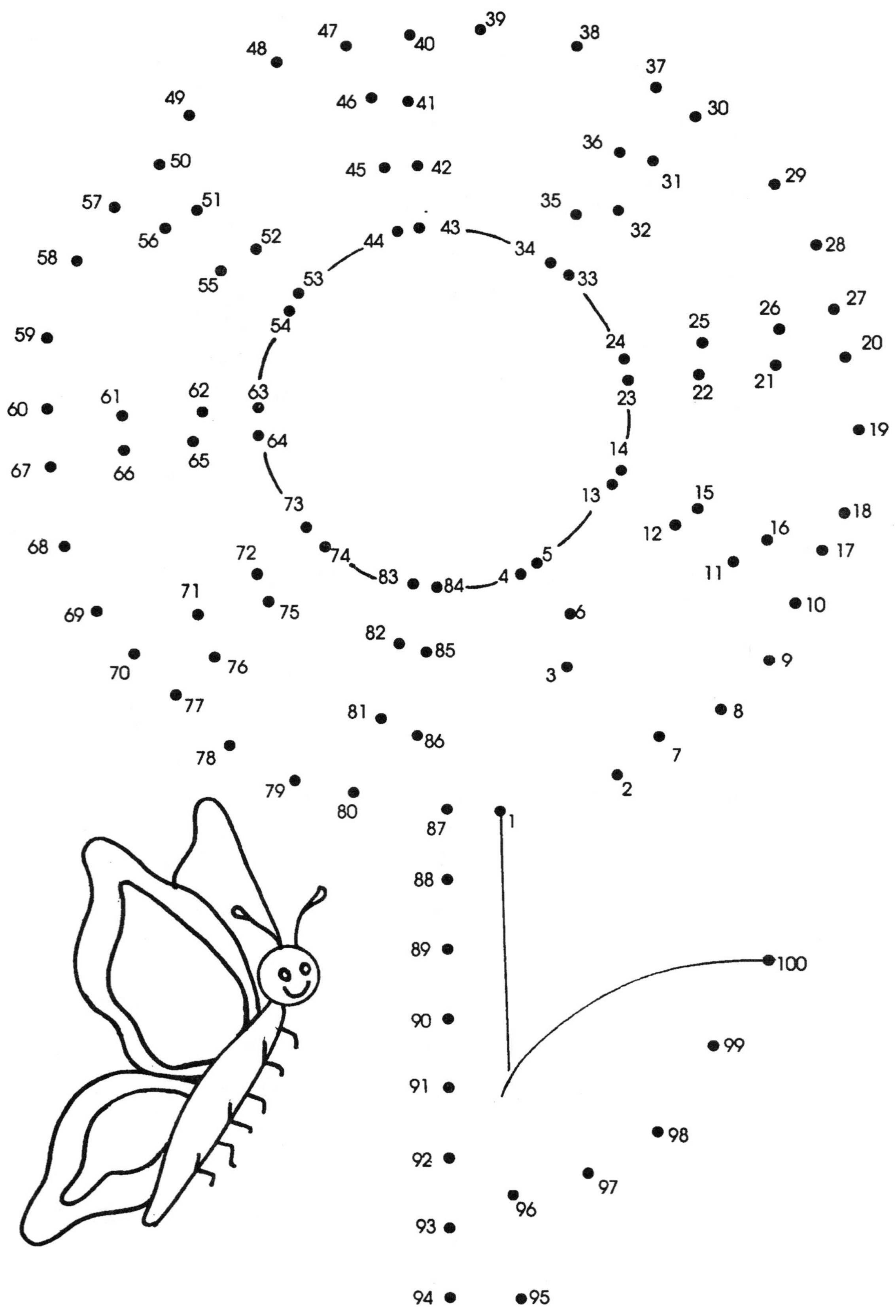

Enrichment Activities for Sound Cards

Assess what your child knows and understands, then use only those activities your child needs.

Two different types of lowercase "a's" are included. You may want to find out which type of "a" your child will be using at his/her school. You could also identify the two different types of "a's" by stating that "a" is the one we use to write with and "a" is the "book a"—the one we find in many reading books.

Parents, when you are working with the letter sounds and the sound blending process, you may exaggerate the letter sounds, but be careful you don't distort them.

When working with the letter sounds, sound blending, and word recognition, you need to help your child learn that these sound words *usually* work this way but there are words that "do not follow the rules."

Consonants

1. Consonant recognition—Start with the consonant sound cards first. Explain that the letters of the alphabet have letter names and letter sounds. Identify the consonant letters and tell your child that these are called consonants because they *usually* have only one sound.

2. Take just a few (1 to 3) sound cards at a time. Identify the letter name on the front and the sound picture on the back. Exaggerate the beginning sound. Now, say two words to help your child choose the word that starts with the same beginning sound as the sound card you are working with. When he/she becomes familiar and successful with this process, you can increase the number of sound cards you are working with.

3. Give your child 3 to 5 sound cards. Say a word or name an object and have him/ her hold up the sound card beginning with the same sound.

4. Play the slap game as mentioned in #2 of the **Letter Enrichment Activities** list on page 47. Say the sounds and/or words and have your child identify the sound card by slapping it.

5. As the child gets better at this, have him/her say a sound and/or word and see if he/she can beat you at the slap game mentioned in the activity above.

6. Have your child label his/her toys by their beginning sound. Give him/her small pieces of paper. Have him/her write down the letter or sound he/she thinks it begins with and place the paper by the toy or on top of it. See if the child can find 2 or more toys that begin with the same sound.

7. Activities 2 through 6 can be used to identify and understand ending sounds (the sound the objects end with) also.

Vowels

1. Explain to your child that vowels have more than one sound. Identify and teach the short vowel sounds before proceeding with the long vowel sounds.

2. Start with the short "a" vowel sound card. Show your child the apple on the back. Say the word "apple," then say it again, exaggerating the "a" sound. Have your child repeat the procedure, then say, "Apple begins with the short 'a' sound."
3. Say 2 or more words and help your child identify those words that begin with the short "a" sound. (Example: ax, astronaut, octopus.)

4. Tell your child there are a lot of words that have the short "a" sound in them, such as "pat," "can," and "man." Next, say two or more words, varying short vowel and long vowel sounds. Then help your child identify which words have the short "a" sound in them.

5. Help your child learn to sound out or sound blend very simple short "a" words (example: can, fat, nap) by writing them on paper, chalkboard, magic slate, cards, etc.

6. Use activities for the other short vowel sounds of e, i, o, and u.

7. Use the consonant sound cards with the short vowel sound cards to put together simple words. Example:

Using the first letter sound of picture side of card.

m a n — Using the letters on the other side of card to make the word "man."

8. Use the same procedure as above, only this time change just the beginning sound or letter card to make new words (rhyming words). (Example: man, fan, ran, can, etc.)

9. Use the same procedure as above, only this time change just the ending sound or letter card to make new words (rhyming words). (Example: man, map, mat, etc.)

10. Use the same procedure as above, only this time change just the short vowel sound or letter card to make new words (rhyming words). (Example: pan, pen, pin, etc.)

11. Say a short vowel word and see if your child can use the sound or letter cards to make the word. Whenever time permits, have your child extend this activity by recording the word on a piece of paper.

12. Word dictation—give your child a pencil and paper. Say a simple word he/she has previously worked on and have your child write it down. Praise your child for his/her efforts and check the word/words frequently as you do this activity.

Long Vowels

1. Talk to your child about how long vowels "say their own name," or sound like the name of the letter. Also, help him/her to understand that when a vowel "says its own name," it usually needs another vowel with it—for example, "cake," "boat," "teeth."

2. Parents, you can use most of the activities listed for short vowel words for long vowel words with a few minor changes.

Long and Short Vowel Sound Cards to cut out and practice with.

ā	ā	ē
ī	ō	ū
ă	ă	ĕ
ĭ	ŏ	ŭ

Consonant Cards to cut out and practice with.

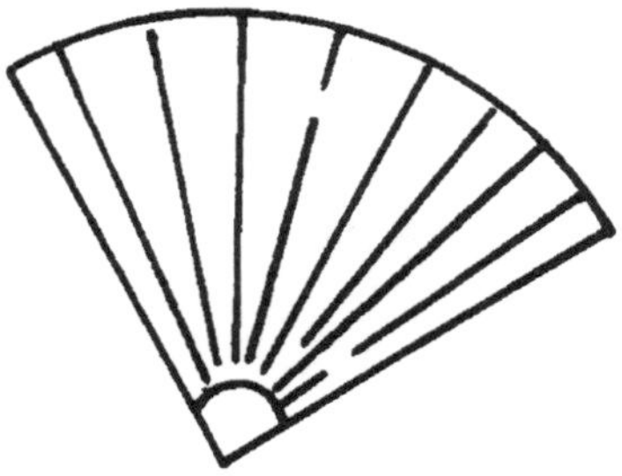

b	c	d
f	g	h
j	k	l
m	n	p

q	r	s
t	v	w
x	y	z

Certificate of Completion

awarded to

for successfully completing the *Summer Bridge Activities*™ Workbook on

date

presented by

Parent's signature

Michele D. Van Leeuwen, author